Wisdom and Folly
Essays on Faith, Life, and Everything in Between

ROB MARCO

Wisdom and Folly

Essays on Faith, Life, and Everything in Between

ROB MARCO

CRUACHAN HILL PRESS
GRASS LAKE, MICHIGAN

Copyright © 2023 Cruachan Hill Press

All rights reserved—no part of this work may not be reproduced, transmitted, or stored in any form by any means—electronic, mechanical, recorded, photocopy, or otherwise–without prior written permission from the publisher, except for brief excerpts in articles or critical reviews.

ISBN: 978-1-957206-21-9
Cover Design by Jessica Fellmeth

Published by

Cruachan Hill Press
12552 E Michigan Ave.
Grass Lake, MI 49240
www.cruachanhill.com

Printed and Bound in the United States of America

O my Jesus, you have said: *"Truly I say to you, ask and it will be given you, seek and you will find, knock and it shall be opened to you."* Behold I knock, I seek and ask that You open my heart to truth."

~Saint Pio of Pietrelcina,
Efficacious Novena to the Sacred Heart

TABLE OF CONTENTS

FOREWORD by Kevin Wells..1
ACKNOWLEDGEMENTS 5
INTRODUCTION 7

ON FRIENDSHIP

Friendship is Always Conditional 11
Online Communities Are Not Real Communities 13
The Ins and Outs of Male Friendship 18
Do Men Need Other Men?..22
I Don't Belong Here Anymore 26
Can People with Different Values Truly Be Friends?................................29
Subversion Through Friendship 33
What Does It Mean to be Faithful?..11

ON DISCIPLESHIP

The Time for Preaching and Teaching is Over...45
Say it with a Smile 49
Why is it so Hard to be Good?...53
"It's Been God All Along"...56
Being the Saint for Your Age 59
Persisting Contra God's Will...62

Want to Suffer Shame for the Name? Start
    Telling the Truth 67
"Everyone Has a Plan Until They Get Punched in the Mouth" 73
Shop Talk..74

ON MARRIAGE

The Gates of Hell Will Not Prevail Against Your Marriage 79
Top of the Sixth, Bottom of the Ninth (And Tenth).......................84
The Principle of Subsidiarity in Marriage......................................88
Arm in Arm 92
The Spiritual Investment in Your Marriage 95
The Flowers in the Corner..98
The Proverbs 31 Conundrum 104
Marriage: A Life Sentence 108
Being Present in the Marital Act...111
The Threats to a Catholic Marriage...116
No Country for Married Men 124
Laugh Your Way to Heaven..128
When Your Wife Doesn't Respect You 131

ON FAMILY

That's the Good Stuff...137
What Should a Good Catholic Family Look Like?......................141
The Most Ordinary Things..143
A Father's Eye View of Motherhood 149
My Son, Where Have You Gone?..152
Mountains and Homepaths..156
Saint Joseph's Pain...159
Have All the Babies..163
Second Generation Catholicism..166
A Wallet Full of Memories 170

ON MANHOOD

Do the Hard Thing..175
Sex is the Snare..179
Spiritual Direction: Men Need Not Apply..................................184
The Stay at Home Dad Dilemma Revisited.................................188

Don't Fear the Heart 194
Led Like an Ox: The Effeminacy of Carnal Capitulation 196

ON FAITH

Trad Piety vs. An Abasement of Trust 203
"I No Longer Fear God, But I Love Him" 206
Consummation 211
What's Old is New 215
The Mammon of Iniquity 218
Make Room for Mystery 223
"He Who Lives Well Dies Well" 226
Wherever Truth May Be Found, It Belongs to His Master 229
I Will See You There 233
What You Live For: Drafting Your Death Wish 239
Scrupulosity: A Thousand Frightening Fantasies 242
When You Can't Take the Stairs 246
On Secret Faults 249

ON PRAYER

The Art of Listening is An Act of Charity 255
I Will Celebrate Before the Lord 260
We Are All a Mess 265
Life by a Thousand Aspirations 269
The Pet Project of Spirituality Without Mortification 272
All I Hear is Silence 275
Let's Be Honest: You're Just Not That Into Him 278
You Have Ten Fingers 283
If the Love of the World is in You 285
In Desperate Need of a Friend 289
I Will Not Rise From Here 294

ON THE CHURCH

Getting on Base 301
The Church is Hierarchical for a Reason 307
The Faithful Bishop: A Meditation 310
Beauty Will Not Save the World 316
Bishops are Born of Families 320
Healing the Church from the Ground Up 325

Spare Not the Rod: A Letter to Our Bishop 328
The Church Will Hurt You 332
A Revolution of Saints 339
Converts Are Made by Witness, Not Pastoral Letters 343

ON WRITING

Why Do I Write? 347
The Witching Hour 351
Letter to an Aspiring Writer..357
What Makes and Artist an Artist 362
Reasoned Order and Creative Mess..368
Letter to a Housewife 373

FOREWORD
Kevin Wells

Mankind needs more books like *Wisdom and Folly*. We are in dire need of more writers like Rob Marco. Why? It is no mystery that factions are growing in the Church and the world. This isn't the time or space to comb over splintering in the Church, but it *is* time to highlight the greatness of what Marco accomplishes in his first book (we hope this is the first of many). Simply, he does this: his compilation of essays is kind, gentle, and humble. Marco is like Christ, who searches out nuance with sinners without ceding an inch of His Father's Will or compromising the majesty of the Church's thornier teachings.

Oddly, the more deeply I waded into Rob Marco's broad and often piercing considerations, I found myself being hand-led into what seemed an uncorrupted garden. In the same fashion a farmer must beat back earwigs, gophers, and nibbling rabbits from befouling his bounty, Marco leans on his philosophic bent, vulnerability, and ferocious love for God to ward off temptations to cede ground on illuminating the raw Truth of Christ's pilgrim Church. These exceptional essays are a demonstration of pure grace, given by God to one of his humble writers.

Each of the essays herein seem to subliminally scream for readers to repent, to lay their heads against Christ's heart, and to begin anew.

WISDOM AND FOLLY

As Marco himself has attained a settled peace after his *searching years*, he urges readers toward the same sacred blueprint of renunciation of self and total union with Christ into which he's bought. A large part of sainthood demands humbling oneself and baring all, and the married father from Pennsylvania does this and more in these often nakedly vulnerable, raw, and penetrating essays.

It is no surprise that St. Philip Neri—the patron saint of Joy—is among Marco's favorites. He writes: "St. Philip took the organic approach to cultivating friendships and relationships across social and class lines…He loved going out into the streets and talking with people; he took a very personalist approach to this…Humility, humor, and a love of people—these are the things I find myself so drawn to in St. Philip Neri. We are living through a great leveling of the Church in the culture, and we need those on the ground to go out amidst the rubble and get to work rebuilding from the ground up."

Although Marco was writing about the Italian saint, make no mistake he was writing about himself. Since opening himself to the fullness of the Father's love after his conversion to the faith in high school, he's been a serious-minded but joy-filled and radical evangelist who, in his Kerouac-like travels across America, has often seen a worldly absence of joy. In *Wisdom and Folly*, Marco is unafraid to write about the joylessness to which he's paid witness while using his own life as a test subject and buffer. Over and over in these essays, he points to the various ways of attaining lasting joy. The cross, a commitment to sacrifice, a Marian mindset, a proper understanding of conjugal love, and adoration of the Eucharistic Face of Christ are just a few of the holy icons Marco identifies as having brought himself closer to God's embrace.

For those unfamiliar with Marco and the countless hundreds of articles and blogs he's written, you're in safe hands. Why? Each of these essays stems from where the Holy Spirit led him in prayer. Marco is intensely devoted to meditative prayer, scripture, spiritual reading, and ordered living. He is the least arrogant man you will ever meet, the kind of neighbor who seems to sit in wait for you to ask for a cup of sugar or

FOREWORD

a stick of butter. Those who know him say he is a happy old soul with an unbudging devotion to Christ and His Church.

This book will lift you into the richness of storytelling and into the soul of a man with a zeal for God. His unique perspectives on modern Catholic life and the jarring manner of his candor will stick to the ribs of your memory and conscience. My advice, as one who has read Marco for years now, take in an essay or two with your morning or evening prayer, close your eyes, and meditate on where the Lord "took you" through Marco's words. In time, you might see where a particular essay/s in *Wisdom and Folly* has become a personal invitation from your Heavenly Father to see a blind spot, convert, and to come to know Him in a more intimate way.

"We are being ransomed, all of us, in dribs and drabs," Marco writes of the movement of God's grace. "The best we can do is labor, scatter, till, and fertilize…But isn't it a wonderful thing to see a flower bud, a tree bear fruit, in its due season?"

In *Wisdom and Folly*, chances are you find these "wonderful things" budding or becoming lodged deeply into your own soul. It did for me—and I am grateful to Rob Marco for having planted and scattered that seed. Over and over, I was led to go about the business of purchasing that treasured field and to never look back.

ACKNOWLEDGEMENTS

I'd like to first and foremost thank Mr. Phillip Campbell for his generosity and willingness to take a chance on me. Publishing today is a tenuous business, especially when you are dealing with someone who doesn't fit well into prescribed boxes, Catholic or otherwise. Yet it is that very quality that drew me to Mr. Campbell's own writing and my affinity for his work. Although I know he does much more than simply blogging, I can say in all honesty that his Unam Sanctam Catholicam is the only Catholic blog I feel compelled to read regularly. Beyond just writing though, I have been edified—in the Faith, in my spiritual journey, and in my family life—by his extending the hand of friendship to me during a time of need.

I'd also like to thank Kevin Wells, another man of faith and integrity whom I am honored to count as a friend, for joining my wife's chorus of "Write the book. Write the book. For Pete's sake, WRITE THE BOOK!" No stranger to the ardor (and arduous) work of writing and publishing himself, Kevin's encouragement and trust over the past few years have meant a lot to me, and I owe him a debt of gratitude for his mentorship.

Additionally, there are many untold friends in the Faith who, like the unnamed martyrs and not-yet-canonized saints, have prayed for me and suffered much on my behalf. Part of that suffering might entail reading essay after essay I have sent to them over the years, by text or email, and their responses have always been charitable, uplifting, and encouraging. This book is as much for them as it is anyone. You know who you are.

Since the last shall be first, as it says in scripture, I would finally like to give glory to God for the gift of my wife, Debbie. It is truly an honor to walk the road to Calvary with her, hand in hand, with our eyes together fixed on Christ. I hope this book will serve as a lasting testament to our children, and an encouragement for them to follow the Lord Christ wherever he leads.

INTRODUCTION

My wife was reading a collection of essays recently by naturalist Henry Beston while we were on vacation. She relayed to me a passage from the Introduction of his bestseller *The Outermost House:*

> Despite this idea of himself as a writer-naturalist (the phrase he used to describe himself), Beston seemed to have no clear idea of producing a book from his year of living on the beach. Not so with his fiancée, Elizabeth Coatsworth, herself a writer and a woman with formidable belief in and ambition for Henry's talents. He left the beach in the fall of 1927 with several notebooks full of material but no publishable manuscript. When he proposed setting a wedding date, Elizabeth replied, "No book, no marriage." *The Outermost House* was published in the fall of 1928; the Bestons were married the following June.

My wife is not a writer, but I can say with full assurance that she is my biggest cheerleader. Before we even met, she found my blog online and felt it was an embarrassing secret she kept in her heart—that she knew me by my writing even before she set eyes on me in person. She never gave me an ultimatum as Ms. Coatsworth did to Mr. Beston, but it seems implied that writing would weave its way like an unbroken thread throughout the tapestry of our relationship and eventual marriage. She has also been gently trying to get me to write this book which is now in your hands for the past ten years. The funny thing is, I had just finished the manuscript the morning of the day she read me that particular passage.

Part of my reluctance in compiling these essays for publication for so long has been that I don't think of or refer to myself as a writer, but rather insist that I'm "just a guy who writes." For better or worse, though, it's in my blood, and I lament with the prophet Jeremiah, "I will not make mention of him, nor speak any more in his name: and there came in my heart as a burning fire shut up in my bones, and I was wearied, not being able to bear it" (Jer 20:9).

I have had my Jonah moments, my Jeremiah moments, my moments of being the servant with the single talent that buries it in the yard. Thankfully the Lord is patient with me, and He did the heavy lifting of bringing this work into being even when I didn't want to. This is the miracle of His abundant grace: He sent friends into my life who opened doors, offered services and encouragement, and spent countless hours reading the words I put to page. He gave me plenty of material to work with: my marriage, my children, and my Catholic faith, to name a few. He gave me the unmerited gift of faith. He has filled my cup to overflowing (Ps 23:5).

This collection of essays is really the outpouring of that cup, to give back to the Lord all He has given me and entrusted me with, albeit in a small drummer-boy offering. It is the product of forty-three years as a man, twenty-five years as a grateful Catholic convert, thirteen happy years of marriage, three awesome children, and many late nights and early mornings before work pecking away at a keyboard trying to quench the fire shut up in my bones.

In our family and marriage, we ascribe to the natural order which orients everything else in our life: God first, spouse second, children third. This book is really just a compilation of reflections on these three "big stones," with some additional smaller pebbles interspersed in the

INTRODUCTION

spaces between. But they all work together, as different sides of a prism, to hopefully reflect back the glory of God to those who read them.

In many ways, I have questioned whether people even have the ability to read and digest the kinds of books I used to read as a teenager: Dostoevsky, Hesse, Augustine, Wilde. Our collective attention spans have been steadily wilting in the blazing sun of smartphones, the internet, social media, podcasts, and YouTube. I myself am as much a victim of my age as the next man. And so the question for any writer becomes "How does one effectively communicate?" Do we adopt the spirit of the age and play into it? Or do we try to recreate something that man seemingly no longer has the capacity for?

I see this book as a kind of middle path: I don't have the intellectual, academic, or literary wherewithal to write something in the vein of *War and Peace*. I don't have any formal training or education in writing or English. But there may still be some scraps of flesh left on the bone here to satiate a hunger. That is how I see these collection of essays: strings of meat, sips of table wine, small morsels of passed-over sweets which are easily digestible but (hopefully) don't leave one feeling bloated. They can be read independent of one another and are grouped under general themes that I hope many Catholics can identify with.

In *Sins Of The Tongue*, Monsignor Landriot, Archbishop of Rheims, wrote:

> Man is born for companionship, and he feels within himself a sweet but irresistible power, forcing him to cast in his life with the common lot, to unite it with that of others, to give to his brethren, and to receive from them in his turn, the superabundant treasures of heart and intellect. The tongue is one of the principal organs marked out for transmitting them. It is the bridge of communication, suspended between two worlds, which loses itself on one side in the invisible regions of the spiritual, and rests on the other on the world of the senses, that it may reach the opposite bank of the stream. (76)

Though he is speaking of the tongue as the "principal organ" here, I would say the pen (or the keyboard in modern nomenclature) also serves the same purpose: to unite with man, to give and receive the heart and the intellect, which bridges the chasm between the spiritual and the sensory world. At least that is what has always pushed me forward, even when I didn't want to go—that "irresistible power" compelling me to unite with that of others and with God through words on a page. I'm not a writer…just a guy who writes. I'm not a teacher…just a fellow traveler, a local beggar showing a brother and sister where I've found bread.

ON FRIENDSHIP

FRIENDSHIP IS ALWAYS CONDITIONAL

One of the hardest pills for me to swallow in my adult life has been that none of my friends will be there with me through thick and thin, when things get ugly and I get ugly. No one will be with me to the bitter end. One of the hardest pills to swallow is that friendship is always conditional.

I have always struggled with this, from high school on. Maybe I was spoiled by a family and parents that loved me unconditionally, even at my very worst. In an ideal world, we would have friends stand by us even when we change, when we do unconscionable things. In reality, I have not found this to be the case.

And maybe for right reason. Employers don't like pension funds because they put them on the financial liability hook to their employees for life. Is it reasonable for them to incur that risk when people are living longer, and markets are volatile? Maybe not.

Likewise, maybe my idea of people that will not distance themselves when you become a public embarrassment or a ghoul or a Democrat or an apostate is not reasonable. Maybe the conditional logic and clauses *are* the appropriate response: we are friends as long as you are Catholic. As long as you don't commit a crime. As long as I still like hanging out with you. As long as you don't get weird.

I've made and lost a lot of friends over the years. Very, very few people will stand by you when you are being crucified. If that's the case, these are the "friendships of utility" in which a *quid pro quo* unspoken understanding is that we have permission to peel off when we are not being fed by the other, or finding a lack of common bond as things change over the years.

Again, I think this is just a matter of misplaced expectation. I don't have a friend in my life who has pledged to be there for me unconditionally, nor have I been that friend to others. It's a Catch-22, isn't it? When we are younger, we do not have the virtue to be concerned about the ultimate good of another but are concerned mostly with the emotive and utility (benefits) of the friendship.

Yet, as we age and acquire virtue, the opportunities to develop true friendships—whether utilitarian or those based on the good—begin to wane. Aristotle considered friendship a virtue, and "necessary for life." Whereas in the modern world, however, we get set in our ways, have familial and work obligations, and most men simply deduce that friends are a luxury one can do without.

Given that a true friendship founded on the good of the other requires trust, intimacy, virtue, self-deference, and vulnerability, it becomes like a needle in a haystack trying to find a male friend to which we can confide and bear burdens for. As a married man, I'm obviously precluded from seeking such friendships with those of the opposite sex. And among those of my own, it can be very difficult to come by a man willing to enter into something like this.

Realizing that I will probably never have a true friendship based in filial love and virtue to the level in which I would like is, as I said, a tough pill for me to swallow. Like realizing you'll never be a pro basketball player, or that you'll never do great things in your career. I feel foolish for waking up to it so late. So now it's a matter of adjusting expectations and coming to terms, in a kind of dark night, that maybe unconditional friendship really just is a luxury we are simply not afforded on this side of eternity.

ONLINE COMMUNITIES ARE NOT REAL COMMUNITIES

Recently I joined an online community as a way to connect with other Catholics, hopefully deepen my prayer life, and have some support in my spiritual journey. After twelve years on Facebook, I deleted my account two years ago after witnessing the growing disease with both the platform and online interaction as a whole. And so there was some vacancy for me, both in terms of mental space and new-found time, that I found I had after giving up social media. Maybe it was time to revisit the online space and get engaged again?

I went through a kind of module orientation (virtual, of course) for this particular apostolate, watched the videos, learned the rules and etiquette of this particular community as well as its charism, and was approved as a new member. The website was very well-done, professional, and interactive; I made a profile, and within a few days my inbox was starting to be populated with "New Activity" or "New Discussion" notifications—people posting asking questions about prayer, or sharing something they had read, or bringing up topics for conversation. I joined in on a few discussions, even, and attended a Zoom meeting with hundreds of people involved in the apostolate to discuss a spiritual book.

After a few months, though, I started to feel the lack of real-world connection. My inbox filling up each day with people posting this or that, lots of topical "activity" but no real meaningful connection with individuals, and just feeling like it had the potential to be a repeat of my years on Facebook—posting, checking, dinging, engaging, scrolling, and feeling ultimately unsatisfied and sometimes even agitated at the end of the day. I tried to remember the original reasons I got off in the first place and saw that this was just a differently packaged experience from the same type of factory.

Before I got off Facebook, I connected with people I hoped to stay in touch with and got their phone numbers before jumping ship. Some of these people became real-life friends, whom I have met in person and/or talk or text with regularly. There are a few, though, that I find it strange I have no idea what they even look like in person, having never met them, and the fact that they never had an online photo of themselves. I go back to this question of "what makes someone a true friend?" and, by extension, "what makes a bonafide community?"

I know for some people who are isolated, introverted, or geographically remote, online-internet-virtual communities may be a lifeline to assuage loneliness and feel connected with others of like-mind, even if it's through a strand of ethernet cable. They look forward to waking up and logging on to their computer and getting down to the business of posting, discussing, and engaging.

I've thought about this a lot, and I keep coming back to this Matrix-like situation in which a collective of individuals online (on social media, in chat rooms, in online-only apostolates, etc.) feel like it's so real, so true, and yet still only a mirage. It is a kind of mannequin-like reality, approximating what's real and true, and yet still a counterfeit separated from the vitality of life by a profound and impassible chasm.

For someone like myself who is searching for deep, meaningful friendships that are of course Catholic, but even go beyond the topical to approximate the "communing of souls" that St. Augustine writes about so elegantly, it's a constant source of frustration and disappointment. It reminds me of that film *Her* with Joaquin Phoenix in which the protagonist falls in love with an Operating System (OS) A.I. that seems to know him more intimately than anyone else. And yet, it's still the latex hangover of waking up and realizing that those feelings of intimacy are "always real, but never true."

I think Tommy Killackey in "Talking At Each Other" (Fraternus/*Sword & Spade*) nails it here:

> Friendships of virtue, by contrast, require a much deeper commitment and investment than those of utility of pleasure. The facade of the screen might not just limit things like physical encounter, but it also helps us avoid the vulnerability required of true friendship. [Roger] Scruton [in *Confessions of a Heretic*] again helps us here:
>
> "By placing a screen between yourself and the friend, while retaining ultimate control over what appears on that screen, you also hide from the real encounter—forbidding to the other the power and freedom to challenge you in your deeper nature and to call on you here and now to take responsibility for yourself and for him" (Scruton, 96).

Put simply, intimacy and control cannot coexist. Social media always renders us in complete control, and whether we choose to click, scroll, watch, reply, like, or close our tab, we individually always have the power within our fingertips. Scruton goes on to say—

> "Risk avoidance in human relations means the avoidance of accountability, the refusal to stand judged in another's eyes, to come face to face with another person, to live yourself in whatever measure to him or her, and so to run the risk of rejection" (Ibid, 108).

We might call this Scruton's warning against the risk of avoiding risk. The "risky" friendships that "call us out of ourselves [to] take up our crosses" were not built online, nor could they exist there exclusively. We may still interact online, but the soul of virtuous friendship where we risk encountering another can only occur offline.

Friendships of utility may exist on LinkedIn, friendships of pleasure may exist in double-tapping our friend's latest post on Instagram, but as long as we maintain perfect control over the encounter, we cannot truly share life, encounter, risk, accompany, and be with anyone behind a screen, full stop.

The maintenance of control, the lack of vulnerability, the inability to read body language, the unwillingness to engage outside the platform, absence of accountability—these are all things that I think lend credence to the position that online communities are not real communities. Or rather, maybe better stated, online communities are real **but not true** communities.

When I was quitting smoking I attended a Nicotine Anonymous meeting. I tried to find one in my area in person, but the lady who ran them formerly said there just wasn't enough interest in it in person. I went to a Zoom NA meeting instead. I can't describe it, but it left a lot to be desired, and I quit on my own without going to another one. Post-Covid, I have come to loathe Zoom for anything but the most utilitarian of work meetings.

Have you ever asked yourself why people are more lonely, more socially stunted (especially Millennials), more disconnected, more despairing today? You don't think maybe, just maybe, this type of contracepted "social" internet space contributes to that? Like, that your body could really use a hearty loaf of good bread to satisfy your hunger but instead you are sitting down with a bowl of Fruit Loops because that's what's in the pantry? We need to admit this "era of social media" was the Cultural Revolution of social engineering, a novel experiment that was bad for society, failing to deliver on its promises and better suited for the scrap pile of history.

I feel like I have enough years—decades almost—of skin in this game and experience in the online world to be able to reflect on it with some street cred. I've played the game and been around the block, and

ON FRIENDSHIP

I have nothing much to show for it, kind of like past one-night stands and hookups where one looks for connection, love, and yes, gratification and afterwards leaves emptyhanded. Always real, and never true.

I don't know where this leaves me currently, only that my time in prayer and time with my family has become deeper, heavier and yes, lonely at times, but in a good way—not empty, but real and painful because we are not meant solely for life here on earth but Eternity. I'm less willing to settle for counterfeits and Pavlov-like distractions now that I know what they promise and fail to deliver on, and I'm much less inclined to vainly attempt to fill up that loneliness with discussion/engagement/zoom/distraction for the sake of feeling connected to an ethereal community.

THE INS AND OUTS OF MALE FRIENDSHIP

My twenty year high school reunion is this weekend, at a bar in my hometown. I want to want to go, but I just don't. I didn't have a bad experience in high school; I had a good group of guy friends, and we would hang out in each other's basements shooting pool and watching Saturday Night Live reruns, take off after school on Friday afternoons to hike in the woods and walk the railroad tracks, play backyard football, and cruise around town in our cars. I wasn't a Christian then, and so it seems like another life when those things were what we were really living for. Our common bonds were, for the most part, external; it was what we did together that bound us.

I don't, however, remember feeling like I could always rely on them when it came to inner struggles. One close friend in particular was more fair weather than I may have liked. Though we had grown up together, he never visited me when I was hospitalized, and he only seemed to call for his own purposes—when he wanted to hang out, or no one else was around. It was never completely without some kind of self-gratifying ulterior motive. We reconnected a few years ago and I had hoped all that had changed, but I saw relatively quickly that it hadn't. I was someone to hang out and have a good time with when it was convenient or suited him, but beyond that there wasn't a whole lot that bound us together. It still kind of stings to this day.

ON FRIENDSHIP

Men are often pegged as simple, uncomplicated creatures. This is generally true when speaking about our needs—when we're fed, working, feel respected, and having marital relations regularly, we are 98% taken care of. It's not rocket science.

However, if there's one variance between men and women where the inverse proves to be true, it's in the realm of friendship. From my vantage point, making and maintaining female friendships as a woman appears to be vastly less complicated than what it takes to forge lasting male friendships. If women are really more relational in general, *being* relational comes naturally. For men, however—even the most normal, well-adjusted men—forming lasting friendships can feel akin to what it takes to dismantle a bomb. There are a lot of wires, and touch one to the wrong cathode and BOOM! Show's over.

Men tend to view friendships as optional and ancillary—good things that they may long for but not know how, or be willing, to forge. And yet we see article after article identifying the biggest threat facing middle-aged men isn't smoking or obesity, but *loneliness*. As I approach middle age, I can relate to this. It seems harder and harder to make friends. We are in a busy season—working, trying to advance in our careers, raising families, yard work and house maintenance.

Making friends as a guy can be tricky, though. There are a lot of factors and conditions that need to be right for the kernel of friendship to find good soil and take root. These are a few of the things that I have noticed:

1) Men do not just pick up the phone and call with a desire to relate their struggles or connect. If that is the objective, there needs to be an external modus operandi to facilitate the internal, something to "do." It could be going camping or building something, some activity to couch it in. Generally speaking, men do not call each other to get coffee and talk. Having a beer at the bar may be the exception to that rule, but it would have to be clear that the reason for getting together is the beer and not the talk.

2) Protestant men seem better equipped to support one another in their faith journey by means of "fellowship" and bible studies. I have heard Catholic men speak of such gatherings as effeminate (sharing,

talking, etc.); I don't necessarily think that is always the case, but the Catholic paradigm is one in which it is commonly posited that "the sacraments are all I need" or "I go to Mass to worship, not to meet other people." Men stand alone, as the thinking goes. If you're not isolated and holding your own on your own, there's a deficiency, a weakness, in your inability to stand on your own two feet.

3) You have to be mindful of the "weird" or "gay" factor. Men (and boys, generally) have a pretty strict code of conduct when it comes to revealing weakness and emotions in a group. No man, generally speaking, wants to be associated with effeminate men, because you might be regarded as effeminate by association. It sounds so stereotypical but there is truth in it, like it or not. Now, that being said, I feel pretty strongly that men with same sex attraction can benefit from friendship with heterosexual men, and that heterosexual men can extend such invitations to friendship as a mutually beneficial act of Christian charity and brotherhood. But the "maleness" aspect needs to take precedence over sexual identity, and that can sometimes be difficult for men with SSA to adjust to, because they don't know always know the codes and inner ways of relating in that way. That's okay; they are men first and foremost.

4) The mentor/mentee model works well with men. Again, it may necessitate revolving around some rite of passage or activity (working on a car together, for example), but the opportunities to pass on wisdom and life lessons are appreciated by both the one passing it on and the one receiving it.

St. Augustine had such a high regard for friendship that he posited it as one of two things in the world that are of the utmost importance:

> In this world two things are essential: life and friendship. Both should be highly prized and we must not undervalue them. Life and friendship are nature's gifts. God created us that we might exist and live: this is life. But if we are not to remain solitary, there must be friendship. [Sermon 16:1, Denis Translation]

ON FRIENDSHIP

As tricky as making friends as a guy in middle age can be, and as much as I have always wanted more from a friendship than seemed possible in this life, I still think it's indispensable for our social and spiritual well-being. No man is an island, no man is completely self-sufficient. It's perfectly fine to share common interests like sports and activities, but how much more so a common desire to cast ourselves on Christ and live the virtues? Friendship with other men, when it is built on the foundation of Christ, helps us to grow in holiness and shoulder each other's burdens. It doesn't have to be weird or awkward, but it more likely than not does require a degree of intentionality. As St. Thomas wrote, "There is nothing on this earth more to be prized than true friendship."

DO MEN NEED OTHER MEN?

Every now and then I will hear a story of an old lady who lives alone who passes away. Sometimes it is days or weeks before the super gets wind of it or anyone notices, and when they open the apartment, it's a dreadful smell of weeks-old death. I hate hearing stories like this, and yet I think it's more common than we think.

I'll confess to feeling a bit of resentment sometimes when my mind gets to speculating. I feel like I'm always checking in with people, but people rarely check in with me. Aside from my family, if I passed away in my room, how long before anyone would notice?

One of my personal Achilles' heels is being a relational person. Whereas most Catholic men are content to just be with their families and go to work, I feel I benefit from outside relationships. This often makes me feel like a defective archetype, a "less-than" man, and a shameful weakness. It's not normal to be like this. It's kind of womanly.

There was a helpful article I came across in Catholic Exchange on this topic. I'll quote a bit of it, as the author and I seem to be on the same frustrated page:

> "Do men, Catholic men, need the support of other Catholic men?" A few years ago, I asked this question of my friend, and

fellow parishioner, Jack. "Of course they do," he replied. "I couldn't get my job done at work without the support of the men in my department. And I'd go crazy from all the stress I'm under if I didn't go out every Sunday with my buddies from St. Mary's and play golf. You know, 'All work and no play makes Jack a dull guy.'"

"I see your point, Jack," I responded. "But that's not what I mean. Do Catholic men need to share their lives with other men on a personal level? Do men need to be part of a group in which they can build close relationships by sharing their personal and common struggles, pray for one another, support one another, and hold one another accountable to live an authentic Catholic Christian life of integrity?"

"Well, now you're talking about a whole new ball game," Jack replied. "What you're describing goes against the whole grain of who we are as men. By nature, men are created to be individualistic, strong, independent, self-reliant, self-sufficient, and guarded. We keep our distance from other men. We have to. Remember, men have always been the protectors of their family. Why, the highest compliment a man can receive is to be called a 'self-made man.'"

"I agree with you, Jack, that men have certain God-given characteristics so they can fulfill their roles as protectors and providers of their family. But let me ask you a couple of questions: Have there been times in your life when you felt helpless or lacked the power or wisdom to change things? I'm talking about destructive behavior in one of your kids, grave disagreements with your wife, or a splintered relationship with a family member. Have you ever felt powerless to fight certain temptations or sinful habits?"

At this point Jack got very quiet. Then he said, "How about the playoffs so far. I don't think the Yankees or Red Sox are going to make it. Wouldn't that be something?"

Jack is not alone in believing that when it comes to our personal lives, men are not called to share them with other men. Yet, if we are honest with ourselves, we all know how difficult it is for men and their families to thrive in today's culture. The ever-increasing demands on men's time and energies and the collapse of traditional values and support structures underscore this challenge. Yet, I do not believe that God intended for Catholic men to live out their faith on their own.

Times have indeed changed. We're working harder, our schedules are tight, and what little time we have is often used for television, sports, or activities that help us unwind. This has led to men having even more superficial relationships with other men. In spite of this, I do not think most Catholic men even consider that they need to be part of a group that prays together, or to have committed brothers in Christ who could offer prayer and sound advice to help them through difficult circumstances.

I will confess to feeling frustration with my local men's group, but it's not their fault—I find we connect well over "things"—events, shooting guns, worship events, bible study, social things, etc. But rarely do any of us get "real" enough to share our struggles with one another. We struggle alone. Part of me understands this, and part of my frustration bubbles up in saying, "well, what's the point of this, then?"

Years ago there was a guy from our old parish, a few years younger than me with a large family who had some struggles with the common sins for men, as well as scruples. He was a blue collar guy, but sensitive enough to reach out and share a degree of vulnerability. I was doing my best to give him support and some guidance, sharing resources, etc., but eventually like a rubber band the relationship snapped back into the "I only need my family and not other men" mode. And I never heard from him again.

I think all this goes back to that issue of expecting more from people than they may be willing to give. Just because I find I need support and relationships with other people, doesn't mean other men do. Part of me gets in this "well, screw this" mode and retreats, trying to be more like them: self-contained, not reaching out when struggling, keeping to oneself, etc.—but it's just not how I'm wired. So I end up getting resentful—both that I'm not more like the other guys, and part that they're not more like me (and that I'm able to relate to someone on the same level).

Augustine writes beautifully on the need for friendship, and that Christian friendship is the highest ideal. The love between two men is a beautiful thing, but many men are uncomfortable with it because it feels gay and too vulnerable. But Augustine had this with Alypius (as he recounts in his *Confesssions*), and that love was not superficial or surface level. Today this is a rare thing indeed; if it exist, I have not found it.

So, the question remains: do men really need other? Their wives might say, "yes, totally." And maybe a man might even think deep down inside he could benefit from it. But I rarely find a man willing to say, "I need a brother in Christ to help me be accountable, help carry my cross, push me, etc." We have these group things like Exodus 90, etc. where there's this warrior/knight/soldier archetype which is kind of generic and works for a lot of guys, but I find I just don't operate that way. I have a lot of guys I know—but not "one good friend" who I feel I can confide in, or if I can, that he would feel the same way. Like the U2 song goes, "I still haven't found what I'm looking for."

I DON'T BELONG HERE ANYMORE

In getting ready to appear as a guest on EWTN's "The Journey Home" next week, I have been going over the past twenty years in my head. Why did I become a Catholic? What attracted me to the Christ, to the Church? Where did I come from, and what does it all mean?

My story is a bit of a "conversion wrapped in a reversion." In outlining it in chronological order (so I can keep things straight in my head for the show), I realized that the timeline looked like a weightlifters barbell—two significant years on the beginning end, two significant years on the other end, and long stretch of "in-between" floundering to live the faith with integrity from age 18 to 36. I'd like to shelve the beginning part of that journey for now and focus on a detail I had forgotten about until I started writing it down.

It was the summer of 2016, and I was in Colorado for a bachelor party. Now, ever since high school I have loved to party, and even as a new Catholic I never stopped. I went to parties, threw parties, and would party into the morning with friends. I never had a drinking problem, but temperance was a virtue I had trouble developing. I prayed, went to Mass every Sunday, read spiritual books, but was "friends with the world" (John 15:19), trying to have my cake and eat it too.

ON FRIENDSHIP

This particular bachelor party I was not really looking forward to attending, but I had to, for various reasons. The guys were younger, and I knew they partied hard; I was getting older, but still susceptible to influence. The first day I tried to not partake in any of the revelry, but concupiscence and appetites are a funny thing, and by day two I was crushing the opposition in drinking games. I found myself mirroring Paul's words, "I do not understand what I do. For what I want to do I do not do, but what I hate I do" (Rom 7:15).

At one point near the end of the weekend I went in my room in the mountain house the crew had rented and sat on the bed. I wasn't in full on praying mode, but I was really hoping God could get me out of being there. Nobody else there seemed to have any pangs of conscience or problem with going full tilt since they weren't believers, and yet here I was, feeling the tension of having one foot in the world and one foot in the Church, not living as a good example as a Christian, and not be able to go in with full abandon either.

I always carried a small Gideon bible with me whenever I traveled. I took it out and sat on the bed and prayed a quick prayer for help. I remember to this day, I opened it and the first thing I read was

> Put to death, therefore, whatever belongs to your earthly nature: sexual immorality, impurity, lust, evil desires and greed, which is idolatry. Because of these, the wrath of God is coming. You used to walk in these ways, in the life you once lived. But now you must rid yourself of all such things as these: anger, rage, malice, slander, and filthy language from your lips. Do not lie to each other, since you have taken off your old self with its practices and you have put on the new self, which is being renewed in knowledge in the image of its Creator. (Col 3:5-10)

I was struck dumb. I recalled the story of St. Augustine in the garden, picking up the scriptures at the words he heard from a child, "Take up and read, take up and read." What he read was this:

> Not in carousing and drunkenness, not in sexual excess and lust, not in quarreling and jealousy. Rather, put on the Lord Jesus Christ, and make no provision for the desires of the flesh. (Rom 13: 13-14)

I called a Christian friend back home, a man of integrity, and told him what had happened when I opened the scripture, what I landed upon, and how it cut to the heart and left me exposed to my inconsistency. He was encouraging, but in that room I felt alone in a crowd. I didn't belong there anymore.

In the *Imitation of Christ*, Thomas à Kempis wrote about this wretched "in between" state of a lukewarm religious in a way that hit home:

> A fervent religious accepts all the things that are commanded him and does them well, but a negligent and lukewarm religious has trial upon trial, and suffers anguish from every side **because he has no consolation within and is forbidden to seek it from without**. The religious who does not live up to his rule exposes himself to dreadful ruin, and he who wishes to be more free and untrammeled will always be in trouble, for something or other will always displease him. (Chap 25)

Fence-sitting had never born a lot of fruit in my life. Reading the Word of God in the passage in Colossians made me realize it is a lousy place to be, and that friendship with world makes one an enemy of God (James 4:4). Who was I kidding? I had to get off the fence. The past two years has been a series of grace-encounters and renewal that have sifted weeds from wheat in my life and introduced me to people that don't make me feel like so much of an outsider in my faith.

We all need that from time to time, being called to be in the world but not of the world. I pray for the grace to take that to heart, and to never go back to straddling the line. Now when it comes to my faith, I'm invested. It informs my choices, even when they come with costs. I'm in too deep. Thankfully, there's nowhere to go but deeper.

CAN PEOPLE WITH DIFFERENT VALUES TRULY BE FRIENDS?

This morning I texted an old friend of 15 years something I saw on the topic of bachelor vs. married life. My friend is not a Christian, but we've always stayed in touch and hung out. We spent our twenties and early thirties in the city, so I guess he just came to mind. I thought it was an interesting diatribe on the shallowness of material living (specifically, in this case, young urbanites) that is fun at first but gets lonelier as one ages if they stay in it. I thought it gave some food for thought. He responded that he thought it was judgmental, negative, and narrow minded.

I don't have an issue with people being of different opinions about things. But it did give me pause and made me kind of reflect on the life cycle of our friendship. What bound us together? Was it that we went to bars together and lived in the same geographic locale? Was there anything deeper? I kind of assumed there was, just by virtue of the years, but I'm not sure. We live near each other, and we like riding bikes. Beyond that, I'm not sure.

It also made me think more fundamentally, "Well, what is a friend? What is friendship, really? What constitutes a friend?"

When it comes down to it, I am an Augustinian at heart. My conversion to the faith came by way of dissatisfaction with the temporal nature of the world—I wanted something true, something beautiful, something that would last. "Love is real, not fade away," as Jerry Garcia said. My friendships in high school were solid but, looking back, shallow and utilitarian; I wanted more than my friends could give, I think. One of my closest friends in particular I realized years later really didn't care about me, as close as we were. I was just someone to occupy time with.

Years later, I would lose another good friend of many years over the issue of gay marriage. I remember Jennifer Fulwiler when she still talked and wrote about Catholic things recounting this elephant in the room with one of her close (gay) friends when he asked her, "So, what do you think of gay marriage?"

> At the end of the evening—way too late, as always—we all exchanged hugs and promised that we'd do this more often. I watched Andrew and Tom walk away, holding hands, and prayed that I hadn't done a totally terrible job of articulating my beliefs. I hoped that, if nothing else, he understood that there is no contradiction between me being a faithful Catholic and a close friend of his. I have converted to the religion of the crucifix, a belief system that promises joy in exchange for losing it all. Most people don't want to sign up for that. I get that. I hope they consider it, for their own sake, since their lives would be better if they did — but it doesn't change how I feel about them if they don't. As the guys disappeared down the street, I hoped Andrew knew how much I loved him and Tom, and I hoped they still loved me too.

I'm not sure if "Andrew" is still in Jen's life, but I would be surprised if he was. Not that it's not possible. But at some point, there is a degree of eggshell naiveté the older we get when belief systems, race, class, religion, and politics are different. We tend to homogenize over time according to our values. My sophomore year of college I read a book *Why Are All the Black Kids Sitting Together in The Cafeteria?* by Beverly Tatum. The title alone suggests that it's not an uncommon sociological phenomenon. Race, like friendship, is complex.

While I hate to say it, but I'm no exception. I have no gay friends, no Muslim friends, no African American friends, no truly poor friends. It's not for lack of trying or desire. I consider myself pretty open minded. But it just seems like the natural state of things. Perhaps you're in the same boat.

Friendship is complex, and for some individuals (like those, I imagine, with Autism or social anxieties) it can be frustratingly elusive. Cicero defined friendship as "a perfect conformity of opinions upon all religious and civil subjects, united with the highest degree of mutual esteem an affection." Augustine adopted this pat definition early in his life as a rhetorician, but as he aged and matured the subject became for him more complex. Mike Aquilina of the St. Paul Center notes—

> It's not the agreement of religious and civil subjects that makes friends. It's the grace God gives us that allows us to love others and become friends. That means **the only real friendship is Christian friendship.**

That's something, isn't it? "*The only real friendship is Christian friendship.*" I'm at the point in my life when my time is in short supply, and I have to make sure it's being utilized judiciously. Why waste time with what's not authentic? I want the real deal, and if that means that the only real friendships in my life are because they are built on a Christian foundation, then so be it. Some men don't have any friends, or maybe one or two....and sometimes by choice. It might not even bother them—their family and their job and their solitude may be enough for them. The Age of Social Media adds an additional layer of obfuscation. We were not meant to have 1k+ "friends." The term itself in this context is a misnomer.

As for me, like the way our unhinged society is debating "What is a man? What is a woman?", I am wrestling with this question that is maybe bigger in my life than it should be: What constitutes a friend? Do I have any true friends? Why have so many people come into my life...and ultimately exited as well? Does anyone truly know my heart, is there for me unselfishly? Am I for them? What does it mean to love someone? To be a true friend?

SUBVERSION THROUGH FRIENDSHIP

Daryl Davis is a fascinating man...my kind of guy. The R&B musician, who made a point of befriending members of the KKK as a way of coaxing the white hoods out of their grip, said this:

> The most important thing I learned is that when you are actively learning about someone else you are passively teaching them about yourself. So if you have an adversary with an opposing point of view, give that person a platform. Allow them to air that point of view, regardless of how extreme it may be. And believe me, I've heard things so extreme at these rallies they'll cut you to the bone.
>
> Give them a platform.
>
> You challenge them. But you don't challenge them rudely or violently. You do it politely and intelligently. And when you do things that way chances are they will reciprocate and give you a platform. So he and I would sit down and listen to one another over a period of time. And the

cement that held his ideas together began to get cracks in
it. And then it began to crumble. And then it fell apart.

I've seen the Socratic method in action, mostly on social media and through those who are steeped in logic and love to debate, like Ben Shapiro. I'm sure it works to change minds on issue in some cases and there's a place for it. But most people steeped in ignorance are not thinking logically, not connecting on that level. It also belies the adage that I find to be true, "no one cares what you know until they know that you care." So, Davis' unorthodox approach to winning someone over is attractive to me, and after going into the lion's den and leading more than 200 Klansmen away from their formerly racist life, it's hard to argue that it doesn't work.

I think this approach could have potential in the work of pro-life activism. It's a different approach, for sure. Most of the time, the escorts and pro-abortion activists are dug in because they see us as the enemy. They are on the defensive. And we see their actions and ideology as abhorrent (which it is). But rarely do we "cross the aisle" with an open mind—not to agree with what they believe, but to say, "you know, let's suspend that for a moment and just meet on a human level." There would be many that wouldn't agree; you don't sit down with murderers or invite them into your home to share a meal. You hold up your signs and yell from the sidewalk in order to get your point across. In it, you make clear what side you are on.

There is one of Aesop's fables that speaks to this:

The North Wind and the Sun had a quarrel about which of them was the stronger. While they were disputing with much heat and bluster, a Traveler passed along the road wrapped in a cloak.

"Let us agree," said the Sun, "that he is the stronger who can strip that Traveler of his cloak."

"Very well," growled the North Wind, and at once sent a cold, howling blast against the Traveler.

With the first gust of wind the ends of the cloak whipped about the Traveler's body. But he immediately wrapped it closely around him, and the harder the Wind blew, the tighter he held it to him. The North Wind tore angrily at the cloak, but all his efforts were in vain.

Then the Sun began to shine. At first his beams were gentle, and in the pleasant warmth after the bitter cold of the North Wind, the Traveler unfastened his cloak and let it hang loosely from his shoulders. The Sun's rays grew warmer and warmer. The man took off his cap and mopped his brow. At last he became so heated that he pulled off his cloak, and, to escape the blazing sunshine, threw himself down in the welcome shade of a tree by the roadside.

What if we just suspended our disgust and did this kind of dirty work of risky engagement? I like Davis' out of the box thinking. He's not about the sides or the image or caring what team people think he's on or doing things just to be seen as putting in the effort: he's doing what he's doing to get results. Davis again:

> I had one guy from an NAACP branch chew me up one side and down the other, saying, "You know, we've worked hard to get 10 steps forward. Here you are sitting down with the enemy having dinner, you're putting us 20 steps back."
>
> I pull out my robes and hoods and say, "Look, this is what I've done to put a dent in racism. I've got robes and hoods hanging in my closet by people who've given up that belief because of my conversations sitting down to dinner. They gave it up. How many robes and hoods have you collected?" And then they shut up."

What can we learn from this kind of unorthodox method of converting those most "out there?" Well, for one it seems to square with the Christian ethos of "Love your enemies, do good to those who hate you, bless those who curse you, pray for those who mistreat you." (Lk 6:27-28). So it's a betrayal of nothing, except maybe what we are used to doing in conventional ways. Christ walked straight through Samaria. He picked up a woman from the dirt rather than stone her. He tells the parable of the Good Samaritan to illustrate the point of those who love the unlovable in spite of the convention that says not to.

Two, it gives new meaning to the dirty word "dialogue." I don't think dialogue is necessarily a bad thing, except when it becomes masturbatory. Part of Davis' background as a child of foreign service workers was exposure to and being educated in different cultures from all over the world at an early age. So, there was a lot to learn from others. And the more extreme cases, the better it works. But, as Davis says,

> There are a lot of well-meaning white liberals. And a lot of well-meaning black liberals. But you know what? When all they do is sit around and preach to the choir it does absolutely no good. If you're not a racist it doesn't do any good for me to meet with you and sit around and talk about how bad racism is.

Third, it challenges our faith in a way that gets us out of our bubbles and echo chambers. If you are strong in your faith, you don't have to fear. We are not given a spirit of fear, but of power, and of love, and of sobriety (2 Tim 1:7). It gives us a missionary heart in our own wicked country. It allows us to work one by one in the work of converting the culture. Because you are putting yourself out there with the potential of embarrassment or failure, it tests your resolve. Then again, what do you *really* have to lose? If you invite a pro-abort to have coffee, or a rabid atheist over for dinner, the worst they can do is say no.

Finally, I think this kind of technique works well when you are very open-minded, and not invested in the outcome, but willing to just ride the boat to wherever it drifts to. Not everyone is open to friendship or being open minded—but some may be. Some may be on the precipice of changing their mind about what they are involved in, but no one has extended a hand to them. That hand could be yours. Bubbles are safe, comfortable. We know what those in our bubbles believe, and you are "let in" because of that.

But walking into a lion's den filled with those who hate you and extending your hand—there's something to that, something admirable. Something that requires not only Christian faith, but faith in humanity and a willingness to think outside the conventional box. I wouldn't believe it if Mr. Davis' didn't have the hoods to prove that it has potential. But he does. And so I do.

WHAT DOES IT MEAN TO BE FAITHFUL?

Something occurred to me when it comes to Calvinists: no one who attends your run-of-the-mill Presbyterian church on a typical Sunday would consider themselves reprobate. According to Calvin's theology of double predestination, God chooses some to be saved (the Elect) and some to be damned. If one is not part of the Elect (and, thus, reprobate or damned), there is nothing you can do about it. No point in attending church on Sundays or living a moral life, because this is not a matter of free agency, but God's salvific grace that has passed you by. You're damned if you do and damned if you don't, so to speak. It would logically follow then that those in the pews listing to Rev. Lovejoy's sermon at First Presbyterian must presume themselves as part of the Elect because, otherwise...well, why bother?

Of course, as Catholics, we know this "double predestination" is heresy and not the true nature of God, for 'The Lord delayeth not his promise, as some imagine, but dealeth patiently for your sake, not willing that any should perish, but that all should return to penance" (2 Peter 3:9). It is the mystery of the cooperation with grace and that man may be redeemed by choosing the good—not the total depravity purported by Calvin—that gives Catholics hope. No one is beyond His terrible mercy. We are not pre-determined to damnation.

On the other hand, you have the "once saved, always saved" contingent among Evangelicals who, unlike Catholics, do not believe that one can lose their salvation once they have been "born again." "Wherefore he that thinketh himself to stand, let him take heed lest he fall" St. Paul tells the church at Corinth (1 Cor 10:12). To these Christians, perdition is not possible for a child of God to sin in such a way that he will be lost. And yet, they may find themselves on the outside of the door on account of failing to carry out God's will, being told "I never knew you" (Mt 7:23). "And all the people shall hear and fear, and no longer act presumptuously" (Deuteronomy 17:9-13).

Somewhere in the middle, the Catholic finds himself. He knows he is a child of God and member of His family by nature of his baptism. He "has been saved, is being saved, and hopes to be saved." He knows "none is righteous, no not one" (Ps 14:1) and yet he knows if he has sinned mortally he is one confession away from Paradise. He knows even should he ascend the heights of sanctity, like the Ladder of Divine Ascent icon of Mt. Sinai, though he may be two rungs from the gates of Heaven, demons stand ready to pick him off by way of pride, presumption, and other temptations to drag him to the worm that never dies waiting for him below. The Catholic recognizes this tension, and the mystery of salvation, that we can't wrap up in a box-and-bow and put in our back pocket.

As a married man, I am always cognizant of the fact that my faithfulness, or that of my wife's, is not a guarantee in which one can sit back on their laurels in self-assurance. When the Lord tells Joshua after the death of Moses to lead the people he instructs him "to be careful to obey all the law my servant Moses gave you; do not turn from it to the right or to the left." (Joshua 1:7).

In marriage, it is the "looks to the left and to the right" that can get you in trouble. We make these vows when we stand on the altar "to be true...in good times and in bad, in sickness and in health...to love you and honor you all the days of my life." There is an exclusivity there that can be undermined in a moment, even after years or decades of faithfulness. One lie makes a liar. One affair makes an adulterer.

Aside from the Lord, and my parents and immediate family, I have put all my eggs in the basket of my wife that she will be with me, and I with her, til death. That radical kind of exclusive trust—faith even—

in another human being who has the capacity to hurt you more than anyone on earth and is privy to your darkest secrets, allows for a love that surpasses that of common relationships.

I have always been faithful to my wife for the eleven years we have been married, and she has always been faithful to me. What would it take to drive her away? Infidelity? Violence? Financial Ruin? We have not been through these trials to date. I trust her with our children, our finances, and my very life. She has a greater capacity to hurt me than anyone I know. And yet she refrains from doing so for the most part, out of faithfulness. I, for my part, try to do the same.

My issue, however, is not with my wife, but questioning what it means to be faithful to the Lord in the context of my relationship with Him. I can only think of this relationship as it relates to marriage, because my faith and my marriage are my two bedrocks when everything else seems to be shifting beneath my feet, particularly when it comes to friends.

I had a text exchange with a close friend the other day that got heated. It affected me more than I thought it would, and I was out of sorts for days. I have friends who I rarely talk to anymore who I thought I was close with on account of all this stupid vax 'n mask stuff. I'm realizing that these are not unconditional relationships, but dependent on a minimum of congealing factors that can fluctuate depending on circumstances.

"We should esteem highly health and friendship," St. Augustine writes, "and we may never despise these. Health and friendship are natural goods. God created the human being so that he or she could exist and live a life that is healthy. But in order that the human being should not be alone, he or she desires friendship. Now, friendship begins with wife and children, and then reaches out to strangers." [Sermon 299D.16.1]

It has always been hard for me to accept that friends or people I am close with now may not be here in five or ten years. I may slight them in some way, step out of line, and without the assurances of the kind of bond I have in my marriage, that they will always be there. I once got very angry at a friend in high school who said they loved me unconditionally, because I took it as a lie. Friendship almost always comes with conditions and can be hard to be faithful to through thick and thin. "The saddest thing about betrayal is it never comes from your enemies," as the saying goes.

I even question how faithful I am to the Lord these days, and how I show Him that faithfulness and how I love Him. This comes by way of comparison, I think, when I see principled people taking morally admirable stands at great costs to prove their fidelity to what they believe, and publicly so. They have a tribe, small as it may be, but fiercely loyal. I have been mediating, instead, on the words of the Lord, "who has no place to lay his head" (Lk 9:58).

As much as I started this post with thinking about Calvinists and their presumption of being part of the Elect, I had also been giving a lot of thought to the *traditors* and the Donatists of the 4th century. Donatists adopted "Deo laudes" ("God be praised") as their slogan to counter the ancient Catholic "Deo gratias" ("Thanks be to God"). This was the rallying cry with which they harangued Catholics. One distinctive characteristic of the Donatists was their desire for martyrdom. Donatus taught that death for the "cause," even death by suicide, was holy and merited a martyr's crown and eternal life. They did their best to incite Catholics and pagans to kill them. When their provocations failed, they sometimes took their own lives, a favored method being to leap from high cliffs with the cry "Deo laudes!"

It is not sin that turns us into *traditors*, Judases, but kisses. We exchange our loyalty in the inner circle for silver pieces offered by outsiders, enemies. And when we realize the depths of the betrayal, a Judas does not weep as Peter does, but despairs unto death. He is cast out, but also casts himself out into darkness.

What does it mean to be a faithful friend, a faithful Christian, and a faithful spouse? To not betray with a kiss? It may be too much (I have always been "too much") to think one could be loved and befriended "unconditionally." I have been hurt, and I have hurt. I have always wanted my friends to (unrealistically) stay awake with me perpetually in the garden of my dark night.

WISDOM AND FOLLY

And yet all my friends become strangers at some point, and I mourn it every time like the seasons. Like the dunes that remain after the tide rolls out, my faith, wife, and family remain.

ON DISCIPLESHIP

THE TIME FOR TEACHING AND PREACHING IS OVER

 asked a friend this evening, "Do people read books anymore?"
"No. They don't," he replied.
"What's the point, then?" I asked.
"The people who read books like those that you or I or anyone of like mind might write have all read what we have to say by better people. And the thing is, nobody who needs to read your words ever will. The target audience is immune."

I thanked him for the reality check and confirming what I already suspected. "Everyone is over exposed and over published," I said. "The like-minded end up having conversations with the same pool of people. It's all been heard."

This friend of mine, I know, has eyes that see—maybe too much sometimes. But I know I can turn to him to get it straight. Then he went on to say something that stopped me dead, because I had been thinking it for a long time without the words to express it:

"I once had a vigorous disagreement with a religious, who was absolutely right. He said, 'The time for preaching and teaching is over.' I was shocked by that, but...he was profoundly right."

"What did he mean by it?" I asked, still reeling a bit from the cold stiff truth.

"He meant it on a large scale, a metaphysical scale, a historical epoch scale. Not that one couldn't teach and such...but that the preparations now are not evangelistic. They are one hundred percent witness and prayer."

I had to take this to prayer. I crawled on my hands and knees into the "hidden room" (which is really just a three foot by twelve foot pipe closet) where I had moved my kneeler and crucifix and icon, to have a little bit more hiddenness to finish my rosary. I joke with my priest friends that it can double as a priest hole if things get bad, or a kind of spiritual entombment where no one would even know where you were in the house if you wanted to be so hidden. Though I crawl in in the middle of the night for late night prayer, I could probably make better use of it. It's like a writer's desk—you get the perfect desk, and then you find yourself with writer's block all of a sudden.

What did this religious mean, "the time for preaching and teaching is over?" My first reaction when my friend mentioned it was YES. But then, why? Haven't the Word on Fire videos brought many spiritually curious people to intellectual assent of the faith? Haven't we been learning to make "intentional disciples" in parishes and through workshops and conferences and retreats? Haven't we been DOING something to address the "failure of catechesis" by LEARNING more about what the Church professes, TEACHING more about the truths of the Faith, EVANGELIZING by having discussions on social media with non-believers? Haven't we been preaching the good news to the poor, the imprisoned, as a kind of spiritual product to be considered to improve one's life, gain eternal life, attain peace?

I'm sorry to be so negative, but I'm in a bit of a stripped down state of being right now. The words my friend shared by the erudite religious—the time of preaching and teaching is over—point to a harsh and unsettling reality we are faced with as followers of Christ in war.

In fighting off demons of despair shooting arrows in my back, another wise friend also sent me a scripture that made me exclaim, once again, "Wow":

> And the places that have been desolate for ages shall be built in thee: thou shalt raise up the foundations of generation and

generation: and thou shalt be called the repairer of the fences, turning the paths into rest (Is 58:12).

But we are not in this state yet either, I suspect. We are in an in between. The well-produced teaching and catechetical materials, the preaching to a pagan culture—I have lived through these endeavors and been a part of them myself. I don't know how effective they are, or if they are making wrong assumptions about things. I do have a friend who makes rosaries and plants them for people with instructions on how to pray it; he does is clandestinely. Someone he knew even picked one up and considered it a sign to come back to the faith. So you never know.

But we are not saving masses here, we are pulling stray bodies on the ark who, I'm sure, are ultimately grateful to be there. Like writing a book these days, it is, I'm afraid, ultimately futile. Not to those who have been saved, who would consider it anything but. And there is it's place—of course, we need to preach and teach when called for, one on one. But we are not going to convert the world by well-produced series on the history of Catholicism or using any of the tools of the modern age. Those going to the front lines are getting *mowed down* by the culture because they are ultimately going alone with no shepherds to have their back, no critical mass to support them long term. The Steubenville degree and Thomistic defenses of Natural Law in a disordered society, I'm afraid, may not hold their weight against the breaches.

"We are living in the age of witness and prayer." Bold witness and confident prayer, the kind that works miracles. What does this mean? What does it look like?

I attended First Friday Mass this evening and there was a new face, a young woman who has fallen away from the faith and somehow found the only Latin Mass in the state and showed up. She seemed moved, hungry, but just mostly willing to recognize it as an outpost in an otherwise harsh wasteland, one that she seemed especially grateful for. We made small talk after Mass, and I told her we all hope to see her again and when Mass times were, that she was welcome, that it is a respite from the war. I think she will be back. "That some might be saved," as St. Paul writes to the Corinthians, being all things to all men.

Do we really need more books? More blogs and podcasts? More catechetical materials? More parish programs? Everything is being stripped down around us, maybe it's time to strip our faith down to the essentials as well, the powerful essentials rather than tepid peripheries. To pray well, to witness boldly. To strip out what is not needed, to enter into the loneliness of stepping outside the kind of matrix-esque mirage of technical engineering and just get back to square one. Then count the cost and do the work ahead of us but knowing that our time is running short, and things are ramping up—a time in which teaching and preaching may very well fall on deaf ears, and in which prayer and witness is all we have.[1]

---

[1] This essay appeared in *Catholic Stand* (catholicstand.com) on January 28, 2021

SAY IT WITH A SMILE

At our bible study last week, one of the guys' wives made a delicious zucchini bread. Zucchini is one of those vegetables that's relatively easy to "hide and sneak" into a recipe without your kids being the wiser. Nobody's a big fan of vegetables, though we all know they are good for us and that we *should* eat them.

Hard truth can an unpalatable thing, difficult for many people to swallow. Perhaps on account of their blindness, trauma, or even social conditioning, people often reject obvious truths reflexively and before even considering its merits.

As I have observed, it is often the unfortunate tendency of orthodox Catholics who love and live for Truth to adopt the same outrage reflex as the Left when it comes to things like heresy, hypocrisy, and societal dishonesty. Fr. James Martin tweets "pastoral" heretical garbage? Get up in arms. Twitter war started by the SJWs? Get the clubs, bro.

I once took issue with a friend over the place of "tone" in truth-telling and, by extension, evangelization. My friend was a big fan of the Timothy Gordons and the Fr. Altmans because they didn't mince words. I can't listen to these guys, even though they sometimes have the right message. My friend thought tone didn't matter; that is, *how* you say what you're saying shouldn't matter if what you are saying is true. I thought that was simplistic.

The truth is, I think we were both kind of oversimplifying things. St. Augustine initially preferred Cicero to the dull sheen of the Christian scriptures because in his eyes the gospels lacked sophistication and rhetorical beauty. And yet, it is the Word that is the way, the truth, and the life (Jn 14:6). Its essence is not in its beautiful language or power of persuasion, but because it is the Truth itself. To my friend's credit, there is a place for the unpolished John the Baptists of the world, of whom there is none greater born of woman (Mt 11:11).

That being said, I still hold that there is a case for *how* one says something; i.e., that tone matters. The old adage rings true here, I think: no one cares what you know until they know that you care. A stranger can quote all the bible verses and catechism at a person they want; if the person doesn't trust the messenger, however, it is likely that the ground is not fertile for the seed of faith to sprout. St. Paul did not write one blanket epistle to all the communities of believers irrespective of their cultural and religious context but tailored each letter specific to that particular church. St. Damien did not endear himself to the lepers of Molokai simply because he was a priest, but because he showed genuine love and concern towards them, caring for them not in the abstract but in the wretched physicality of their illness.

Those opposed to Truth, who are blinded to it, are conditioned to adopt a posture of resistance. The light has come into the world, but men prefer the darkness, as scripture says (Jn 3:19). Force-feeding zucchinis, even if it did work, tends to diminish the dignity of the person having it rammed down his or her throat. You can't make people love truth and beauty, but you can present it as something worthy of love. When an enemy of Truth is locked into a rigid, defensive stance of opposition, they are anticipating locking arms in battle. It is an art of war, then, to flank their sensibilities where they least expect them as a way of disarming. When they are stunned and vulnerable, it is then that one moves in to lay the lethal blow.

We are Christians, not mercenaries. We do battle first with ourselves, seeking to smother our own egos and selfishness in our cell with the pillow of virtue and mortification. Infused with the grace of faith, hope, and charity and having obtained a modicum of mastery of our own wily natures, we approach our enemies in self-defense, not active aggression. We heap coals upon their heads by opposing our lower natures and instincts--feeding them when they are hungry, giving them drink in thirst (Rom 12:20). In the face of aggression, we turn our cheek to take a blow on the other side.

What does this look like practically, this "stun and gun" method of Truth-delivery? We must always speak the truth, but to sweeten the spoon we should do it...with a smile.

We already know that our culture supports the "empty shell" (as Pope Benedict XVI said) of love without truth, which is filled with emotional influences which in the worst case can result in love turning into its opposite. "The individual who is animated by true charity **labours skillfully** to discover the causes of misery, to find the means to combat it, to overcome it resolutely" (Pope St. Paul VI, *Populorum progressio*, emphasis mine).

Imagine an instance in which we are put on the spot in our place of work to affirm that, say, abortion is a kind of healthcare, or that one's sex is irrelevant to their personhood. We can refute their assertion with firmness but disarm them with the smile of charity. In doing so we imitate the Savior, whom Isaiah prophesized would

> not shout or cry out, or raise his voice in the streets. A bruised reed he will not break, and a smoldering wick he will not snuff out (Is 42:1-4).

For those poised to fight, a smile is the last thing they expect to see. It is important that it is not a self-assured smirk or an insincere saccharine gesture. Our charity must bleed through the lips to stun and melt the hearts of our adversaries in that moment, to transmit that like our Savior, we have not come to condemn but to save. They may resent us for our presumption to claim to not only know the Truth but to possess it; they may spurn our outstretched hands extended from the lifeboat and choose in pride their own demise. They may hate us.

And yet if we love them in that moment, and let our charity bleed through our eyes, lips, and hearts to communicate that love in that opportune moment of disarmament when they are most vulnerable, we may have the chance to win our brother. In this case, tone does matter because the tone is charity itself. Charity is not a force easily argued against. Because by its nature it is not composed of rhetoric or empty words, but indisputable action which flows through the current of grace. It proves itself, rests on its own two feet. "True virtue is not sad or disagreeable, but pleasantly cheerful" (St. Josemaria Escriva).

Love completely confounds its adversaries. It may not completely appease the mob. It may not keep us from getting strung up a tree. But if we can display our charity in a resolute smile during such attacks as a means of momentary disarmament, it may be enough to blind and confound so that we can slip in a letter of Truth in that moment. And once Truth takes hold in a soul, nourished by the light of grace and sprouting in the darkness, there is no telling the lies it will untie in the process. We may win our brother in the end.

WHY IS IT SO HARD TO BE GOOD?

In titling this post I was primarily reflecting upon my own experience, specifically with regards to this awful-lousy-no-good-very-bad whole food/plant based diet I've been trying out. My intentions were good—to cut out animal products, eggs, dairy, oil, etc., for my health and heart—and the science seems to back it up.

But my inner foodie-concupiscence has been rearing up. I started out well for the first few weeks—lots of leafy greens, beans and legumes, quinoa, sweet potatoes, vegetables, etc. Then I got kind of...bored. I would catch myself grouchily thinking "I just want a freaking burger, is that so wrong?"

Admittedly, I hadn't acquired a good habit of "eating clean," so it felt onerous. I would get cases of the "Screw-Its" more frequently, where I would just throw out my good intentions, knowing whatever it was I was going to eat was not especially healthy. A book I listened to on audiobook about this diet extolled how it can extend your life for years. I was thinking to myself, "why would I want to do that, when this doesn't feel like living at all?" Ha.

I always go back to the pivotal epistle of St. Paul (Romans 8) when it comes to this mystery of knowing the good and being unable (or unwilling) to carry it out with regard to sin. "I do that which I do not want to do." When I would teach and give lessons in the prison, I would read from Romans often. So many of the guys in there seem to know what is good and simply feel unable to carry it out based on their past or their lack of acquired virtue and good habits.

St. Thomas defines virtue as a good habit bearing on activity. But it was interesting to me to realize that Aristotle was wrestling with this as well way before that, before Christ, as he said, "it is no easy task to be good." I only read that after titling this post, but it affirmed this consistent struggle with concupiscence that affects all men and Christians, from the sinner straight up to the saint.

According to Aristotle, the aim of all virtue is the mean, to avoid what he calls the "excess and defect;" i.e., too much or too little. Excess would be considered "a form of failure, and so is defect, while the intermediate is praised and is a form of success."

For St. Thomas, "the act of virtue is nothing else than the good use of free will." Knowing the good comes from grace, from the Holy Spirit, and from the teachings of Christ, the Church, and the Commandments. Carrying out the good is within our power when we cooperate with grace, but this is where habit comes in.

I have always regarded our inherent concupiscence as the attraction which takes resistance to overcome; that our natural inclination deep within is towards what is good, true, and holy; but that because of the Fall, we are like leaves that float where the current takes them because...well, let's face it, it's easier to go with the flow. Acquiring virtue is arduous, because it depends on the work of developing habit, and it is called work for a reason. To know something is possible—our sanctification—does not make it immediately attainable. If it was, why would our Lord say the "straight is the gate and narrow is the way which leadeth to life, and few find it?" (Mt 7:14).

I love St. Philip Neri's exhortation to his followers: "Well, brothers, when will we begin to do good?" This is the essence of our work, our habit, and our calling as Christians: to acquire virtue not as an end in itself, but to carry out the work of the Lord in our own lives, and to show others the way as well. He gives us the grace to "be good" (i.e., virtuous) because "those who ask, receive" (Mt 7:7). To do so leads to our own happiness in this life, even when we suffer, and sets us up for it in the next life as well.

ON DISCIPLESHIP

The 'work' of Christian living is knowing that what is not always pleasant or pleasing to the senses is often in effect good for the soul, and so our task in overcoming concupiscence by the exercise of the will (the work) helps to develop this good habit St. Thomas talks about so that we begin to love the pursuit of virtue, rather than seeing it as something onerous to overcome. In the spiritual life, St. John of the Cross and St. Teresa of Avila speak of perfect union with God in the seventh mansion as the point in which the gravitational pull of sin loosens and rather than being subject to the strengths and wily nature of the tempting demons, the demons rather fear the saint and leave them alone. We may perhaps draw the same analogy when virtue has become perfected in a soul, that it is practiced out of love, rather than by grit, because of both habit and grace.

Whether it's a diet or trying to remain in a state of grace, we need to be mindful of the "Screw-Its" that bubble when we "grow weary of doing good." It can drive us outside of the means Aristotle references, to the vices opposed to temperance, prudence, liberality, etc. This is the struggle for me in dieting, of course (JUST GIVE ME THE BURGER!), but also in my prayer life where I may be tempted towards apathy, or doubt, and falling out of the good habit of regular prayer, spiritual reading, and intimacy with the Lord; or in falling into one minor sin, we figure "well, might as well go big or go home at this point!" The Devil will leverage this thinking and our propensity towards concupiscence against us. How hard it is to be good! But then again, all things worth something, cost something.

"IT'S BEEN GOD ALL ALONG"

I have always told the Lord, "If I have brought but one person to you, I will die happy." All glory to God, I think I can say that has happened, though I was only about one percent of the equation.

A few years ago a friend from high school—I will call her Kay—reached out to me via Messenger. Though I couldn't find the original message, I remember that this friend was being drawn back to the Church and had reached out to me, I think, because she knew so few Catholics.

I always knew her as an extremely perceptive and intuitive person, but I hadn't seen her since high school. She was living in a metropolitan area on the West Coast now, married with two children. She had been taking her kids to a Protestant church, but kept being drawn to Catholic churches, especially those with Latin Masses, and adoration chapels. In an email exchange we had a few years ago, she tenderly noted that she could not bring herself to go in but lingered outside the doorway. "No words really to describe the experience," she'd said.

For me, there is honestly nothing more moving than to see a soul being stirred by grace, but especially when it's someone you know. I have had people and friends I've tried to share the Gospel with who I thought were open to it; not in an aggressive way, but just by planting seeds, and it can be deflating when they never seem to sprout. But Kay was different. I didn't really do anything or play much of a part, besides maybe offering some material to read by way of my blog. Rather, I just had the good grace to witness the Holy Spirit nudging and moving her to come home. A true privilege worth living for.

Her last Confession was also her first, some 30+ years ago. She shared in that email from a few years ago that:

> My Confession is scheduled for Thursday morning. I feel like I'm standing in two worlds. Just recently I found Flannery O'Connor's quote "Grace changes us and the change is painful." I had no idea. My whole life I've walked through the world seeing "meaning" and "beauty" everywhere I looked, and now I know it's been God all along.

I hope she will forgive me for sharing that, but it gives me hope; we are being ransomed, all of us, in dribs and drabs. The days of the mass conversions of St. Francis Xavier are not so common in our culture today. Maybe souls escaping the Titanic of our culture and finding their way to shore on life rafts, or pulled upon rescue boats, is as much as we can hope for. I take to heart St. Paul's words to "become all things to all people...so that I may save some." (1 Cor 9:22)

But again, it has little to do with me or you except that we are foot soldiers, pencils, instruments in God's hands to sow the seed. We have little capability to make it rain, shine the sun, pollinate the buds. The best we can do is labor, scatter, till, and fertilize. The rest is grace. But isn't it a wonderful thing to see a flower bud, a tree bear fruit, in its due season? It is a miracle of nature.

We can never force or manipulate grace, however. God is loving but wholly sovereign, and the Holy Spirit is like the wind that blows where it wishes (Jn 3:8). The featherweight pods of grace are carried across the fields, floating until they rest on a tender heart. But a heart cannot be rushed or hurried along. It reminds me of a passage from Nikos Kazantzakis' *Zorba the Greek*:

> I recalled one dawn when I had chanced upon a butterfly's cocoon in a pine tree at the very moment when the husk was

breaking and the inner soul was preparing to emerge. I kept waiting and waiting; it was slow and I was in a hurry. Leaning over it, I began to warm it with my breath. I kept warming it impatiently until the miracle commenced to unfold before my eyes at an unnatural speed. The husk opened completely; the butterfly came out. But never shall I forget my horror: its wings remained curled inward, not unfolded. The whole of its minuscule body shook as it struggled to spread the wings outward. But it could not. As for me, I struggled to aid it with my breath. In vain. What it needed was to ripen and unfold patiently in sunlight. Now it was too late. My breath had forced the butterfly to emerge ahead of time, crumpled and premature. It came out undeveloped, shook desperately, and soon died in my palm.

This butterfly's fluffy corpse is, I believe, the greatest weight I carry on my conscience. What I understood deeply on that day was this: to hasten eternal rules is a mortal sin. One's duty is confidently to follow nature's everlasting rhythm.

When I think of my friend Kay, I think of the mercy and goodness of God first and foremost, and then the privilege of witnessing grace working to flower faith in its due season in my friend's heart. Her marriage and her relationship, in her words, has completely transformed. Meaning and beauty is everywhere, but now with the eyes of Christ the Divine Artist, my friend's heart has been able to fully bloom and recognize the threads in the tapestry of her life. A contrite heart, O Lord, you will not spurn.

When I think of my friend, I breathe a sigh, because I can go to my eternal rest a sated man, can enjoy a happy death. Because the Lord has done great things for us, and we are glad (Ps 126:3). As she noted, it's been God all along. I was just glad I was able to be gifted a ticket to the show.

BEING THE SAINT FOR YOUR AGE

The witness of the saints who have gone before are a great gift of the Church for our benefit. Often we think we don't possess what is needed to attain sanctity, when it fact, there is only one thing necessary in this life, and that is to be a saint. As someone said, "What else is there?"

The fact is, we have been given all we need by grace to carry out our calling. And we often sell ourselves (and the power of the Holy Spirit) short. There is a story in the lives of the Desert Fathers that stuck with me over the years:

> Abba Lot went to see Abba Joseph and said to him, "Abba, as far as I can say, I do my little office, I read my psalms, I fast a little bit, I pray and I meditate, I live in peace with others as far as I can, I purify my thoughts. Tell me, Father, what else, what more can I do?" Then the old man, Abba Joseph, stood up, stretched out his hands toward heaven, and his fingers became like ten lamps of fire, and he said to him, **"If you will, you can become all flame."**

Although I haven't read much of his life, the recent beatification of Bl. Carlo Acutis lends itself to this witness for the millennial generation. He was cheerful, devoted to the Eucharist, and was a whiz with computers. He was a teenager being a teenager while keeping his Catholic faith at the forefront and using his gifts for God's glory and the benefit of his fellow men. If sanctity seems to be the thing of dusty volumes of patristic ascetics, Bl. Carlo's life, witness, and canonization would offer an argument to the contrary.

There is a tendency when we are younger and trying to find ourselves and who we really are to emulate our heroes in the faith. For me, it was St. Anthony the Great, who wrestled in the desert alone against Satan himself and lived a life of solitude and asceticism. I have an icon of St. Anthony (next to Our Lady of Guadalupe) in my prayer station to come to my aid when war is waged against me. But as I've gotten older, I've sought a spiritual father in the Church Triumphant who can maybe serve as a special patron given how God made me. As much as I love St. Anthony, God did not make me a solitary or an ascetic.

As I go through my spiritual rolodex, there are many, many saints (those canonized and those who have not yet been but may be on the way) whom I love and whose diversity spans the breadth. I have written about many of them, and often invoke their intercessions depending on the intention and situation. There is great diversity among the saints.

Were there one I had to choose for my own life, though, to be a kind of "older brother" or mentor—a kind of "spiritual buddy system" whose gifts and personal charisms strike a chord, I think it would have to be St. Philip Neri.

There are many things I love about St. Philip, and many things about his life that have inspired me.

First and foremost, St. Philip had a burning love for our Lord, especially in the Eucharist. He was often taken to ecstasy with a heart on fire. He was spontaneous and impulsive. But he knew that the cornerstone of all virtue begins with humility. He cultivated this humility by sabotaging himself—like purposefully mispronouncing words in the presence of the bishop or wearing ridiculous clothes or shaving half his beard off. Though he spent hours in prayer, he was also found by visitors to be reading joke books, which he loved. The lesson—to not take yourself so seriously—is one I find so important today.

St. Philip was also an evangelist. He took the "organic approach" to cultivating friendships and relationships across social and class lines. For one thing, he was a layman for many years, but engaged in this apostolic work for many years before he became (was encouraged, actually) to become a priest. He loved going out into the streets and talking with people; he took a very personalist approach to this. He was not a systematic thinking or master planner. The origins of the Oratory began with these informal meetings in his room, where those he invited could engage in edifying discourse, but not without action either. He encouraged frequent reception of the Sacrament of Penance and Communion and made himself available at all hours for it.

St. Philip lived in the wake of the Reformation and was one of the great saints of "rebuilding" called to renew the Church, especially in Rome, where he found it full of spiritual laxity and clerical worldliness. Remember, he did this as a layman, as he was not ordained until 1551 at the age of 36.

Humility, humor, and a love of people—these are the things I find myself so drawn to in St. Philip Neri. His organic approach to cultivating friendships and leading people to Christ as a layman are also creative and inspiring. If I were able to be matched up with any saint in history to learn from and identify with, it would be him!

We must be saints. The age is wicked, but despair serves no one well. In a time of confusion, we can offer clarity. In a culture of outrage, be lighthearted. In an age of great sinfulness, make known the great gift of mercy in Confession. We are living through a great leveling of the Church in the culture, and we need those on the ground to go out amidst the rubble and get to work rebuilding from the ground up.

We are given different gifts and talents, but we must first and foremost be ourselves! St. Frances de Sales gave a simple retort to the unattainability of sainthood, "Be who you are, and be that well. So that you may bring honor to the Master Craftsman whose handiwork you are."

PERSISTING CONTRA GOD'S WILL

I remember very distinctly when my idealized vision of my life in my twenties came into stark confrontation with the reality of my situation. Whereas most people during this time are getting started in their careers post-college and working their way up the ladder, meeting people to match up for a future together, and buying their first house, I was going in the opposite direction—quitting my job, giving away everything I owned, and buying not a house but a school bus to live in.

For ten years, from the age of 19 to 29, I wanted more than anything to be a monk. Not just wanted to be a monk but wanted to be *called* to be a monk. The pursuit of what I thought was a calling seemed like a noble one—not from a worldly perspective of course, but from a spiritual investment standpoint. Objectively, I had "chosen the better part." And so surely it must be God's will because it was what I wanted. Or what I *thought* I wanted.

I was thus crestfallen when I actually did apply to be a postulant at a contemplative Benedictine community and was turned down after my observership. As an alternative, I decided to go the "DIY monastic" route and bought a school bus to convert to an urban hermitage where I would eat, sleep, read, and pray in monastic fashion. I worked for weeks outside of my apartment as my lease expiration loomed. I removed the seats, built cabinets, bed, and desk, laid flooring, and had everything set (except a place to park it). When I actually got down to the quasi-monastic life, though, I realized something: fundamentally, I was not happy.

The analogy I have always used to describe this experience that seemed to describe it best was akin to finding the shirt you always wanted at the local thrift store, trying it on, and finding that it's one size smaller that what you typically wear. You can make it work if you walk out of the store with it. But then you begin to notice it chaffs under the arms, rides up an inch too much at the waist, and is just snug enough to be uncomfortable. It looks great—it just doesn't fit. Because it wasn't made for you.

You could use the "trying to fit a square peg in a round hole" analogy, but it doesn't quite work because no matter what you do in that situation, you can't ram it through. It would be almost easier if it was like this because the fact that you have the wrong piece would be apparent from the start. You wouldn't spend ten years trying to make it so. That would almost be an apt description of a kind of insanity!

You could use the puzzle piece analogy, which is closer to the mark, but that isn't quite it either. You know, when you find a "close but not cigar" piece in a puzzle, and it's *almost* the one you are looking for, but you'd have to slam your fist down on the table to force it, which would distort the edges and present an inaccurate picture.

No, I think the shirt analogy works best in this circumstance. You want to look good. You found a good deal on a great brand. Surely, it *should* fit, despite the label saying 'S' rather than 'M.' The stitches aren't breaking, the buttons aren't popping off. You can tolerate the discomfort to an extent, but it's far from fitting like a glove. You always kind of feel it, even if you convince yourself otherwise.

When we don't pay attention to these things, these little chaffings, we can sometimes miss the ways in which God is telling us, "This isn't for you. I have something set aside for you. But you have to trust me." Because God rarely speaks to us audibly, we have to rely on these signs and signals to discern whether we are trying to conform our will to God's, or God's will to our life.

St. Alphonsus speaks of this when he writes of the difference between *conformity* and *uniformity* with God's will—

> Conformity signifies that we join our wills to the will of God. Uniformity means more—it means that we make one will of God's will and ours, so that we will only what God wills; that God's will alone, is our will. This is the summit of perfection and to it we should always aspire; this should be the goal of all our works, desires, meditations and prayers.

Uniformity is the "more perfect way," the better part (between good and better) that our Lord relates to Martha and Mary. It is beholden to the attainment by saints and mystics, but that doesn't mean it shouldn't be our aspiration as well.

Here in the world, in the day to day, our seemingly noble and holy actions of attempted abandonment can sometimes be held up so that we present them to the Lord expecting Him to bless them, when in fact, He wants something else of us entirely. Like saying, "I will prepare the altar for you Lord," when He really needs the monastery toilets scrubbed. Or whatever.

Think of the testing of Abraham. The Lord tests his faith by demanding his most precious property—his son Isaac. At the moment of sacrifice, when there was no doubt Abraham had the butt of the knife ready to bury within the flesh of his son, an angel comes to tell him to back it off. Would Abraham had responded, "No, begone demon who appears as an angel of light! For it is God's will that I slaughter, though I do not understand it, and I will do God's will as He has asked."

But that's not what happens. Abraham pivots and is awash in relief. Not only that, but He has also pleased the Lord by His obedience and abandonment to the Divine will as it was given to him. If the news media were there to throw shade, they may take a snapshot out of context and print, "God told you to sacrifice your son Issac with the knife, and that didn't happen, so obviously you did not follow through and accomplish His holy will."

Did God's will change? Well, yes and no. God was seeking faith and obedience, and that Abraham supplied in full measure. And yet the action to accomplish and live out that faith and obedience did change. Were Abraham to plow through with what he thought to be God's will after the angel holds back his arm by decree, he would have lost the blessing of such obedience, and the subsequent inheritance for generations to come.

This is what can be so deceptively difficult in following God's will, compounded in proportion to the extent that we are not praying and paying attention. We may charge ahead with our ideas—"I will become a monk and be holy!" "I will marry John because he is such a good Catholic man!" "I will become a missionary in Africa and save God's orphans!" But maybe God wants you to be a father; maybe he wants you to marry Maurice, the air conditioner repairman; maybe he wants you to get your rear end back to work at your computer programming job. Who knows. But you get the idea.

"The shirt that never was" can be a painful experience, because it scrambles our holy expectations of our life the way we envision it. When we think we are doing God's will, and God says, "No, not this way," we can feel the pain of the virtuous plate of doing God's will being pulled off the table. And so what are we left with? Often something unexpected, or more waiting (which causes suffering), or something not in accordance with our own will. When we pray for x and get y instead, it can be hard to reconcile. This is why it takes an attuning of the heart to be assured that doing something contra to God's will, even something holy and virtuous, will not ultimately give us the peace we seek, but will chaff ever so slightly.

Remember, Abraham pivoted in faith. He was not "rigid" (again with the rigid!) so as to keep God's command in this instance immovable and sealed in amber. Amber-ensconced artifacts belong in museums. God's Word and command is not a dead historic letter, but a living, speaking language that is alive and speaks to us differently in different circumstances of our life. God's will for you yesterday may not always be His will for you tomorrow. If we persist in our will contra to God's, we will not have the peace we seek, we will only have a pious veneer. But if we conform and unite our will with God's and are willing to pivot and carry it out even when it bears no resemblance to what we think it was supposed to look like, we may in time know the peace of Christ that surpasses all understanding.

Our spiritual growth is part of a process. Sometimes we follow what appear to be dead ends, but we must view them through the eyes of faith. The reason God leads us down a road isn't always about merely getting from point A to point B. Sometimes it is about learning why we should *not* go down that road, or about what we see along the way. Rather than dead ends, we should consider these side journeys as steps by which we ascend the ladder of God's will.

WANT TO SUFFER SHAME FOR THE NAME? START BY TELLING THE TRUTH[2]

Have you ever wondered how many Jane and Joe Catholics are walking around, working, raising families, and wrapped up in the day to day who have no idea what road they might be on? Have you ever thought that maybe, just maybe, the majority of the average Catholics you might encounter on the street have *no idea* that it is a sin to miss Mass on Sundays, to practice contraception, to get remarried without an annulment (adultery), to have an abortion or live a life of totally ignoring the poor?

There are two Spiritual Works of Mercy that are very hard to practice today, and I see them as going hand in hand: "Instructing the Ignorant" and "Admonishing the Sinner."

Here's the thing: with regard to the former, we all know where this has gotten us. Being ignorant or "in the dark" is sometimes happenstance ("You know, I never thought about that before!") and sometimes it can be willful ("I don't know, and I don't want to know.") A shameful example of men remaining willfully ignorant to abuse in

---

[2] This essay appeared in *Catholic Stand* (catholicstand.com) on June 30, 2020.

order to acquit themselves of culpability can be seen with regards to Cardinal Donald Wuerl's desire to remain "in the dark" when confronted with instances of abuse:

> [Fr] Zirwas informed the diocese in 1996 that he knew of other Pittsburgh priests' involvement in illegal sexual activity, the report found, and "demanded that his sustenance payments be increased" in exchange for that information. Wuerl replied with instructions to provide the names of the priests involved or to "state that he had no knowledge of what he had previously claimed" to get any additional assistance. The priest then disavowed any knowledge of priests being involved in illegal sexual activity in a letter to the diocese. "Zirwas was granted an additional financial stipend and his sustenance payments were continued," the report said.

A scandal, indeed! But sometimes the case is not so nefarious. It is possible for people of general goodwill, due to faulty or insufficient catechesis, to really be effectively ignorant of the teachings of their religion. If a Catholic couple is fornicating or living together before marriage, they might just think this is normal in today's culture and be going along with their lives with a skip and a smile. One might be afraid of turning them off altogether, or shutting down and hating you. But when opportunity presents itself to speak the truth in love (Eph 4:15), you are presented with an opportunity to save your brother or sister.

We know that the divine law is written onto the hearts of men, even for pagans and unbelievers. We know conscience is an endowed gift of God:

> For when Gentiles who do not have the Law do instinctively the things of the Law, these, not having the Law, are a law to themselves, in that they show the work of the Law written in their hearts, their conscience bearing witness and their

thoughts alternately accusing or else defending them. (Rom 2:14-15)

How, then, does one do this work, practically speaking—this instructing and admonishing? Well, I have always been bad at it, because, well, I'm not that different from most people in that I like to be liked and have thin skin, generally. But God is working on me, and I'm giving less figs about that these days, so I'm more inclined when presented with the opportunity to bring attention to these things.

First: get your own house in order. No one likes a hypocrite, and no one likes to be judged. Truth be told, we should not be judging people at all, but that does not mean we cannot judge actions as objectively right or wrong. Live a life of integrity yourself before admonishing others to do the same.

Second: When delivering hard truths that have the potential to knock someone off their rocker of ignorance, have some humility, and remember that you were there once too. Expunge all sense of self-righteousness because people can smell this a mile away. Make it clear by your thoughts, words, and actions, that you care for the person you are speaking to, and you speak out of love.

Third: pray for grace and for the Holy Spirit to give you the words and speak for you. Do not rely on your own power. You are not a heart or mind reader like St. Padre Pio, so don't try to act like one. If God tells you by the Holy Spirit in prayer that now is not the time to speak, now is not the time to speak. If He tells you to speak the truth in love, speak the truth in love. Do whatever He tells you.

Fourth: always with a smile. I don't know if this is kosher or not, it's even counter intuitive, but I think it can be disarming and helpful to smile, intentional and genuinely, when admonishing. The message is important. HOW you deliver the message may be even more so. Not all of us can pull off being a John the Baptist. But we can deliver his message to repent in concrete ways without being sour pusses. Our faith is motivated by the JOY of being saved from sin and death, and we need to communicate that concretely when dishing up hard truths if we want a greater likelihood of the medicine going down.

Fifth: suffer derision for their sake. They may curse you or strike you even, ignore you or cut ties. They may mock you or accuse you. Take it upon yourself to pray and do reparations that they may have eyes to see, and experience a new heart, a changed heart, a born-again heart. Christ took on suffering and derision for the sake of blind and ungrateful men, and so if we want to follow him we may be wise to get used to this feeling of being rejected and our love thwarted. That's ok. God does His part, you do your part, and the rest is out of your hands.

The image that comes to mind of standing in the midst of such derision and shame is of the Woolworth's sit-in during the Civil Rights movement. Blacks exercising civil disobedience had sugar, ketchup, and mustard poured on their heads when they refused to move. They knew what was right, were willing to take the hits for it, and refused to be moved or intimidated.

You don't have to go looking for suffering. Speak the Gospel truth to those who are resistant to it, and it will find you. Stand for the truth when it hurts and you *will* experience it. Love anyone, and you will suffer for it; it is only a matter of time. But who knows—if you speak out and accept the consequences, they may hate you and simultaneously wake from their fatal slumber at the same time. You will have popped their balloon of ignorance, and they will no longer in good conscience be able to fly it into the careless clouds. You will start them on a hard road, perhaps, and they will hate you for it, at least initially.

And you, my friend, don't you scorn this shame, but relish it, as the apostles did when "they left the Sanhedrin, rejoicing because they had been counted worthy of suffering disgrace for the Name" (Acts 5:41). You know you are doing something right, earning your keep and on the narrow road, when you are covered in the mess the world pours on your head in its hatred of you. No matter. For then you will attest, with St. Dominic Savio, "If I can succeed in saving only a single soul, I can be sure that my own will be saved."

"EVERYBODY HAS A PLAN UNTIL THEY GET PUNCHED IN THE MOUTH"[3]

A few months ago I was following a thread about how people of faith would respond if faced with martyrdom. It generated some good discussion, but I couldn't help remembering the words of Peter to Jesus, "Even if I have to die with You, I will not deny You.' All the disciples said the same thing too." (Mt 26:35)

And what does Peter do? Well, he does die for Christ, eventually. But not before denying him, not once, but three times. The disciples scatter when the soldiers come to arrest Jesus. One guy even leaves his underwear behind (Mk 14:52). Who was with Jesus in his last hour? Mary, his mother, the other Marys, and the disciple whom he loved—the strong and silent types.

Peter eats his words in a bitter shame, weeping over having said them with such bravado. But we should not overlook that while Peter does not die *with* Christ at his hour, he does go to his death for him at Peter's appointed time. This is, of course, after Pentecost, when Peter and the other disciples are given the *grace* and courage by the Holy

---

[3] This essay appeared in *Catholic Stand* (catholicstand.com) on April 30, 2019.

Spirit to suffer and die, and to do it well. But their high-minded words prior to that are just that—words.

I appreciate quotes from the saints who have walked the walk and have the street cred to give credence to their words. I don't have much use for nicely crafted words from inspirational speakers making the daily memes for their social media postings. But every now and then I come across a blunt little nugget from someone having no intention of being a JV philosopher, and are not necessarily religious, but are just speaking from life experience. Life carries weight.

Mike Tyson was that guy this morning when I read his words, "Everybody has a plan until they get punched in the mouth." He once spoke about the origins of that quote:

> People were asking me [before a fight], 'What's going to happen?,' " They were talking about his style. 'He's going to give you a lot of lateral movement. He's going to move, he's going to dance. He's going to do this, do that.' I said, "Everybody has a plan until they get hit. Then, like a rat, they stop in fear and freeze.'

Like a rat, they stop in fear and freeze. Can anybody relate to that? It's easy to talk a good game about dying for Christ and being a martyr, and we should in fact desire that. But I dread that day. A person wrote me the other day crediting me with some religious points for my interview on "The Journey Home" and asked if I agreed, and all I could tell him was that I can only identify with Peter who said to the Lord after sinking in the sea, "Depart from me Lord, for I am a sinful man" (Lk 5:8). Grace is the only thing I have. My faith is smaller than a mustard seed, by a lot. Grace keeps me from drowning. It's all I have.

I'm not used to being in the public eye, so to speak. It's a little disorienting. After the airing of the show I spent a good amount of time in prayer, arms extended like Moses to feel the burn, because I felt like I deserved a good smarting, a sharp thorn, like Paul, to keep my face close to the dirt. I was scared of it, and still am. I've seen big names fall.

ON DISCIPLESHIP

I've seen the devils shooting arrows at the saints on the ladder of divine ascent, and pride brings every one of them crashing through the rungs.

If you want to die for Christ, suffer for Christ, save your words. Sacrifice, but do it in private. Pray, and pray some more, with tears. Peter would tell you the same, I suspect. God will give you what you want when you are focused on Him. Just make sure it's what you really want. Converts are made by witness, not pastoral letters. Live your life as a witness. But go easy on the words and saber rattling because you never know what that day is going to look like when it comes. Faith and character are proved by fire, as gold through the furnace.

"If you're good and your plan is working," Tyson said, "somewhere during the duration of that, the outcome of that event you're involved in, you're going to get the wrath, the bad end of the stick. Let's see how you deal with it. Normally people don't deal with it that well."

There's truth there. Sanctity doesn't come cheap, and nothing really goes according to plan. Stay focused, do the work in front of you, and roll with the punches so you can persevere to the end. Don't make an oath, just let your yes mean yes and your no mean no. Anything else is from the evil one (Mt 5:37). No one plans to get punched in the mouth, after all. How you respond when you do will be the mark that matters in the end.

Please pray for me.

SHOP TALK

Pablo Picasso once noted, "When art critics get together they talk about Form and Structure and Meaning. When artists get together they talk about where you can buy cheap turpentine." I'm not an artist and don't hang around artists. I write, but I don't get together with other writers either. The only thing in my life these days that really seems to matter is following Christ and submitting to His will. Much of that walk is unaccompanied, but I am always scanning the horizon to meet other followers of the Way to be fortified by, and to fortify if need be.

Do you know what my favorite Mystery of the rosary to meditate on is? It is the Visitation. Why? I've often wondered that myself. I've never been pregnant. I don't have cousins I'm close with. But there is something about the scene and motivation of Mary, pregnant with the Savior, who set off "in great haste" (Lk 1:39) over 80 miles on foot (pregnant!) to pay her relative Elizabeth a visit right after the Annunciation. Who can she share with about this unbelievable event? Who is going to "get it?" It is a moving communion scene when Mary arrives—Elizabeth cannot contain her joy and "cries out in a loud voice" while Mary's soul exults, and her spirit rejoices in God. Mary stays three months, presumably until John is born.

In our lives, as we get older, our friends—the ones we trust, the ones to whom we share with deeply and intimately—tend to thin out.

If we have one or two, we should count ourselves fortunate. Many do not have even that. In a religion such as Catholicism, that preaches unpopular truths, these genuine friendships in faith can be a much-needed balm for weary travelers following the Way.

When I meet another Christ-follower on the road who "gets it," who wants the same thing for themselves and their family—holiness, living for God alone, to love and serve Him exclusively—I feel a deep joy. It doesn't come right away, but only after a gentle dance together to test each other's steps, to see if the other can complete them, not unlike those early Christians who clandestinely celebrated a common brotherhood on the road by, as the story goes, "completing the fish":

> Greeks, Romans, and many other pagans used the fish symbol before Christians. Hence the fish, unlike, say, the cross, attracted little suspicion, making it a perfect secret symbol for persecuted believers. When threatened by Romans in the first centuries after Christ, Christians used the fish mark meeting places and tombs, or to distinguish friends from foes. According to one ancient story, when a Christian met a stranger in the road, the Christian sometimes drew one arc of the simple fish outline in the dirt. If the stranger drew the other arc, both believers knew they were in good company.

Once a comradeship is established, it affords an opportunity to "talk shop." From the outside this can look like Catholic nerd speak, but among believers, it is a moment of reloading magazines, comparing maps, and exchanging messages while in asylum.

"I'm in need of a miracle for my sister in law, but I don't have nine days," says one.

"Have you tried Mother Teresa's emergency novena? My visa wasn't going to arrive in time and she came through for me!" the other responds.

"My scapular is wearing thin, and I'm almost out of Miraculous Medals. Do you know someone who can wholesale? We've given out a lot this month."

"Yes! I know a guy, he's got nine kids and runs a distribution center out of his garage in Cleveland, faithful guy..."

Etc.

Saints are both idealists and realists—they realize that they are incapable of anything apart from God, and yet trust in His ability to do great things, miraculous things, in the world and in their lives and the lives of others. They realize that sanctification comes as much through the daily faithful observance of mundane works of cleaning toilets and restocking shelves as it does through the loftier occasions of consolation and communion in prayer and contemplation. They realize their cross is a "reservation for one," and yet with the communion of saints and those who have gone before whom they can call upon anywhere at any time, they are never really alone.

When you start walking the difficult and lonely path and meet a sincere fellow believer on the way, don't pass him by without an embrace and an encouragement, after he proves himself trustworthy. It may be for you or for him or for the two of you, but in pagan land, we can't afford to travel alone, since "two are better than one...if one falls, the other can pick his companion up" (Ecc 4:9). Stop and talk shop, exchange notes, reload each other's sacramentals, and pray for one another—after all, you are soldiers heading to the same destination over the same treacherous terrain. Let the theologians and the doctors discuss Form and Structure and Meaning. You in the trenches? You figure out who sells the cheap turpentine and go get it. There's work to do.

ON MARRIAGE

THE GATES OF HELL WILL NOT PREVAIL AGAINST YOUR MARRIAGE[4]

If there were one analogous example of Christ's promise and commitment to the Church in scripture, it is that of marriage. This union of Christ and the Church is not strictly friendship, not strictly ownership (as a master to a slave), not strictly contractual. Rather the Church is the BRIDE of Christ which encompasses all these elements. This is why Christians can claim divine intimacy as part of our spiritual adoption, and why we can call the God of the Universe *Abba*, Father. Just as Genesis tells us that Adam "knew" Eve and produced progeny, so Christ knows us and propagates in us spiritual fruit through sanctifying grace.

In his masterful encyclical *Casti Connubii* Pius XI says, quoting the Council of Trent:

> ...By raising the Matrimony of His faithful to the dignity of a true sacrament, [Christ] made it a sign and source of that peculiar internal grace by which 'it perfects natural love,

---

[4] This essay appeared in *Catholic Stand* (catholicstand.com) on December 3, 2022.

> confirms an indissoluble union, and sanctifies both man and wife. (*Casti Conubii*, 38)

That is, for two validly married, baptized Catholics united in a consummated marriage*, there is no force on earth, no solvent that can dissolve this bond…not even the Pope.

For one who is in a dysfunctional or trying marriage, this can be a source of despair, because it can become a kind of hell with no hope of a valid exit. But because of the effect of sacramental grace in the Sacrament of Matrimony, no marriage is beyond repair when one cooperates with that grace made available in the Sacrament. As Pius XI notes:

> Since men do not reap the full fruit of the sacraments … unless they cooperate with grace, the grace of matrimony will remain for the most part an unused talent hidden in the field unless both parties exercise these supernatural powers …(41)

Even though some may despair at being "stuck" with the person who has become their cross for a lifetime, one can also find great solace in this indissoluble character of the sacramental bond. And what does it relate to, in terms of the analogous example of Christ's wedding to His bride, the Church? For He said that the Church was founded on the rock of Peter, and "the gates of Hell will not prevail against it" (Mt 16:18). In the darkest hours when all seems lost, we can have faith that Christ is not lying and that he will not abandon us to the dark powers.

Because we have this same assurance with a sacramental marriage—that no force on earth acting outside of it can break it apart—we can have the assurance of stability when we cooperate with grace. St. Paul alludes to this continence when he says that nothing can separate us from the love of Christ:

> For I am convinced that neither death nor life, neither angels nor demons, neither the present nor the future, nor any powers, neither height nor depth, nor anything else in all

creation, will be able to separate us from the love of God that is in Christ Jesus our Lord. (Rom 8:38-39)

Because of concupiscence, our wills have been weakened; the Devil cannot enter into us except through the portal of the will. And so, though he is like a wild dog on a leash, when we voluntarily walk into his circle, we have the potential to get bit. But nothing compels us to do this...except our own will. Therefore, when we cooperate with grace, we are choosing to stay in a state of sanctifying grace and the safety of divine protection as it relates to our souls. That is a good place to be, and especially in a marriage.

Not long ago I wrote an essay entitled "I Liked You the Way You Were Before," wherein I explored what happens when one partner "changes" in a marriage, and radically so. In this instance it involved an autistic married man who went from being "autistically even-keeled" emotionally (which his wife, as a chronically depressed person, appreciated) to someone "joyfully shedding the cloak of disability" and being in tune with not only his own emotions and social cues, but others as well—something foreign to him as an autistic man.

There was also that interesting historic case of Phineas Cage (1823-1860), who seemed to be transformed into another person altogether after a railroad spike went through his skull. You marry one person, and the next morning you realize you seem to be married to a stranger.

Of course this can happen also with those married to someone with Alzheimer's. It can be very difficult and trying. But, despite all evidence to the contrary, this is still the same soul you married, that you were joined to as one flesh—even when they regard you as a stranger.

I was disgusted to hear my parents recount a friend of theirs who had started dating a man whose wife was in this situation. I don't know the details, but objectively speaking any justification of such an adulterous action has no grounds and is a deplorable dereliction of duty rooted in selfishness. When we think carnally, we act carnally.

It's interesting when one speaks of this, "You've changed...I know longer know you" phenomenon (which is so common in marriages), but as it relates to the current "marriage" of Christ to his Church. We have attended Mass in the Extraordinary Form as a family for the past five years. Our kids do not even know the New Mass; it is akin to a foreigner for them.

But what would happen if the vicar of Christ puts the boot on the neck and, overnight, this form of the Mass was practically abrogated for us as a family? What would we do? For some, this has already happened in their diocese. I was speaking with a priest friend last night over dinner and flushing this out. What would it look like? Would we take up at a Byzantine parish? Fly to the FSSP? Stay at our diocesan parish and attend the Novus Ordo (celebrated *ad orientem*, but still)?

I don't have the answers, and just pray for the grace to stay faithful if and when we are faced with this conundrum. Christ will not abandon his Church, just as the marriage between my wife and I cannot ever be dissolved, under any circumstances. Were she to change overnight, become unrecognizable, I would still be bound to her, though it seems as if I were bound to a stranger. And yet, we are called still to be true, to be faithful, till death do us part.

God will give us the supernatural grace to do that when it seems impossible to accomplish it through human means alone. Just as in a marriage the grace of the Sacrament is strengthened through regular marital intimacy and conjugal union, so in our lives of faith we are strengthened by regular reception of the Holy Eucharist. Just as we continually ask forgiveness in a marriage and do not hold sin against our own flesh, so are we strengthened in faith in the sacrament of Penance. Just as our witness as a married couple gives courage and our love be like holy chrism, so to with the sacrament of Confirmation as it relates to faith.

The gates of Hell will not prevail against God's Church, though the Bride be disfigured in her purification. And the gates of Hell will not prevail against your marriage, because you are assured that the bond which hold you together as one flesh is indissoluble, if you trust that God can sanctify you through it. Every marriage goes through a crucible in which each party is refined; perhaps the Church is preparing to enter that ultimate test as well in the coming days.

TOP OF THE SIXTH, BOTTOM OF THE NINTH (AND TENTH)

"Thou shalt not covet thy neighbor's wife: nor his house, nor his field, nor his manservant, nor his maidservant, nor his ox, nor his ass, nor any thing that is his" (Deut 5:21).

If there was a Family Feud: *Catholic Edition*, Steve Harvey might pose the question to the contestants: "What Commandment do *men* confess to breaking the MOST?" Most people would intuitively answer "The Sixth Commandment." And they would most likely be right. As Our Lady told St. Jacinta of Fatima, "The sins which cause most souls to go to hell are the sins of the flesh." Sexual sin is a major problem for men, and difficult to get under control!

Ask any woman the same question, though, and unchastity may make the list, but as a collective it's most likely not near the top. I'm not a woman, but based on my observations I suspect a sin many women struggle with involves the 9th and 10th Commandment: jealousy, envy, and covetousness.

The Catechism links greed and envy (§2538-9): "Envy can lead to the worst crimes...It refers to the sadness at the sight of another's good and the immoderate desire to acquire them for oneself. Envy is a form of sadness that comes from lack of charity."

But where does this sin of envy come from? For men, sins against the ninth and tenth Commandments are relatively straightforward. Generally speaking, men crave power and wealth more than women do; if they seek to acquire more in terms of goods, it is because of the kitchy adage, "He who dies with the most toys wins." The sixth and ninth Commandments are linked, of course, since our Lord warned that "whoever looks a woman with lust has already committed adultery with her in his heart" (Mt 5:28).

What about for women? I would wager that this happens more subtly, more internally, and is more weighted towards the inherent inward *sadness* more than the immoderate desire to acquire. Insecurity is a breeding ground for envy. New moms, and even some seasoned moms, face the temptation of *comparison* and when it is indulged, can lead to sin. This may involve projection, speculation, inane "mommy wars," or simply an inability to be secure in one's parenting abilities. Comparison poisons the well of contentment.

A two-for-one consequence of this sin of envious sadness involves the close but distinct link between the ninth and tenth Commandments. For when a woman is preoccupied with what other women/moms/wives are doing, it may be less that she is "coveting another woman's husband," and more that her envious, preoccupatory sadness is crowding out the attention that should be reserved for her husband. This "mental absence" can contribute to an emotional (and sometimes physical) distancing from their husbands they might not even be aware of. Husbands must take ownership of their sexual faculties which are reserved for their own wives, of course.

But wives, too, must be on guard against creating an environment in which they have put other "things" in the seat which should be reserved for their husband. Wives are not directly responsible for their husband's sins. Then again, why do men look outside the marriage chamber? Is it perhaps because they seek to be acknowledged, elevated, and yes, put first and given undivided attention by their spouse? And when she fails to do so, is she blameless? Were you to notice the danger of putting your children, your envy, your jealous sadness before your own husband...would you view this temptation to sin differently? "The heart of her husband trusteth in her, and he shall have no need of spoils" (Prov 31:11)

St. Paul has strong words on this matter:

> Not that we dare to classify or compare ourselves with some of those who are commending themselves. But when they measure themselves by one another and compare themselves with one another, they are without understanding. (2 Cor 10:12)

What is the antidote to this sin, the antecedent virtue which serves as the beachgrass which stabilizes the dunes and prevents erosion of the spirit? "Rejoice in your brother's progress," St. John Chrysostom says, "and you will immediately give glory to God. Conquer envy by rejoicing in the merits of others." And again, pursuant to the woman of worth's domain, King Lemuel notes (emphasis mine):

> She is clothed with **strength and dignity**;
> she can **laugh** at the days to come.
> She speaks with wisdom,
> and **faithful instruction** is on her tongue.
> She watches over the affairs of **her household**
> and does not eat the bread of **idleness**. (Prov. 31:25-31)

Men, be on guard against the temptations of the flesh, that seek to drag you to Hell through voluptuous seduction of the mind, laying traps and greasing the skids with the oil of covetousness. Keep custody of your eyes, your members, and your heart!

But women, you too must be on guard against temptations of petty jealousy, envy of other women, of sadness at the state of others' good affairs, of comparison and looking outside your own sphere of the home! This usurpation, renting out the room which should be reserved for your husband and family inoculates the bacteria of unchastity in the home and enthrones a kind of Jezebel spirit which sows seeds of discord and strife where there should be good order and peace.

ON MARRIAGE

Resist this spirit! Focus on your own spouse, your own home, your own affairs, your own business. As the old saying goes, comparisons will lead you to be either vain or bitter in the end; for there will always be greater and lesser persons than yourself.

THE PRINCIPLE OF SUBSIDIARITY IN MARRIAGE

A few months ago I stumbled across a critique of Stephanie Gordon's (wife of YouTuber Tim Gordon, *Rules for Retrogrades*) book *Ask Your Husband: A Catholic Guide to Femininity* in Catholic World Report by Dr. Abigail Favale, PhD. I think the crux of the intense disagreement in the combox as to the merits of the article hinged on Gordon-supporters arguing that Catholic feminism is an irredeemable term that should be abandoned in favor of the patrimonial deference implied in the title of Mrs. Gordon's book.

Dr. Favale takes an orthodox but more nuanced approach that sees the value in the roots of authentic Catholic feminism to get at what it means to be a woman (and man). Granted, this approach takes a bit more reflection and thoughtfulness to keep the knee-jerk tendency to dismiss "triggering" words like *feminism* outright and consider the merits apart from the baggage.

I have not read *Ask Your Husband*; apparently TAN pulled it after Timothy Gordon's brother David claimed Stephanie plagiarized sections of his own manuscript, so I can't speak to its contents apart from the general premise. While I may be biased (I am not a Gordon fanboy and have just settled on the conclusion that we all have our own particular styles of delivery), I did think Ms. Favale's article offered a balanced and fair critique. I happened to stumble upon her Pints with

Aquinas sit-down last night, and found her conversion to Catholicism interesting and authentic, her respect for nuance refreshing, and her recognition of the problems replete with feminism in the culture today honest and thoughtful. She is married to a Catholic convert and has four children.

What does any of this have to do with the Catholic principle of subsidiarity, especially as it pertains to marriage? In reflecting on the Gordons' approach, which Ms. Favale claims is "legalistic and ideological," I felt there were some parallels worth exploring.

In this context, we can see marriage as that *social organization in which the human person is the principle, subject, and object*. In this one-flesh union, husband and wife lay the building blocks of society through the generation of new life and the raising up of families. Even in the Sacrament of Matrimony this subsidiarity is respected in that the parties consenting to the union—the husband and wife—are themselves the ministers of the Sacrament.

Subsidiarity is concerned mostly with economic systems and governments. With regards to the higher orders participation in that of the lower orders, it essentially means that higher levels of government should not intervene to solve all problems if they can be handled locally. The government has many necessary and indispensable functions to play, roles that cannot be accomplished by individuals acting alone or even by smaller groups in society. Yet states and governments often exceed their legitimate role and infringe upon individuals and groups in society so as to dominate rather than to serve them.

The affairs of marriage are best handled at the lowest possible level, closest to the affected persons. There is a macro scope of vision (leading each other to Christ, how to live out one's vocation, etc.), but the majority of marital decisions are those that take place in the day-to-day decisions spouses make. It would be unreasonable for a higher agency is this context to formulate top-down approaches to these kinds of decisions—a "micro-managing" if you will.

Violations of the principal of subsidiarity *decrease economy, efficiency, liberty and the personal character of the social order*. This "personal character" of the social order (the marriage) depends upon a degree of liberty and leeway in discernment between the individuals as to the affairs of work, dress, charity, and child rearing at the lowest level.

So, let's circle back—what does this have to do with the Gordons' book and their particular constitutions of "authentic Catholic femininity" and "the case of patriarchy" in more pragmatic terms? Well, my first reaction (again, based only on my viewing of Tim's channel and not having read the books, so take it for what it's worth) is that it is heavy-handed and a bit top-down in their proscriptions of what "real Catholic" men and women have to do and be in their particular roles that does not allow for the liberty and personal character of the social order referenced above.

As I see it, a healthy marriage in the modern age builds from the bottom up on a (hopefully) firm, sacramental foundation. One lives within the vows, which come from above and are consented to. So there is a restriction there, but for the sake of liberty and the respect that comes with it. One pledges to be faithful—in sickness and health, for richer or poorer—but the spouses are not handed a set of blueprints of how to build the house of their marriage from a higher authority. They are not told how many children they are to have, how much to give to the Church in offering, how to school their children, where to live or how to live out their vocation in legalistic dictate. They are given that freedom to build and live in it as they see fit.

I respect my wife enough not to dictate to her what she can and can't do. I certainly don't expect her to "ask me" for permission to leave the house or for any hundreds of minor decisions we have to make in the course of our days. I do expect her to consult with me for big financial decisions, or with things related to our children (schooling, friends, etc.). But we do this in consultation with one another, not me making ultimatums.

There is a great deal of contention about "working women" in Catholic circles, which I choose not to wade into. Part of this is that my wife does work, albeit minimally and not in a way that interferes with family life or her primary vocation as a wife and mother. I have seen the struggles full-time working mothers go through, especially with regards to daycares and balancing everything, and I feel for them. I don't think it's ideal in any sense, though some do seem to pull it off.

With regards to dress, my wife has common sense and a natural modesty that I don't interfere with much. Veiling is a good example of how one could "command" their wives to veil, citing Scripture or Church teaching. I have left it up to my wife, and she naturally took to it over time. But it wasn't by threats or shaming on my part. I think this is a better and more respectful way of approaching matters of modesty.

When it comes to roles, I don't think my manhood is diminished by doing an occasional load of laundry or loading the dishwasher. There was a time when my wife was working full time in which I was doing the majority of housework and daycare pickups, and that didn't work particularly well. There was a degree of doing it for the sake of getting it done, but that it didn't fit my sense of role in the marriage. But again, this was on the lowest level of subsidiarity in which we lived out this way of delineation of duties and learned what worked and what didn't. It wasn't handed down to us from a higher authority in which we were mandated our duties. Like the invisible hand of capitalism, it worked itself out naturally over time when we brought things more in accord with a traditional model of duties.

I could go on with other examples, but I think the point I'm trying to make here is that a healthy respect for freedom and dignity of spouses is not "effeminate" but more in line with authentic Catholic social teaching at the fundamental level of society—the family. I will admit it is a social overlay onto an economic and political model, and it may or may not work in this context. We're all trying to figure out how to live authentic Catholic lives in a confusing modern age. But to the degree that the case for patriarchy and authentic femininity is dictated from above by self-proclaimed "Catholic retrogrades" looking to restore the monarchy and abolish feminism in their spare time by writing books and doing podcasts, we may have to ask if the latitude and freedom of discernment the Church provides in these matters to individual couples is perhaps a better model to adopt. A principle of subsidiarity in marriage, if you will.

ARM IN ARM

Those who know my wife know she is an extremely affable, kind, and just a plain *good* soul—beautiful inside and out. I know this too, but I also know all the day-to-day foibles behind the scenes that also makes her human; this is my exclusive privilege as a husband, to *know* her in the flesh and in the spirit.

One of the greatest gifts and graces of our marriage is that my wife and I have been walking together, serving the Lord, since our beginning. I know it can be a painful cross for many, including those I know, when they are "unequally yoked" to either a lukewarm Christian or an unbeliever. But this is not our cross.

In my essay "The Matter of Life and Death," I wrote about my father in law in his final days. As those days are now drawing down to hours, I have been reflecting more about the role my wife is playing in my father-in-law's final chapter of life. She has always been a dutiful daughter, but her care for her father these past few weeks in his final decline has exemplified the life of a Christian. It is a period filled with grace and intimacy. Wiping and cleaning him up when he needs to be changed. Arranging appointments and coordinating care. Reading him the Psalms as he sleeps. Attending to his every need. Living the Fourth Commandment as a witness to the man who gave her life.

I have done my best to hold down the fort while she's been away. I do a lousy job, and it's been a strain trying to work, watch kids, homeschool, and cook/clean/wash even for just a few days. Where my wife's sanctity excels, mine staggers in survival mode pettiness and an embarrassing self-centeredness. I can't do what she does on a daily basis, and it's glaringly apparent.

The only thing I can figure in all this is to meditate on "the helpers" throughout scripture, the supporting cast, the sideliners: Simon of Cyrene, conscripted to help Jesus carry his cross when he had no strength to; Joanna the wife of Chuza, the manager of Herod's household, Susanna, and many others who were helping to support them out of their own means; Silas, Priscilla, and Aquila who aided Paul in his ministry; Simon Peter's mother-in-law. They didn't have a big role to play, but they did have a role. Even mighty Moses needed his arms held up by Aaron and Hur to win the battle against the Amalekites (cf. Ex. 17:12-14).

Marriage is a school. You learn to love each other, but you also walk arm in arm—sometimes edging ahead, sometimes falling behind your lover. Sometimes you need them to pick you up or sit with you in the mud on the side of the road. Sometimes you need to carry them on your shoulder. The important thing, though, is that you are facing the same direction.

The Lord saves, but we sit at his feet to learn how to love. Then we practice on each other in the most intimate and mundane of settings as husband and wife. We learn the subtle cues, the unspoken signals, the ways of forgiving, and how to support one another. We learn the depths of our own selfishness, and the root of sin. Sometimes it is our spouse themselves who become our cross, the enemy that has dipped his hand in the cup with us, who betrays and denies us before men.

But because we walk not eye to eye, but arm in arm to our Golgotha and new Jerusalem, we play a supporting role in each other's sanctification. In observing my wife living out her role as a daughter, I am strengthening my own vocation as a husband and father. In praying together with her at the kitchen table in the early morning before sunrise, her robe becomes perhaps a future relic that brushes up against my arm.

For us married people, the witness of our faith can happen on our knees in the pew, but that's a fraction of it. It's more often than not at the kitchen table, the bedside, the bathroom, the hospital room. The places we visit in order to live out the love that has been poured into us from Christ himself in our marital sacrament. He has stooped down from Heaven to teach us how to stoop down ourselves. He humbled himself and opened not his mouth to show us what humility looks like in the flesh. He gave us our life so that we can pour it out for not only each other, but the world. The world right in front of us. The world we walk through together, arm in arm.

I know her secrets. I know her weaknesses. I know her little foibles. But I also know her love—for her Christ in the sky, and for her father in the bed before her whose muscles are atrophying and who can no longer swallow. She wipes his brow, holds his hand, consoles his heart for the passage ahead. She has given me and my children the privilege of witnessing it from the sidelines with the other helpers, teaching us what an ordinary holiness, and a commandment lived out, looks like in real time.

THE SPIRITUAL INVESTMENT IN YOUR MARRIAGE

One of the blessings of now being able to work remote two days a week is my morning time with my wife. We usually both get up around 6 A.M. or so (a little bit earlier on my office days), while the kids are still sleeping. Sometimes one of us is up before the other and has some quiet time to themselves.

Whoever is up first will put the coffee on, and we convene at the kitchen table, our de facto domestic community chapel. There we have our Lady of Guadalupe candle, blessed salt and epiphany water, a couple of rosaries, and a 1st class relic of St. Maria Goretti.

Depending on the day, we will sip our coffee and catch up on things either before or after prayer for about half an hour. We talk about the kids, the day-to-day stuff and to-do items, but also anything that needs to be discussed as it pertains to our marriage. It's time "set aside."

When we pray, we bless ourselves with holy water, make a morning offering, and read a chapter of the Carmelite book of meditations, Divine Intimacy. If we have time, we will pray our daily rosary together as well, and then do intentions and pray for those who have asked for prayers.

One of the greatest blessings in my marriage has been my wife as a partner in faith; that we are walking together shoulder to shoulder. But like other aspects of marriage, it requires continual fertilizing and attention. Daily life with a family can get so busy that it's easy to neglect the time set aside to pay attention and connect on the nuts-and-bolts stuff, but also the deeper issues of goals, where we are at individually and collectively, and being open to (and recognizing) grace working in our marriage.

When I was growing up, there was a framed photograph in my parents' bedroom of a Colorado river, with the words "Nothing is ours, but time." Time is hard to substitute. God asks everything of us—our whole heart, mind, strength, and soul—but you can't enter into that relationship without giving Him that precious resource.

In our married lives, time is the exercise of love. Because of the busyness of life, it needs to be intentional, set aside. It's always an unsexy shocker to newly married couples when they hear of people who have married for a while "scheduling" intimacy. But that's another example of investment in your marriage. Hard to believe for newlyweds, but you can get so busy sometimes that you neglect or sometimes forget about sex. Sex is the oil in the engine or marriage...and you can't run an engine for long without oil! To the degree you are investing the time in your marriage, your sexual relationship will act as the barometer. So it's good to keep an eye on the gauge.

Marriage is multi-layered: it's emotional, intellectual, physical, pragmatic, and not the least of all, sacramental and spiritual. For some people, especially if one or the other of the couple is not on the same page, prayer together can be an awkward thing and is sometimes avoided. Like, what do we do? Because my wife and I are on similar pages with our faith, it's relatively natural for us.

But even when it's not, and it feels awkward to pray together, it's still good to do, and pleasing to God. God gives grace to the simple and humble, so make your prayer mirror that characteristic. Set aside time, preferably in the morning for one another, and the evenings for family prayer. Remember the words of scripture, "Behold, I stand at the door and knock; if any man hear my voice and open the door, I will come in to him, and will sup with him, and he with me" (Rev 3:20).

ON MARRIAGE

One thing we know about Christ from the Gospels is that He will enter any home where He is welcome, be it that of a sinner or saint. Think of your marriage itself as a "home" into which Jesus Christ can enter. If you and your spouse reserve time and make a place for Him at the kitchen table, He will honor your request.

THE FLOWERS IN THE CORNER

I'd like to say of the day I proposed to my now-wife, "I remember it like it was yesterday." But the truth of the matter is, I only recall snippets—vignette-like petals of memory, the shards of window glass lying on the doorstep after a break-in.

I remember the name of the coffee shop downtown where we had our first date. It was an establishment trying to figure out its identity: was it a coffee shop? A gourmet food bar, where you could fill half-quart plastic containers with pricey olives and egg salad? A sit-down establishment or a grab-and-go? I had arrived there early; I was wearing corduroy carpenter pants and nervously killed time penning a Metro crossword puzzle I kept in my back pocket. I had more hair on my face than I did on my head.

I don't remember her walking in, or what she was wearing apart from a slightly conservative knit sweater, which she would tighten around her chest as we talked. She ordered a tomato basil salad—cherry tomatoes because she offered me some and I popped them in my mouth like gobstoppers. We talked about our faith, our respective conversions, and reversions. She was so nice, though, so easy to be around. She may have been the kindest person I had ever met.

We got engaged five months later. I proposed on top of a hill at a park in the city over a picnic. It was nothing fancy or contrived, but I had some roses and a ring. Afterwards, we stopped at the grocery store for toilet paper and instant pudding since she was out of both.

Everything related to my memory is bits and bobs, but a complete aberration of timelines and markers. I'm not so bad as Guy Pierce in *Memento*, but it's a struggle. I attribute it to two and a half decades of anti-psychotic medications, but I guess you never know. It scares me some; I'm not a reliable witness of anything. I wonder if I will suffer from Alzheimer's in old age. I write to remember because I so easily forget.

We went through the toilet paper and the instant pudding we used to make friendship bread that afternoon in mid-summer twelve years ago. But the roses remained, now dried and retained in the corner of our family room. Most days, we forget they are even there. If you were to touch the dragon's breath interspersed among the roses, it would explode like a puff of dandelion spores, fall to the carpet like a brush of dandruff. So we don't touch them. They are a museum piece to that iconic time in between my first date with my new love and my last day as a bachelor.

As the years pass, one after another, like the mosaic of leaves that fall year after year around this time, this material memorial remains inconspicuously in the corner of our family room. One kid, then two, now three. The baby of the family, now almost four, still has his baby voice, but I wonder for how long. I try to pay attention to the moments when he speaks, so I can mentally catalog the audio, but I know it's no use. I will forget, just like I forget what time of day or night they were all born.

I remember with our second, our first daughter, getting some air outside the hospital while my wife rested after the birth. There was slush on the ground, and as I smoked a cigarette in a Wawa parking lot I remembered saying to God, "I can't do this," and telling Him that He would have to handle it all because otherwise I would just worry about everything.

I don't know where the days go. Everything bleeds together. That was almost nine years ago. In six years my oldest will be driving. Eventually those voices will deepen and fade out. The noise and mess will be replaced with something else (order? quiet?) and I think then the sadness will settle in because I will want to remember every detail and won't be able to. Just these little snippets of memories.

Someone will breathe on the dragon's breath of my mind and the spores will just flutter off. We'll have the solid gold bands on our fingers, the hardened foundation of our vows, and hopefully the aquifer of our love for one another that will not have run dry. And we'll have the dried flowers in the corner, the museum piece of our beginnings that shouldn't be moved too quickly or carelessly, for fear of it blowing away like crimson powder into eternity.

THE CHALLENGES OF AN INTERFAITH MARRIAGE

I grew up in a mixed-faith household. My mom came from an Anglican background, and my dad was an Eastern rite Catholic. Though neither of them was especially religious, it was a point of contention in their marriage; my dad did not respect the Episcopal church, and my mom didn't feel especially comfortable with the exclusivity of Catholicism. I guess that is why my brothers and I were not raised in either faith tradition and left to our own devices.

Love has no walls as they say. You can't always help who you fall in love with. Love is blind, and its embers often jump the circle of the fire pit. But marriage is almost the opposite—it is a conscious choice, informed by reason and a healthy dose of pragmatism. After eleven years of marriage—not quite veterans, but not quite newlyweds either—I'm still amazed how much of building a life with someone is largely nuts-and-bolts stuff.

Because of the way I grew up, when I became Catholic at age 18, I had it in the back of my mind that I would never marry a Protestant if I could help it. My now-wife had more temptations to marry outside the Catholic faith, though it was not her preference. Her faithful Christian friends encouraged her to consider "widening her net" to include faithful non—Catholic Christians in her dating pool. She prayed to meet and marry a Catholic whom she could share her faith with though, and God honored that prayer. It has been a major point of unity in our marriage that we are grateful for.

Marriage is hard. Faith is hard. Faith within marriage is no exception. The living out of love within marriage is expressed in the daily routine and sacrifices marriage calls for. The living out of one's faith, likewise, is expressed in works, which looks different for a Catholic and a Protestant, especially when they are both faithful to their respective traditions.

What seems to happen more often than not is that one partner concedes things to keep the peace. It could be in obvious ways (not attending Mass) or subtle ways (not expressing devotion to Mary, "holding back" in prayer, etc.). Some couples make it work—they agree to raise the children Catholic, as one example, or attend Mass every Sunday as a family. But there is still something missing that creates a longing in one or both parties, namely, the ability to share something they love with the person they love, fully and without reserve. There will always be a part of their soul which lives in loneliness in these instances.

Can a Catholic marry a Protestant and make it work? Sure. Should they? That's another question entirely. Even as a child, I never doubted my parent's love for and commitment to one another and their vows; they have been married for almost fifty years. But there was an element of unity which was lacking in our family with regards to faith.

For this reason, for any young fervent Catholic who falls in love with a Protestant Christian, I would say be very discerning. Just because you love someone, doesn't mean it always makes sense to marry them (though sometimes the wind of the Holy Spirit blows where He will, and will use it for God's glory). You will undoubtedly have challenges in an interfaith marriage that two Catholics marrying will not have to deal with, and you will need to go in with eyes wide open.

Personally, I would always caution a young Catholic against marrying a Protestant. Marriage is different from any other relationship. It is not just rooted in love and commitment to the vows, but in creating and sharing a life together…for life! And we are called to love and serve the Lord through our spouse, but to put Him before them. "You shall worship the Lord your God and him only shall you serve" (cf. 1 Sam 7:3). One also cannot serve two masters, for "either you will hate the one and love the other, or you will be devoted to the one and despise the other" (Mt 6:24).

Marrying another Catholic does not magically solve all your problems and no marriage is immune from difficulties, but it does create a unique environment of fertile ground for the seed of faith to be nourished in unity by the Sacrament. To quote the great Cardinal Raymond Burke, "There is no greater force against evil in the world than the love of a man and woman in marriage." How much more so when they are one flesh, united in the true faith!

THE PROVERBS 31 CONUNDRUM

When we went to see *A Hidden Life* after it came out in the theaters, my wife said afterwards, "I feel like a wuss." She was referring to being "soft" as a wife, seeing how hard Bl. Franz's wife Franziska worked as part of their daily life as farm laborers. It seemed like every scene she was doing some kind of manual labor, working, being resourceful, often alongside her husband. Life was work. Leisure was an anomaly.

Of course this was one hundred years ago in rural Austria. Franziska seemed to exemplify the Proverbs 31 wife, the "wife of noble character":

> She gets up while it is still dark; she provides food for her family. She considers a field and buys it; out of her earnings she plants a vineyard. She sets about her work vigorously; her arms are strong for the task. She sees that her trading is profitable, and her lamp does not go out at night. She watches over the affairs of her household and does not eat the bread of idleness. (Prov. 31:15-18, 27)

In the scripture, none of this is merely for show. The wife of noble character increases the bottom line of her family in tangible ways. She lets no moment waste—she is strong, resourceful, smart, profitable.

ON MARRIAGE

Today, in 21st century America, I think our women are trying to figure out what it means to be a Proverbs 31 wife. Some weren't taught how to cook and are learning. FemCatholics have adopted the sentiment to say it's okay to work. Traditional Catholic wives wear their aprons and tend to the children as their husband heads off to work. Some wives try to start some kind of home business selling essential oils or LuLuRoe or other multi-level marketing schemes (which exploit the vulnerabilities of homemakers) so they can contribute or start a little garden to "feed their family."

I know some women who married young, and their entire identity is being a mom. They tend to their households and take pride in their roles but have no tangible skills that are employable in the workforce aside from minimum-wage unskilled work.

We live in the tech-era, no longer an agrarian society. Anyone can cut wheat or milk cows, but how many families live in such a way today? Should a traditional wife even want to help her family financially, she finds herself stymied of how to actually do so. It's not for lack of desire.

I had an interesting conversation with a friend from India who works in supply-chain management, who told me recently in a conversation, "Indians are conservative in morals and values—most dress modestly, have strong faith irrespective of the religion they practice, we look after our parents until they die in our homes—but believe in the value of work and independence. To be on your own feet." When I asked her why that was, she replied, "I think it's because we do not have Government handouts. No one will look after you if you don't look after yourself."

It's different for sure, I replied. Women working in the U.S. here has probably led to greater divorce, since they are no longer dependent on their husbands.

"Ah yes," she replied. "The difference with us is the money earned by the wife is still managed by the husband. He is still the leader of the family—currently India is like this. The husband makes the financial decisions most of the time. There is a lot of wisdom in how we Indians have navigated the women contributing financially to the family. But with the onset of U.S. influence (TV shows, primarily) we are seeing an erosion of our values. The working wife usually has her in-laws living in the same house. Usually, the mother in law (who would have retired from her own job) would help the daughter-in-law with the chores of the house and the grandkids when the wife has to go to work."

It was an interesting perspective outside my own culture as an American. Two main differences I saw: the lack of a societal safety net, and the commonness of multiple family living in India. This is not common in American households today. Women are obviously in a bind—they can't necessarily work in an agrarian sense, and to leave the house to work often necessitates daycare, a difficult proposition. Some may live in areas where they have little family or community support, contributing to feelings of isolation. It would seem we don't live in a culture anymore that makes it very easy to live in a way more conducive to family life. I know my Distributist friends have been cognizant of this, and also critical of the breakdown of this possibility of family life where all worked together, as a result of industrialization.

It is a scary prospect for a wife who has no real skills aside from homemaking, should something happen to her husband. I would imagine for such families it would make sense to have at least a $1M life insurance policy should anything happen to the husband, so she does not have to work.

Before anybody jumps down my throat, we all know wives who tend the home work the equivalent of two or three full time jobs. Their husbands often have it easier (in some ways) by going off to an office or whatever all day.

I think the tech-heavy society we live in today makes it difficult for unskilled workers to eek out a living; many wives may be reticent to admit that their home lives are afforded by their husbands being successful members of this tech-class, and many working-outside-the-home wives may be reticent to admit that it is not an ideal situation for homelife without the additional support of a live-in family member, as my friend in India noted. Perhaps the Proverbs 31 wife of noble character is a pragmatic composite portrait of the "ideal wife" and that no one woman would possess all these qualities.

ON MARRIAGE

What then makes a Proverbs 31 wife? Is the model presented by Proverbs ultimately unattainable? Does it place unrealistic expectations on women as an unobtainable ideal? What does "work" for a 21st century American Christian wife and mother look like today? How does/can she contribute to her family so that her husband "has full confidence in her?"

MARRIAGE: A LIFE SENTENCE

It is strange that we have forgotten in the modern era that the very nature of marriage, its essence, is that it is meant for life. Marriage is a primordial good. It is contractual from a civil standpoint, but from a sacramental standpoint, it is more than that; it is a covenant. Modern man tends to think today that, like other obligations, marriage should be temporal with built in exit-clauses when his sensibilities are violated. But this is not marriage. Sacramental marriage is a lifelong commitment, and as such is indissoluble.

And yet for many young people approaching the dawn of marrying age, a large percentage of whom have come from divorced parents, the concept of marrying and being with the same person for forty, fifty, sixty years seems like the stuff of fantasy. Impossible. Much like the attainment of sainthood.

Christ elevated matrimony to the dignity of a sacrament—an outward sign, instituted by Christ, to confer grace. This sacrament bestows upon the spouses the grace necessary to attain holiness and to accept the gift of children. Married people work out their salvation in fear and trembling in their respective state of life—that is, the married state.

By virtue of the sacrament, they are given everything they need to remain married till death and attain the crown of sanctity in the next life. Marriage is their proving ground where the faculty of the will is ground down and exercised every day, sometimes through clenched teeth. It is the school in which Christian spouses learn how to carry out their vocation, which is to love.

The tenuous prospect for many people is how to trust and put their faith in someone else with the future. Will they be betrayed? Will they leave? Will they be faithful? How can they trust them with their finances, their future, their heart? This can be especially hard for people with control issues who are used to being in charge of their own lives. It does require faith—not just faith in God, who provides the grace, but faith in the vows, faith in the person you are pledging your fidelity to. You can't hold tight to your own life while entering into a life with someone else. You have to loosen your grip enough to be able to trust, because trust is the incubator for love.

Lifelong love and fidelity does not have to be an unrealistic fairy tale. What helps is seeing it lived out by others, that is, the Church. No marriage is perfect; all marriages are full of human defects and minor (and sometimes major) betrayals, selfishness, coldness. But what do the fruit of such marriages—the children—see when they look up for reassurance? If they see the rootedness of permanence, that each parent will stick it out through thick and thin and honor their vows, it goes a long way. Children desperately want to believe in lifelong fidelity and commitment but have been fed by way of example and denigrated language that this is a fantasy.

Faith in the ability for a man and woman to honor their vows is no more a fantasy then remaining steadfast on the cross as Jesus did. It is no more a fantasy than faith in God, which transcends cold, logical reasoning. Lifelong fidelity is possible without a marriage being sacramental, much in the same way we can know God to an extent by the light of human reason. But the sacramental grace necessary to endure during the inevitable trials of marriage is indispensable, the way oil is needed for an engine to go hundreds of thousands of miles.

Part of the downfall of modern man is the built in escape clauses he accepts: If one does not want children, go on the pill. If one does not have the money for something, put it on credit. If one does not feel like attending Mass, he is not obligated. And if the luster of a marriage has worn off, there is always divorce to offer a way out.

Nothing of worth is gained without endurance, and merit is never gained apart from grace. "Marriage is a duel to the death, which no man of honor should decline," as Chesterton said. Christ is faithful to his children—we, likewise, are called to be faithful to our spouses and our vows and exercise our gritty will to actualize it. In his love and desire to see us endure to death, He will give us the grace to do so. And no man of honor should decline it.

BEING PRESENT IN THE MARITAL ACT

Marital intimacy is easy to take for granted, at least (if you're like me) married and your spouse and you are in good health—spiritually, physically, emotionally, and sexually. As Christians, however, we recognize that sex in a marriage is more than just mechanics or routine. As the Church teaches, marriage is for the dual purpose of procreation and bonding—both of which the marital act, thankfully, accomplishes well in most cases. But even beyond that, the spiritual elements of marital intimacy are so closely tied to the communicative and life-giving nature of the Godhead that they are integral and necessary for a marriage to be considered sacramental. As the *Catechism of the Catholic Church* states:

> Conjugal love involves a totality, in which all the elements of the person enter–appeal of the body and instinct, power of feeling and affectivity, aspiration of the spirit and of will. It aims at a deeply personal unity, a unity that, beyond union in one flesh, leads to forming one heart and soul; it demands indissolubility and faithfulness in definitive mutual giving; and it is open to fertility. In a word it is a question of the normal characteristics of all natural conjugal love, but with a new significance which not only purifies and strengthens them, but

raises them to the extent of making them the expression of specifically Christian values. (CCC 1643)

With such a heavy weight of responsibility to uphold these values and participate in the divine nature with integrity, it is the grace of the sacrament that makes possible what may seem to be, in many cases, impossible—lifelong love and fidelity.

"By its very nature conjugal love requires the inviolable fidelity of the spouses. This is the consequence of the gift of themselves which they make to each other. Love seeks to be definitive; it cannot be an arrangement "until further notice." The "intimate union of marriage, as a mutual giving of two persons, and the good of the children, demand total fidelity from the spouses and require an unbreakable union between them. The deepest reason is found in the fidelity of God to his covenant, in that of Christ to his Church. Through the sacrament of Matrimony the spouses are enabled to represent this fidelity and witness to it. Through the sacrament, the indissolubility of marriage receives a new and deeper meaning." (CCC 1646, 1647)

For the rich young man Jesus encounters in Matthew 19:16-30 who goes away sad after realizing all he would have to leave behind, our Lord turns to his disciples and tells them in no uncertain terms how hard it is for the rich to enter the Kingdom: "Assuredly, I say to you that it is hard for a rich man to enter the kingdom of heaven. And again I say to you, it is easier for a camel to go through the eye of a needle than for a rich man to enter the kingdom of God" (Mt 19:23-24). In no certain terms, it is an "impossible" undertaking for men, and only possible with God (Mt 19:26).

Another seemingly "impossible" standard is the purity of heart Jesus commands in chapter 5 of Matthew's gospel, taking the Judaic law to a whole other level: "But I say unto you, That whosoever looketh on a woman to lust after her hath committed adultery with her already in his heart" (Mt 5:28).

The act of adultery is a grievous injustice to the vows of fidelity one undertakes in a marriage, not to mention to one's spouse. But such acts do not often come "out of nowhere." Our Lord is an astute knower of human nature; for the first causes of such acts emanate a priori to the act itself: "For from within, out of the heart of man, come evil thoughts, sexual immorality, theft, murder, adultery, coveting, wickedness, deceit, sensuality, envy, slander, pride, foolishness. All these evil things come from within, and they defile a person" (Mk 7: 21-22). He also cares for human persons and human souls so deeply that he wants to spare them the hurt of such dysfunction that sin causes. If you want to uproot a tree, better and easier to do it when it is a sapling than a full grown one.

The term "mindfulness" gets a bit of a knee-jerk reaction in the negative sense among faithful, spiritual Catholics, as it is often used in the context of Eastern, New Age spiritualism. But in other ways, it is a neutral endeavor that involves focusing on the task at hand. If one is eating breakfast, one can be "mindful" of what they are eating—savoring the flavors, noticing the textures—if they are doing just that: eating. But often we are multi-tasking: reading the paper or thinking about what we have to do for the day. By the time we have finished our meal, the experience of eating is a kind of afterthought.

In the Eastern tradition, breathing has always been the anchor for existence (after all, if you're not breathing, you're dead, and so meditative practices have been tethered to the breath as a way of grounding the consciousness). As human beings, without exception, we all breathe, though rarely take note that we are doing so. Mindfulness as I see it in this neutral sense is simply being present to the most fundamental things and practicing that by focusing on the most essential to our physical life—breathing—is a way to start.

When it comes to the "task" of the marital act, the temptations for men and women can take shape in very different forms. For many women, sex truly can be viewed as a task—sometimes willingly undertaken, and sometimes grudgingly, but a task nonetheless. The stereotypical joke is that during sex women may be making a grocery list or thinking about something else entirely apart from what is taking place in the moment. They may be "somewhere else" entirely.

For men, sex has the nature of fulfilling an appetite. However, when that appetite seems to necessitate being satiated at whatever cost, it is problematic, to say the least. Compounded by the prevalence of online pornography and the rate, statistically, with which men view it, men themselves may be not only "somewhere else," but with *someone* else. This is the adultery of the heart our Lord warned us to avoid—the cataloging of mental images to be referenced and brought up as in a Microfiche at the very times when they should be the most present to their spouse—during the marital act itself.

Although I don't have data or anecdotes to support it, I have a gut feeling that men mentally "substituting" another actor in this most intimate act is fairly common. It may be a porn star, or a woman on the bus, that they are thinking about or bringing to consciousness willfully (or even unwittingly) while engaging in relations with his wife. Let's be clear: this is a degradation of the sacred space of the marital bed, even though it may only have been occupied by his spouse. It goes beyond the innocuous example of being present while eating a meal to what one is eating—it is a sin, originating in the mind but willfully entertained, and done so without an admission of guilt or even an awareness of the man's wife.

When I speak to my son about keeping our thoughts pure and maintaining chastity, I try to reassure him that sexual urges are normal and that they may be excited by a fleeting image (an advertisement in public, or even an attractive cartoon character on TV), but that while "the first look is free" (meaning, it can sometimes not be helped when it comes across one's path), the second look will cost you. Our consciousness, like our thoughts, cannot always be kept under control (the proverbial "monkey mind"), but we can train the mind in cooperation with grace (especially the grace of the Sacrament in Matrimony) to attain virtues that may seem otherwise unattainable.

This "mental substitution" of another actor for one's spouse during sex is not only bad training, and carrying with it a degree of moral culpability, but it undermines the enjoyment of sex by counterfeiting it with something illusory. It's a kind of hybrid form of virtual and actual pornography by way of this mental substitution and undermines the sacred bond where it is lived out in the intimacy of the bedroom. Not to mention—it makes for bad sex, because the man (or woman) is not fully present to their spouse, and so not cognizant of their needs and the subtle physical cues that fully communicative intercourse depends on.

Rather than see this as a condemnation, or an unattainable state of being (chastity of heart and body), perhaps men and women can rise to the challenge of being fully present during the marital act by putting their partner first, deferring their own needs, and engaging all their faculties (including the mind) to the "task at hand."

Not being perfect, we will fail at times, of course. But it is something worth getting up for again after a fall. Taking custody of the eyes, cutting out things in our lives that lead to unchastity, and self-deferment in the countless daily acts that make up a married life, is a good start. Though it might take a lifetime, spouses may find that as the years and decades go on, a house built on a good foundation of being present to one another inside and outside the bedroom and turning away from the lure of unchastity of mind and heart, will bear fruit in due season one hundred fold.

THE THREATS TO A CATHOLIC MARRIAGE

Yesterday I was reading a financial independence blog post I came across by way of Reddit that was, for once, refreshingly honest. The guy had FIRE'd (financial independence-retire early) in his late thirties and hadn't updated his blog in five years, mostly because he was "living the life" from 2016-2021 and, I presume, didn't feel like he had much to say. Then life took an unexpected turn, and he found himself divorced, diagnosed with a serious medical condition, and back in the workforce.

Life seemed grand at the start. With his newfound time and leisure, he read, wrote, traveled, and did whatever he wanted. The author found, with time, he could not relate as much to his working friends, and vice versa. His then-wife had retired early with him. While he had planned and focused on this particular goal, his wife was having a harder time with it, and found herself unhappy, unfulfilled, and seemingly without purpose. She committed infidelity, and that was the end of the relationship. When he contracted an illness that he hadn't really planned for, it also threw a monkey-wrench in his nest egg spread-sheet aggregates, to the point where he decided going back to work was the best thing he could do. The author admits, with refreshing honesty, that sometimes you can't plan for life going the way you thought it would.

This isn't the first marriage I heard breaking up after early retirement. Two other popular financial bloggers I read experienced the same thing. These are all secular, left-leaning, non-religious types that hold personal fulfillment and happiness as the pen-ultimate goal in life. A kind of soft, civilized hedonism.

Catholics and religious folk aren't immune to the threats of divorce. Though lower than the national average, Georgetown University's Catholic research institute CARA (Center for Applied Research in the Apostolate) notes a 27% divorce rate for Catholics. What makes Catholics different?

Well, for one, there is a cultural-religious dissuasion against divorce, both in Scripture and Church teaching. Of course, one would have to *believe* in these teachings, that the Lord meant what he said and that the Church's teaching on the matter is for our ultimate salvation and well-being. But, again, life happens in ways we may not be able to anticipate, and we need to be prepared for that. Old age, sickness, poverty are *why* we have vows—the temptation to cut and run when they break onto the scene can be very great.

But how we go into a marriage beyond the vows themselves has a large determining factor in how we respond to these challenges and threats to marriage (which will inevitably come). And even if they weren't established from the get-go, there is always room and grace for renewal.

Though I'm no expert, noticing the threat of divorce in these three particular bloggers devoted to enjoying "their best lives" through financial independence, I thought it might be helpful to identify some of the threats we as Catholics may be susceptible to in our marriages, and their antidotes:

One-Foot-In (and No Plan B)

Anyone who goes into a marriage thinking they can simply leave when things get hard is disadvantaged from the start. This can seem reckless (not having a pre-nup, leaving oneself open to financial ruin, not knowing what the future holds, etc.), but marriage is not meant to be temporary, but for life. Like following Christ, if you are putting your hand to the plow and looking back, you are not worthy of the calling of marriage, for in it one "leaves his father and mother and cleaves to his wife and they become one flesh" (Mt 19:5). It's simply too easy to be "subject to the test" when you give yourself an escape route from the start, or open up a door to it down the road. Which leads to the next point.

Apathy (and Stubborn Grit)

Most people do not wake up one day and decide to get divorced. More often than not it is a slow drift apart where bonds and connections are weakened over time, to the point when you feel like you may or may not know your spouse anymore. You may find the inconveniences and threats to your personal happiness and fulfillment are outweighing any potential gains from staying with your partner. Over time, you find you "just don't care" whether the marriage survives or doesn't.

There's something to be said for grit in the life of faith, a kind of stubborn persistence and bullheadedness to persevere in times of trial, despite the cost. Sometimes the way isn't around, but through, which means taking a hardline approach to care, work, and do whatever it takes to plow ahead, together. It may mean holding your spouse's hand when you can't stand to look them in the face, or refusing to listen to those who counsel you towards divorcing and "finding yourself." It may mean counseling, or late nights; fighting is not always a bad thing, if it means it is keeping the lines of communication open. Essentially, it is a refusal to concede to the pressures (which may be temporary) to jump ship, when everything is telling you to do so.

Selfishness (and Selflessness)

The thing I noticed in the three bloggers and their former spouses above was that what they valued was "doing what works for you" and careful planning (often without children that mess everything up, or limiting them) to the point where the ultimate value was self-fulfillment. This is a death-knell to true marriage, since it operates on a faulty assumption; though marriage may fulfill one person by way of the other, it is not it's intended purpose. Christ taught us as disciples to serve, to wash feet, to die to ourselves. Seeking self-satisfaction at the expense of all else is a futile endeavor and a fools-errand. As true Christians know, it is in serving that we find the key to our fulfillment; in emptying ourselves, we are filled. When we lose our lives, we find them.

Marriage is the ultimate test of self-deferment. If you understand yourself as part of a one-flesh union, and also what Christ did for you on the cross, you begin to understand how love works—by emptying itself. Selfishness is a constant temptation in marriage, but often many marriages on the rocks have turned around not by waiting for the other spouse to change, but by changing oneself and exercising the will to act against its selfish nature. This is hard, like exercise. But love is not authentic without something to back it up. Our spouses often know and recognize when we are doing something for our own sake, or for theirs. It can be transformative, but it takes work.

Betrayal (and Forgiveness)

This can be one area where the rubber hits the road. As Christians, we know the grace that comes with forgiveness for our sins; the kicker is we are expected to extend that grace to forgive one another "seventy times seven." This doesn't mean being a doormat, or not setting appropriate boundaries. It can be an inner crucifixion to realize the one who is laying you up on the cross is the one whom you loved the most, who was closest to you and betrayed your trust with a kiss.

Sound familiar? Again, we are only able to forgive egregious sins because we have been forgiven of our egregiousness by God Himself. It happens by grace, with grit sometimes, and often a good amount of time. In any case, it doesn't come easy; but then again, nothing worth fighting for does. It can be the splitting of the Temple, so to speak. If worked through, though, it may bring up issues that were unforeseen previously, out of the darkness, so that they can be addressed and dealt with. You cannot love without forgiving, and by our humanness we screw up, inevitably. A betrayal may not always be in the form of infidelity, by the way. Trust is a delicate thing. But without forgiveness, we cannot live as Christians, and we become prisoners in our own cell.

Taking Things for Granted (and Gratefulness)

It's easy to take things for granted in a marriage or take your spouse themselves for granted; that they will always be there, or always forgive you or be able to provide for your needs. Nothing is guaranteed, not even our lives. Gratefulness is an exercise to take each moment, each day as a gift that we don't deserve, that is not owed to us; essentially, it's a shift in perspective from all the things that may be lacking, to all the things we have been given. It's an easy exercise in the sense that it doesn't take much to compile, even if it's lowest common denominator stuff—like having running water, or a roof that doesn't leak—but it can also lead us into appreciating things about our spouse in a quantifiable way that we may not have seen previously, when one does it intentionally (making a list, for example). You often don't realize the value of something until it's gone (which it will be one day) so the earlier you can recognize it the better.

Sexlessness (and The Marriage Debt)

Studies have shown that married people have more sex more often than single people. As they should. Sex when it is healthy is bonding and a way of expressing love that goes beyond words. But I've also heard of married couples going weeks, months, even years without being intimate—sometimes for valid reasons, some not so convincing.

Sex is a powerful barometer of the health of a marriage. Conversely, what happens outside the bedroom relates to what goes on inside it. Saint Paul in 1 Cor 7:3 speaks to this, that husband and wife fulfill to one another the "marital debt." This is because neither has authority over his body, but yields it to the spouse (1 Cor 7:4).

Pragmatically, I can only speak as a man to other men: always be conscious of fulfilling your wife. Be a gentleman, both outside the bedroom and in it. You should have enough, ahem, practice that you know her needs and how to delay yourself so that you "hold the door for her" in bed, so to speak. Outside the bedroom, this may mean serving her or speaking to her love languages—just because your fulfillment and sense of being loved comes from sex (as is often the case), this may not be equally true for her. So find out what it is she likes—whether it's a backrub, doing the dishes for her, or giving her a weekend to herself by taking the kids—and do it.

Wives, I know this is going to sound a little blunt, but sometimes the best thing you can do for your husband is go full Nike and "just do it." Even if you don't feel like it or would rather by crocheting or watching TV. Of course, there should be mutual respect in a marriage, but you may be surprised how far sex will go for a man's sense of fulfillment. That doesn't mean you're acting like an on-demand wife, or that you don't have limits or reasonable requests to the contrary. But if you understand that in this realm, men really aren't that complicated and that our appetites are relatively unrefined and simple, it can go a long way.

Another benefit of sex to marriage? Kids! Whether accidental (oops!) or planned, children go a long way in pushing you to your limits and giving a sense of shared goals and self-deference. They are also great at distracting you from too much navel-gazing. So have kids, have a bunch if you can, and don't look back. No one ever says, "I wish I could give them back."

Short Sightedness (and the Long Game)

When my wife and I bought our house I was resistant to the idea of moving at first, because it seemed to stretch us financially and was a hassle; it was easier just not to go through the whole process. My father gave a simple but good piece of advice: short-term stress for long term gain.

When divorce becomes a temptation, it's often seen as an out to an undesirable circumstance. One projects the current reality into a prolonged future scenario—"If I'm miserable now, I will always be miserable," or "If it's this hard now, it will only get harder." That may or may not be the case, but often people are surprised when they pull out and hold on, the "golden years" of marriage are the best yet. Plus you have the benefit of not being alone when you get old, sick, and/or die, you can pool your resources, provide comfort and companionship to one another, and learn and grow more than you may have in your early years. But that doesn't come when you jump ship, but only by patient endurance, those who finish the race to earn the crown (2 Tim 4:7).

The Demonic (and The Grace of the Sacrament)

When you are Catholic and see life through a spiritual lens, you realize there are forces working against marriage and the family, because marriage and family are good and virtuous things, and the Devil is the Father of lies. It may manifest itself by way of temptation or misfortune, but Our Lady of Fatima was clear: the final battle against Satan will be over marriage and family.

Thankfully, as Catholics, matrimony is elevated to the dignity of a Sacrament, and with the Sacrament comes grace. I don't know how people survive life without faith, and grace is the oil that keeps the life of faith running smoothly. If marriage is important to you (and it should be), it's good to strengthen and fortify it with regular Mass attendance, the sacraments, prayer (both together and personal), and sacramentals. Ask for the intercession of our married saints, St. Joseph and the Holy Family, and fortify other Catholic families if you are able, as we all need support and one another. Make a retreat if you find it helpful, and pray for your spouse and children intentionally; fasting and doing penance for them is even better.

As Catholics, we journey to Heaven as a collective. In marriage, we work to get our spouses to Heaven (often by giving them crosses, ha!)

while working out our own salvation in fear and trembling as well. We are not fighting against flesh and blood, but powers and principalities. The sooner we realize this, the more we can develop a battle plan under the protection of Our Lady's mantle to make sure the Devil doesn't have the final say in our lives.

NO COUNTRY FOR MARRIED MEN

If you've never had the chance to witness the film *Into Great Silence*, you should; it's a slow, thoughtful, intimate meditation on the everyday lives of the Carthusian monks of Grande Chartreuse monastery located in the French Alps. The filmmaker, Philip Groning, proposed the idea to the monks in 1984 and they said they wanted time to think about it. Sixteen years later, they said he could come and film. Groning spent almost three years editing; there are no commentaries, no dialog, no sound—just the everyday rhythm of the eremitic life lived in community.

Thomas Merton wrote in *The Silent Life* (1957) about the special charism of the Carthusians and the guarding of solitude above all else:

> It is a spirit of solitude, silence, simplicity, austerity, aloneness with God. The intransigeance of the Carthusian's flight from the world and from the rest of mankind is meant to purify his heart from all the passions and distractions which necessarily afflict those who are involved in the affairs of the world-or even in the busy, relatively complicated life of a cenobitic monastery. All the legislation which surrounds the Carthusian, and has surrounded him for centuries like an impenetrable wall, is designed to protect his solitude against

even those laudable and apparently reasonable enterprises which so often tend to corrupt the purity of the monastic life.

I actually wrote to the Carthusians (Charterhouse of the Transfiguration, the only Carthusian monastery in the United States, located in Vermont) thirteen years ago in a horribly brash and self-assured petition to discern a vocation with them. I recall they responded, but I don't have a record of the correspondence to confirm, and I can't remember the details of the rejection. Whatever their reason, it was probably a good one.

In working primarily from home for the past year of Covid, I've gotten a small taste of the "monastic cell" in a strictly worldly setting. There's an old adage from the desert fathers: "Go, sit in your cell, and your cell will teach you everything."

What have I learned in the "cell" of my office (which is usually alone at the kitchen table, or a small desk in the bedroom when I need to hide from the kids), working the secular equivalent of Evagrius weaving baskets and then setting them all on fire at the end of the year to learn detachment?

I have an incredibly long way to go, and am very far from my true home.

Pride, acedia, laziness, vanity, lack of discipline, and, most especially, a lack of inner peace are all my time alone at home have revealed to me.

Solitude, silence—these things are sweet to a someone at peace. It is a marinade for a soul called to it, that longs for it, relishes in it. For the person not at peace with themselves, silence is unsettling, and solitude disconcerting. But in and of itself, it is only acting as a mirror to the soul, neutral and reflective.

Merton continues in describing the antidote to literal insanity that comes with such solitude for the soul not well disposed to it:

> The Carthusians have been preserved not only by their rigid exterior discipline, but by the inner flexibility which has accompanied it. They have been saved not merely by human

will clinging firmly to a Law, but above all by the humility of hearts that abandoned themselves to the Spirit Who dictated the Law. Looking at the Carthusians from the outside, one might be tempted to imagine them proud. But when one knows a little more about them and their life, one understands that only a very humble man could stand Carthusian solitude without going crazy. For the solitude of the Charterhouse will always have a devastating effect on pride that seeks to be alone with itself. Such pride will crumble into schizophrenia in the uninterrupted silence of the cell. It is in any case true that the great temptation of all solitaries is something much worse than pride—it is the madness that lies beyond pride, and the solitary must know how to keep his balance and his sense of humor. Only humility can give him that peace. Strong with the strength of Christ's humility, which is at the same time Christ's truth, the monk can face his solitude without supporting himself by unconsciously magical or illuministic habits of mind. In other words, he can bear the purification of solitude which slowly and inexorably separates faith from illusion. He can sustain the dreadful searching of soul that strips him of his vanities and self deceptions, and he can peacefully accept the fact that when his false ideas of himself are gone he has practically nothing else left. But then he is ready for the encounter with reality: the Truth and the Holiness of God, which he must learn to confront in the depths of his own nothingness.

My vocation is marriage, as it has been for the past ten years. Such relationships are less hidden than a monk in his cell twenty three hours a day, but that one place where married couples enter into that place is in the bedroom. In some ways, the intimacy of the bedroom is where one enters into the "great silence" of marital love where bodies speak to one another without the need for words; perhaps one of the few times in our day in which we can communicate in such a way.

ON MARRIAGE

But as any married couple knows, the fruit and vitality of the martial embrace is not isolated to the act itself as in a vacuum but draws its health from the days and weeks preceding it in the everyday communions and interactions throughout the day. Sexual intimacy serves as the barometer for the health of a marriage. One can't ignore or neglect or fail to love one's wife all morning and then expect sublime communion in the bedroom in the evening.

It is not realistic to expect a married man to behave as a monk, or work out his salvation in the same way a Carthusian would, though it may have appeal at times. St. Paul made it clear that the married man would be concerned with other things—how to please his wife, the affairs of the world. That it is better not to marry. But it is the vocation I was called to. After ten years of discerning monastic life, it became clear that was not my path. If it was, maybe I would relish the solitude, have opportunities to serve in other ways and enter more deeply into silence and all it affords.

Instead, I find myself snapping at rowdy kids and trying to work an honest day in front of a laptop so I can pay our bills and keep a roof over our heads. When I do have time alone, I squander it watching YouTube videos or frittering around in the kitchen eating whatever I see. I have no abbot, no rule, no guide, just my conscience, which has been chaffing me lately at the sins bubbling to the surface from my time alone in my secular cell within my domestic monastery at how far I am from that divine home, and how far I have to go and how far I have fallen, and how muddied the waters of my mind and soul are versus the crystal clear lakes of pristine wilderness. Silence and solitude is a great teacher, but it's only a mirror.

LAUGH YOUR WAY TO HEAVEN

My wife told me once about a friend of hers who had gotten a new Mini Cooper. After fifteen or twenty thousand miles she took it into the mechanic when it was making a funny noise. "When was the last time you had an oil change?" he asked. "What's an oil change?" she replied. Lesson learned.

A car runs on gasoline, but it won't run long without oil for the engine. Humor is the oil that lubricates the cylinders, keeps things running efficiently, and keeps the engine from overheating. Both my wife and I had our "lists" prior to getting engaged of what we were looking for in a potential spouse.

But it wasn't until about halfway through our marriage that I realized that I had neglected to include a sense of humor on the list. It has proven, in fact, to be one of the top three things I appreciate about my wife. I'd also venture to say, it is an important part to marriage as a whole. Thankfully, as I found out not too long into dating, my wife has a good sense of humor.

Another underestimated thing is liking your spouse. Anyone can *will* themselves to love another, but *liking* spending time with them and being around them—that's not always a natural occurrence. So, if you like your spouse and like being around them, count yourself blessed, since not everyone does. The thing is, if you can laugh together, you will usually like being around one another too, so the two complement one another and make your marriage not only easier, but more enjoyable. Laughing with your partner, though—who probably knows you better than anyone—starts with being able to laugh at yourself.

Being able to laugh in a marriage, especially during times of stress and tension, is like a bleed valve on a boiler that prevents explosions. "Letting off steam" with a hearty guffaw at one's own expense can break tension in a healthy way and stave off blowups.

Knowing how to playfully poke fun without hurting feelings can be a discerning art, though. We always have to act in love, even in jest, and respect our spouses' feelings and those hidden parts which might be regarded as "no-go" zones. But self-deprecation can be disarming—its why comedians always lead with it. Hey, if I can laugh at me, I give you permission too. If I'm laughing and you're laughing—well, let's all have a laugh. "He who dwells in Heaven is laughing at their threats; the Lord makes light of them" (Ps. 2:4).

Humor should be tasteful, though, always gentle and mindful. Essentially, it comes down to not taking things too seriously. As the great St. Philip Neri noted, "Nothing in this world is to be taken seriously, nothing except the salvation of a soul." When Heaven is your goal, everything else falls into its proper place as, ultimately, not that important in the grand scheme of things.

My wife knows all my nonsense, my idiosyncrasies and neurosis. What I know of hers I can laugh at as well. When we laugh together (often at each other), it's often followed by some hand holding or a reconciling if we have been fighting.

I don't know if you can teach humor, as in having a sense of one, but if you just remember not to take things too seriously, not wear the dour expressions of a pharisee, and be okay with making fun of yourself from time to time (and inviting your spouse to as well), you may just get a good bit of mileage out of your marriage.

WHEN YOUR WIFE DOESN'T RESPECT YOU

The longer you've been married, the more you tend to associate with married couples. The odd thing is, from the outside, we are largely unaware of the "aquifer of trouble" running through many marriages. People either tend to put on a happy face when in public or even among friends, or you may (as we have) just be sideswiped one day with the announcement of a divorce you never saw coming. The reasons are often repetitive: "I'm not in love with him or her anymore. I'm tired. I just don't want to do this anymore. I've met someone else. This was never right from the beginning." Or sometimes people change, and they aren't the person they thought they married.

As much as we try to nuance every last scenario today, and not confine people to boxes or predetermined roles, biology has a funny way of being stubborn. You try to push it down, and it springs back up the way it was meant to grow. This can often mean stereotyping, which can lead sometimes lead to good comedy fodder (such as Mark Gungor's "A Tale of Two Brains" on YouTube). It's funny because it's predictable and easy to relate to.

There are two basic but vital aspects to a marriage that should come as no surprise, since they undergird the principals of many marriage counselors: Love and Respect. Before you think this is some secular humanist principals at work, keep in mind as Catholic

Christians we rely on Scripture and Tradition to bring ourselves in alignment with God's plan for marriage and family, and not the other way around. And Scripture is clear: "Each of you must love his wife as himself, and the wife must respect her husband" (Eph 5:33).

Notice two things: Paul does not *suggest* that one love and offer respect. One MUST love his wife, and one MUST respect her husband.

The other thing to note, is that the two terms are meant for their respective parties, and not meant to be interchangeable. Husbands must love their wives (as themselves) and wives must respect their husbands.

This is so fundamental and basic but so easily forgotten in the day to day interchange between spouses. Maybe I will do another post on husbands loving their wives, and what that looks like, but for this post I would like to focus on what I see more commonly: the strife and division caused when wives do not respect their husbands.

Now, before I start, I should say that respect (and authority) is one of those heavy handed words, especially in the context of a traditional community; some women may even get triggered by it because of abuses stemming from issues of respect and authority. Fr. Ripperger has some good points to make in some of his talks of the problem of such abuses within traditionalist communities—men shirking their responsibilities while simultaneously using a heavy hand to demand it or exert authority. If Christ is our model, we see he "humbled himself by becoming obedient to death," (Phil 2:8). Men in fact, as disciples of Christ, are called to love their wives in the way Christ loved the Church—to whom, of course, "he gave himself up for" (Eph 5:25).

How would your wife respond to you if you woke up one day and told her, "I don't love you?" Love is a deep seated need for all men, women, and children. Erik Erikson places it in the middle of his Hierarchy of Needs pyramid, but especially in familial context, I would place it much higher. Just as our Lord said that "man does not live on bread alone," (Mt 4:4) and just as love is tantamount to the Christian life, an unloved person (or even a person who feels unloved) will act according to this deficiency. Wives must not only be loved but *feel* loved in order to thrive.

But it is like a Chinese finger trap, isn't it? The more a husband withholds love or does not make it known (even should he possess it), the less the wife is inclined to offer what she knows he needs, namely, respect. It is easier to respect someone you love, and who you know loves you. But also we see in Scripture, "For rarely will anyone die for a righteous person, though a for good person someone might possibly die for. But God demonstrated his own love for us in this: While we were still sinners, Christ died for us" (Rom 5:7-8). Love is not earned. It can't be earned. Love to be true must be freely given. Which is why we have the cross.

But we also have the cross in our own marriages, don't we? And that cross might just be your spouse themselves! Rather than emptying ourselves, as Christ did, we seek to get filled up. This is the paradox of Christian love, and especially so in marriage.

All that being said, if love is true because it is not earned, what about respect? Is respect earned? I would say respect should be earned, but sometimes a wife can help nurture the virtues in her husband by coaxing them the way the rays of the sun coax a seed out of its shell. Often in marriage, we must act contrary to our natural (fallen) inclinations in order to exact virtue from ourselves, and help to grow it in others.

And the "feeling" part of it is even more acute when it comes to respect. A woman may know her husband loves her but may have trouble expressing it (though he should, even if not verbally). But a man who does not know that he is respected by his wife, and in fact doubts that, will usually find his suspicions confirmed. If a wife respects her husband, she is usually quick to express it (as women do). This could be in sex or praise or a gift or physical affection. And most women have no idea the power such affirmations hold, insignificant as they might seem on the surface. When a man is affirmed, even when he is failing, it is often what keeps him afloat or from seeking out someone else to affirm him, from leaving the family, or from withdrawing. When a man is affirmed, and he knows his wife supports him in everything he does and is trying to do, it is transformative. It makes him want to be a better man.

But the more conditions placed on such respect "I will only respect you if you love me," or "I will only respect you if you do such-and-such around the house," the more the husband learns that his wife's love is conditional. These are when the cracks start to develop in a marriage. The thing is, they can often be filled with simple exercises to reintroduce what a man needs most to flourish—love yes, but mostly: respect.

The tongue is a powerful weapon, and women can cut their husbands down with it, whether directly (to him) or indirectly (to their friends, sisters, etc.). Paul reminds us again, "Let no unwholesome word proceed from your mouth, but only such a word as is good for edification according to the need of the moment, so that it will give grace to those who hear" (Eph 4:29).

To gain life, you must lose it. To be filled, you must empty yourself. This is the Christian paradox, and paradox is at the heart of the Christian life, the Christian mystery. Marriage itself is a kind of mystery sometimes, too! But it's not super complicated either. It just takes an iron will and a lot of stubbornness to stay married in the barrage of storms that threaten it. But if I can make a suggestion to wives: find something—anything!—you respect about your husband and let him know it—even if he doesn't deserve it! Do you "deserve" to be loved? You may be surprised you are thinking with this mind. You may also be surprised that a little yeast, a little respect, goes a long way in leavening the whole loaf.

ON FAMILY

"THAT'S THE GOOD STUFF"

I saw this image the other night and it hit me right in the feels. It said very succinctly, in a kind of koan-type fashion, exactly what I have thought on many occasions, and how easy it is not to be present to the blessings right in front of you.

In my article "Looking in From the Outside," I wrote:

> Middle age is a tough time for dads. You're so focused on your career and managing things that time is at a premium. I try to balance having time for myself (time that my wife usually doesn't have as a luxury, admittedly), time with other men, time with my parents, time with my wife, time with my kids, time writing, and time in prayer.
>
> My wife was chastising me a bit last night for not being present with my kids when I have the opportunity. She's not wrong. She is a 'be-er' and I'm a 'do-er.' Every time I do have the opportunity to just 'be' I end up 'doing' something instead. Everyone knows that you can't substitute time together with other things and expect to have a healthy marriage. And the more time you spend with someone, the more you get to know them, and want to spend time with them. I feel like my kids pick up on that I am not as present with them as their mom is,

and so they turn to other 'things' to fill the vacuum that I could be filling if I was more present.

There's an image I have, when I go out on the patio for some time to myself, of looking from the outside in while the rest of my family is inside. I've chosen to take time for myself, but I would be horrified if I tried to come back in the house and it was locked for some reason. Then you realize the place you really want to be more than anywhere, with your family, you're barred from, because of what you've chosen instead. I know it's just a moment but I don't want it to project as a future reality. Moments add up to days, and days to years, and before you know it if you're not careful, you can become a stranger in your own house.

My wife was telling me something she heard from Leila Lawler, some erudite wisdom on homemaking and childrearing, along the lines of "You don't 'make memories' for your children. They make their own memories." I don't know the exact context of what she was saying, but from what I surmised, the trip to Disney World, or the birthday party or whatever is often not the true memory. The memories are those snippets, those scraps of tapestry, that the children make for themselves. It could be the smell of the salt air, a song heard on the radio, laying on the couch with mom, or the salted caramel ice cream cone your dad treated you to.

We played a round of miniature golf yesterday and walked over to the Wendy's afterwards to treat the kids to some frosties and things. It was a great day for them, and it wasn't because of the mini golf or the burgers or any one thing, but because we were together as a family. I don't make much money and I don't have any real professional status or standing. But I realized many people would kill to have what I have. My new core memory as a dad that day was seeing them at the table as I ordered food, and realizing I am not a poor man, but instead very, very rich.

ON FAMILY

The late Robbin Williams has a fantastic monologue in *Good Will Hunting* (part of which I heard was unscripted) when he's talking to the young Will about his deceased wife:

My wife used to fart when she was nervous. She had all sorts of wonderful idiosyncrasies. She used to fart in her sleep. One night it was so loud it woke the dog up. She woke up and went like "oh was that you?" I'd say yeah...I didn't have the heart to tell her...Oh God...[laughing]

Will: She woke herself up?

Sean: Yesssss....aahhh. But, Will, she's been dead two years and that's the shit I remember. Wonderful stuff, you know, little things like that. Ah, but, those are the things I miss the most. The little idiosyncrasies that only I knew about. That's what made her my wife. Oh, and she had the goods on me, too, she knew all my little peccadillos. People call these things imperfections, but they're not, aw, that's the good stuff.

We are coming up on our thirteenth year of marriage, and I have plenty of those memories of my wife—the things that make her my wife. The time she dozed off looking at her phone and dropped it on her head; the particular sigh she makes which distinguishes whether she is angry or just tired, which would be lost on anyone but me; when she laughs and then accidentally snorts at the same time. I try not to take them for granted, either, to recognize and give thanks for that privileged place.

There's a saying I'm fond of, when it comes to your life in Christ as a Catholic:

You have all that you need.

You have the grace of your baptism; the heavenly manna of Christ's flesh in the Eucharist; the opportunity to confess your sins to a priest; a community of fellow pilgrims and those who have gone before you, the saints; the solace of prayer and silence; the assurance of the promise of salvation; the opportunity to become a saint. We are rich in faith, every single one of us. And if we're not careful, there will come a time when you would give all you have to have that again and not find it. You will remember the heavy smell of incense, the flicker of an offering candle bouncing light of the stained glass windows, the solidness of the oak pews where so many hands have been placed, the unlocked door that allowed you to sneak in for a few moments of quiet.

Same goes for our families, or marriages. These are great graces which we can build up, invest in, and recognize them for what they are: moments stitched together in time, moments not promised that can be taken away from us at any moment as the Lord wills. Each moment can be sacred, can be sanctified, especially while the kids are young—if we are paying attention and not letting it pass us by. This is what makes a man rich, establishes a legacy. You have all that you need.

WHAT SHOULD A CATHOLIC FAMILY LOOK LIKE?

Occasionally I get slightly self-conscious because although we are Catholic through and through, and our faith is the most important thing in our life, we don't always comes across as the most "Catholic" of families. We have been known to have family dance parties in the kitchen to top-40 pop songs from the radio. We don't pray the rosary consistently every night as a family (though my wife and I do make every effort to pray it daily on our own). My youngest wears urban hand-me-downs I got from a black family in Philly, and my daughter refuses to wear long dresses. My humor is sometimes off-color.

On the flipside, we home school, my oldest son serves the Latin Mass, we say grace before meals, and we have Catholic books, art and crucifixes throughout the house. We love the Lord, we love our faith, and we try to live it out where it matters.

We are heading to our monthly poetry recitation after Mass this morning with our co-op, and I was joking around with my wife that I should recite Gregory Corso's beat poem *Marriage* (published in 1960), which begins: "Should I get married? Should I be good?" Even though I didn't live through that time period, the Beats were a huge influence in my life growing up—for better or worse. I wanted to write like Jack Kerouac, who threw syntax and conventional form out the window and banged out his epic novel *On the Road* in 1957 on a single scroll of typewriter paper. The Beats were critical of post-war American conformity, typified by jobs, marriages, and suburban domesticity, and I shared Kerouac's affinity that "the only people for me are the mad ones, the ones who are mad to live, mad to talk, mad to be saved, desirous of everything at the same time, the ones who never yawn or say a commonplace thing, but burn, burn, burn like fabulous yellow roman candles exploding like spiders across the stars and in the middle you see the blue centerlight pop and everybody goes 'Awww!'"

But Kerouac died un-enlightened, suffering a massive abdominal hemorrhage at the age of 47. *The New York Times* obit interviewed his wife the day after, who told reporters, "He had been drinking heavily for the past few days. He was a very lonely man."

"I'm not a beatnik. I'm a Catholic," Kerouac used to make a point of telling reporters. And he was. The late 1950's and 1960's were marked by an upheaval of conventional social mores, and Kerouac was no exception to being swept up in this wave of throwing off shackles—of syntax, of dogma, of sexual morality, of what was expected of a good American citizen.

And yet the irony is that as huge an influence as Kerouac and the Beats were on my teenage and young adult years, I saw the writing on the wall: no one was happier, no one was enlightened, and their sexual forays didn't bear fruit worthy of eating. When I met my wife and ultimately got married, I wasn't asking the question "Should I get married? Should I be good?" or feeling like I was succumbing to social convention based on the expectations of others. Rather, I said to myself, "I want to get married, because this is good." And it truly has been.

I do from time to time get a case of the shoulds, mostly related to how we look "on the outside" as Catholics while other homeschool parents are living out the liturgical year with little crafts for their kids, and families are going to Catholic Family Land, etc. But as the saying goes, "comparison is the thief of joy." I certainly don't want to give scandal by doing anything contrary to the faith or in morals, and I think we're good there—because if we weren't, none of the externals matter.

But is there a "typology" of what a Catholic family should look like? I don't think so, and I'm not going to make some bullet point list of things you can do to look more Catholic as a family, either. To be honest, I think the bigger problem is that for many American families who are Catholic and may even go to Mass every Sunday, they are largely indistinguishable from the culture at large.

So, what should a Catholic family look like to those on the outside? I think first and foremost, as we see in today's Epistle from 1 Peter, "Before all things have a constant mutual charity among yourselves; for charity covereth a multitude of sins. Using hospitality one toward another, without murmuring...that in all things God may be honored through Jesus Christ, our Lord." (1 Pt 4:7-11) Catholic families should have charity as their mark, and joy as the plate it is served on.

I do remember that when I was in high school and before I was Catholic going to a friend's house and noticing a picture of the Sacred Heart on the wall. I thought to myself, "What's that?" but it always stuck with me...and I came into the Church a few years later. So, Catholic art is a good thing, and can be an external mark as well that has the potential to lead others to curiosity, and perhaps ultimately, salvation through grace. Saying grace before meals in public, or praying the rosary on the train, can be good things if they do the same.

I do think some people get it in their heads that they have to "dress the part" or use churchy language all the time, or any other number of things in order to stake out their Catholic identity especially if one is trying to figure out "how to be Catholic" and what that looks like externally. That's all fine and good, but to the degree it comes from a spirit of comparison or even a kind of spiritual covetousness, it would be better to eschew those externals and focus on inner conversion, prayer, and charity and let the rest eventually take care of itself. We don't wash the outside of the cup first, but the inside (Mt 23:25).

Writers try to find their voice by borrowing from other writers and trying on their style, as I did with Kerouac. But over time, my confidence in both my identity as a Catholic, a husband, and a writer grew, and I found I didn't need to try to sound like X, or write like Y, or dress like Z. I could just be myself, and be that well, as St. Francis de Sales was so fond of exhorting.

A true Catholic identity is more like a blush that subtly highlights rather than a bright red lipstick meant to draw attention to itself. So, to the extent you are loving the Lord, honoring him in worship, being charitable to your neighbor and the poor, and raising up your children to do the same, you're most likely on a good track.

THE MOST ORDINARY THINGS

There was this thing floating around social media a while back, this little inspirational insight geared towards women and their spirituality. It went something like this:

GOD COMES TO THE WOMEN

Have you ever noticed how in the scriptures men are always going up into the mountains to commune with the Lord?

*Yet in the scriptures we hardly ever
hear of women going to the mountains,
and we know why—right?*

*Because the women were too busy
keeping life going;
they couldn't abandon babies,
meals,
homes,
fires,
gardens,
and a thousand responsibilities to make the climb into the mountains!*

WISDOM AND FOLLY

I was talking to a friend the other day,
saying that as modern woman
I feel like I'm never "free" enough
from my responsibilities,
never in a quiet enough,
or holy enough spot
to have the type of communion
I want with God.

Her response floored me,
"That is why God comes to women.
Men have to climb the mountain to meet God, but God comes to
women wherever they are."

I have been pondering on her words for weeks and have searched my
scriptures
to see that what she said is true.
God does in deed come to women
where they are,
when they are doing their ordinary,
everyday work.

He meets them at the wells
where they draw water for their families,
in their homes,
in their kitchens,
in their gardens.

He comes to them
as they sit beside sickbeds,
as they give birth,

care for the elderly,
and perform necessary mourning and burial rites.

Even at the empty tomb,
Mary was the first to witness Christ's resurrection,
She was there because she was doing the womanly chore of properly preparing Christ's body for burial.

In these seemingly mundane
and ordinary tasks,
these women of the scriptures found themselves face to face with divinity.

So if—like me—you ever start to bemoan the fact that you don't have as much time to spend in the mountains with God as you would like. Remember, God comes to women. He knows where we are and the burdens we carry. He sees us, and if we open our eyes and our hearts we will see Him, even in the most ordinary places and in the most ordinary things.

It irked me then, and it irks me now. And I've been trying to figure out why.

I mean, I get the point. It speaks to the busy Marthas who "find God in the dishes and diapers." Most moms can't go to the bathroom for thirty seconds in peace without a toddler jiggling the lock on the door, let alone find time to themselves the way men do. It's sometimes thrown in our faces as a kind of double standard (usually when our wives are tired and frustrated and running on empty).

Our Lord makes this clear in the ordering of the Commandments—Love God (first), then you will be able to love neighbor as yourself. He makes it clear that Mary has "chosen the better part" in her otherwise useless adoring at Jesus' feet while her sister runs herself ragged with the deets.

WISDOM AND FOLLY

When I was in discernment with the Benedictines, *ora et labora* was everything. This included an attentiveness to the work at hand so that it was not done slovenly or carelessly. And yet, it was clear that the *actual*, primary work (in the monastery) was prayer (i.e., "the work of God").

Cue the eye rolling. "Well, this is a home, not a monastery. And you are not a monk. And while you are at it, do some dishes!"

All true. But back to the mom-post at hand.

What exactly is being conveyed here? I think what it comes down to is that *I am not a woman*. I think what irks me about it is this subtle inversion that the domestic work is, in fact, the "real work" and that men "going up the mountain to commune with God" is somehow secondary. It lists out and numerates all the domestic duties—babies, meals, homes, fires. SAHM: 16. Husband: 1. Not to mention the messaging obviously meant to convey a sense of solidarity: Women stay put; men run off. "Men have to climb the mountain to meet God, but God comes to women where ever they are."

On one level, I can't relate to their domestic work anymore than I expect my wife to be out mowing the lawn and sweating in ninety degree heat every ten days, or taking the car in for inspection and oil changes, or taking out the trash. This is stuff I do, and I'm fine with it. But it's not my primary preoccupation. It doesn't define my identity or where I find my "tribe," and it's in addition to putting 40+ hours in outside the home. *It's just stuff that has to get done*.

My primary vocation, however, is to head my family—spiritually, financially, and corporally. And yes, that sometimes does necessitate "going up the mountain to commune with God." This isn't something to be scoffed at or dismissed as pie-in-the-sky spiritual idealism, pitting women's work against men's work. If I'm not doing that (and believe me, it's not as often as I would like), I'm not following the Lord's model as a man, Jesus "who often withdrew to lonely places and prayed" (Lk 5:16); who was tested (Mk 1:12); who "very early in the morning, while it was still dark, *left the house* and went to a solitary place where he prayed" (Mk 1:35).

I have no issues with women finding solidarity with one another in their domesticity, which often can be their own kind of "lonely place" where they feel isolated and disconnected. There can be a tendency to enshrine the home as their kind of domestic palace where they rule as Queen. And God bless them for it. Let's face it—most men don't know how to do this stuff with the same touch that women do. A monastery, maybe. But without our wives, we'd have a house, but not a home. We benefit from it, and we shouldn't forget it.

But women, for their part, shouldn't forget that it's that very "communing with God" which is what *spiritually fortifies* the home and makes it a sanctuary from the outside world. If we traded those early morning hours, or those times away "up the mountain," we trade away our spiritual fortitude and protection which comes from hearing the word of God in prayer and carrying it out in our vocation as husbands and fathers. Otherwise we don't grow but stagnate in the here and now.

My wife has plenty of opportunities to get up early and pray the Psalms, or meditate on the scriptures, or drive to the Adoration chapel. So do I, for that matter. We just trade these golden opportunities for inferior things—scrolling on our phones, lounging around, shuttling from here to there. We both de-prioritize what should be our top priority—God—we just do it in different ways.

I think where the difference lies is that men need to carve out this time intentionally and separated from others, whereas women, in my experience, enter into those culminated little moments of divine encounter throughout their day, organically, and often in communion with other women. It is natural for me to get up early and "go to a lonely place" to pray with a degree of asceticism, whereas for my wife this may not be necessary. For my part, if all I did was wash dishes and change diapers and make lunches or whatever all day, and didn't work, I think I would want to kill myself. For my wife, she jokes that as hard as it is some days on the SAHM front, she's "living the dream." And she means it.

Men's spirituality and women's spirituality doesn't have to be pitted or scored against one another. We are different for a reason—"male and female He created them"—and find and serve God in different ways. Though I have many women saints I admire, my calling is to be a man, and be the best man God has made me to be. That means prayer and work—*ora et labora*—appropriate to my state in life. Not "my work is my prayer." Prayer AND work. And if I have to go up a mountain for a few days to live that out, then so be it.

We find God when we embrace what He has called us each to live out and who he has made us to be, as men and as women respectively. Mountain or no mountain.

A FATHER'S EYE VIEW OF MOTHERHOOD

On September 8, 2008, a 66 year old father was working outside with his 20 year old son when the son fell into the septic tank on their property. The father immediately jumped into the tank and for fifteen minutes held his son's head above the sewage while he himself remained submerged until help arrived. The son was hospitalized but lived; the father did not.

There are many layers to this story, and when laid one upon another made it hard for me not to be moved when I heard this account of seeming misfortune. For one, the son (the youngest of seven) had Down's Syndrome; at no point did the father weigh the pros and cons or merit of that fact in his decision to dive into the cesspool after him. Nor did he hesitate to offer his own body as a buoy so that his son might have a chance of surviving the noxious submersion. He simply fulfilled what a father, by nature of his vocation, is called to—namely, to sacrifice. It was a noble and memorable example of the depths fathers are willing to condescend to in order that they might give life to their seed.

How I live out my vocation as a parent is refracted through the prism of being a man, a son, and a father. But parenting as a father is not a complete protein. The complementary of this vocation is accomplished in partnership—that is, namely, with my wife, the mother of my children.

From the very beginning, when your child is still incubating in the womb of their mother, there is a latent sense among fathers of being ill-equipped for many of the vital tasks demanded of by children. The bond at that point in development is more psychic than physical—at no point are they attached to or dependent on your body for sustenance in the way they are their mothers. When the child is born, we become late-night waterboys for our quarterback wives during the act of breastfeeding.

As they grow older and are weened, they still instinctually cling and find their way to their mother who provides the comfort and innate nurturing that we can only fabricate. Whereas I was back to work after a week of each of my kids being born, my wife spent every waking hour with them for months, learning their unique needs and temperaments. I would receive this data from her second-hand and store it in my mental repository just in case I needed to corroborate for a doctor or an inquisitive bystander that they were indeed my own children, and I knew enough insider information about them to prove it.

One of the privileges of fatherhood as a married man (much to the chagrin of many a wife) is that I can periodically "check out"—either physically or mentally—and grab a beer at the pub with a buddy, shop for a new circular saw at Home Depot unencumbered, or simply go to sleep uninterrupted. I'm "needed"—but not in any kind of primal, dependent way. Whereas in the Genesis account woman is created from man to be his helpmate in their single state, the roles are reversed in parenthood—man becomes the helper of woman, who is the source of life, the wellspring of Eden, and the eve of creation.

It is a fashionable parody in modern media to portray fathers as hapless gomers with their hands in their pockets when it comes to the rearing of children. As any father involved in the life of his children knows, we play a vital and irreplaceable role in their formation and developmental well-being. But there is something about a mother that goes deeper, like an aquifer. Whereas men of virtue will sacrifice themselves to provide, to protect, and yes, even give their lives for their children (and their mother), a mother will literally *pour herself out* for her children. This applies to married women, single mothers, those who adopt, and widows alike. You cannot gestate an entirely genetically autonomous being for nine months, birth them into the outside world, and feed them with your very body without incurring the status of a...well, a kind of *queen*.

And that is how we should treat the mothers of our children, and the debt to which we should recall when it comes to our own mothers. We remember it with a day in May with cards and flowers, and maybe breakfast in bed. But really, we owe the existence of the entire human race to those called to the most primal and ordinary vocation: that of motherhood. This is why even the most hardened criminal will put you up against a wall for a sleight-of-hand comment about his mama and an orphan will have a hole in their heart that may scab over but never completely heal.

It can be a strong temptation for married mothers to put their children above all else, and at first glance the nobility in this seems apparent. But in fact, just as the birth of a child is preceded by its coital conception, and its coital conception is preceded by its eternal predestination, the order of things matters. For the married mother to overcome this temptation of seemingly noble self-deference to put her children before all else, she must in fact subsume this tendency to a hierarchical ordering and prioritization: God first, her husband second, and her children third. In doing so, she will align her vocation with the natural order that makes everything work—for the glory of God for God's own sake, for the honor of her husband, and for the benefit of her children.

In the Gospel of John it is recounted, "Jesus also did many other things. If they were all written down, I suppose the whole world could not contain the books that would be written." These words sometimes come to mind while observing my wife carrying out her everyday duties as a mother, much of which I would be hard-pressed to undertake for even twenty-four hours. I think if anyone were to do the same, they would echo the apostle's words and say of mothers *"she also did many other things...if they were all written down, I suppose the whole world could not contain the books that would be written."*

MY SON, WHERE HAVE YOU GONE?

Whenever I have reflected on the parable of the Prodigal Son in Luke 15, my focus has been on the younger son. We are presented with two sons, of course, but my life experience has always tracked with the prodigal; the elder son became a kind of peripheral character.

But there is a third figure in this story, and that is the father himself. For the past decade my kids have been little, so our lives revolved around diapers, tantrums, and keeping them from whacking their heads. I was a father, sure, but in that initial stage of fatherhood.

Now that my son is ten going on eighteen, I'm beginning to wrestle with different issues now—the difficulty in relating to him, connecting with him, navigating the moodiness and sometimes disrespect, and sensing a growing distance between us that I struggle to address. I don't think it's anything out of the ordinary for a parent, but it still weighs on me. I'm proud of him in so many ways—he is an accomplished thespian and serves at Mass, among other things—and feel I tell him that I love him and am proud of him often. But suddenly, that archetype of being a runaway son has shifted and I am now sitting in the father's seat bracing for the day my son wishes I was dead already and slams the front door behind him on his way out.

In our circle of orthodox, solid, Catholic homeschooling families I think there can be this temptation that our children are a reflection of us as parents that gets held up in the community. If our kids are "good," we're doing something right—teaching, catechizing, and raising them well, a badge of honor. If one of our kids go off the rails, there's not only the pain of estrangement and feeling helpless, but the shame of what it looks like to those in our circles.

I think this is a projected fear—of being judged or whispered about—that is overstated. Most of the inner shame of our failings as parents is seen in scarlet through our own eyes, and the regret can be bitter, *"If only I had spent more time with him. If only I had been more intentional about catechizing her. If only I hadn't yelled so much, lost my temper so easily. If only I had been a better dad."*

I have a buddy who I get beers with every now and again; I can tell when he needs some encouragement because he feels the weight of his four boys trying behavior and the self-imposed feeling that it reflects poorly on him as a father, that he's doing something wrong. When he loses his patience with them, is forced to discipline them out of love and concern, when he's told them to do something a hundred times and they just don't listen, he says, "This is how God must feel with me."

A friend told me a story of someone he knew back in the U.K. who had gone to Thailand on a trip as a twenty-something and got into drugs; he was in all aspects, a true prodigal living dissolute among the swine. His father had no idea where he was, but his care and concern prompted him to fly halfway around the world to set off and find him. He carried his picture around the streets of Bangkok, asking people if they had seen him, until one opportune moment led him to a drug den where lo and behold, his filthy, sick, strung out son was. He gathered him up and took him home.

You don't know the love and sacrifice you are capable of until you become a parent, the fruit of your vocation. For the father in the Lord's parable, his nobility and tender character would seem to lend itself to the belief that his legacy was good stock. He gave his sons everything, was a good father to them, and still one goes off the rails and the other seethes in resentment. What went wrong? How bitter the recollection of the prophet Isaias' words in his mind, "All your children will be taught by the Lord, and great will be their peace." (54:13) How the townsfolk must have talked when he went into the village.

None of that matters, of course, to the father. He searches the horizon day after day and is willing to gird his loins and run in such an undignified manner to meet his returning son when he sees him in the distance—the son who had no regard for his dignity or respect for his authority—embracing him and showering him with the great good of his household. He had every right to turn from him and disown him, as the son recognizes in his rehearsed speech, "Treat me as one of your hired hands." (Lk 15:19).

The father was not a tyrant-turned-empath. His character was one of compassion, devotion, and paternal love from the beginning. It would seem that one could not blame the father for "failures" of parenting that drove his son away. The father did everything in his power, and still his heritage turned against him and made him the object of murmur within the community. The parable is as much a story of the exercise of free-will as it is of fervent love, longing, and forgiveness.

As fathers and mothers, we all have a heightened sensitivity to our parental failures. We also are subject to the temptation to comparison: "So-and-so has such good kids. They're all doing so well. And look at us."

Part of the added temptation of traditional Catholicism, I think, is "If one simply does X, Y results." Because the liturgy is constant and unchanging, and the rubrics a protection against abuse, I suspect that there may be a tendency to internalize this and apply it to our children. "If we attend the Latin Mass every Sunday, if we don't fraternize with pagans, if we homeschool, etc., our children will not turn away." And for some, that may be the case.

And yet when I reflect on the good father in the parable, he seemed to have done everything right, and his son(s) still strayed...and not only in slight, but in complete dissolution. Is the father the one to blame for the sons indiscretions? Did he spare the rod and pay the price for this dereliction of duty? Was he emotionally distant? Too protective? Not protective enough?

Or is it simply the exercise of that awesome and fearful gift of freewill that God entrusts each of us? That gift that we can use against Him, just as our children may use against us one day despite our best efforts to keep them on the straight and narrow. It's uncomfortable to think that our control as parents is in many ways, illusionary. We set boundaries, we do our best without a Missal for Parents, and still sometimes the rubrics aren't enough, and our children stray for whatever reason. I would ratchet it as one of life's great and tragic mysteries that can even lead some parents to the brink of despair. Parenting is not an "A+B=C" affair. There are a lot of unaccounted for variables.

My darkest nights as a parent are when everything seems to be drifting, and I don't know how to reign it back to the way it was. I experience a loss of control and am driving in the dark with no headlights. I miss my son; I don't want to lose him. In these times, my faith in the paternal love of God is all I have.

Our lives as Christians are founded on the hope of resurrection and ultimate redemption. We know no son or daughter is beyond God's mercy and saving grace, no matter how lost or far gone. As parents, it is our job to never lose that hope, to always be scanning the horizon in prayerful anticipation of that homecoming, to run out and embrace when they are still a long way off and relish the miraculous joy of the dead coming back to life.

MOUNTAINS & HOMEPATHS: REFLECTIONS ON "HAVING A FAMILY TO GO HOME TO"

After I graduated high school I set off to hike the Appalachian Trail for the summer. I started out with a friend who accompanied me for a few weeks; when he had to leave the trail to head back home, I faced a hard bout of loneliness. One night in a lonely A-frame shelter, I was reading the Psalms in a Bible that was left there and feeling especially homesick, quietly crying to myself. Another hiker showed up and I was embarrassed at what I felt was a weakness of character. I confessed to him that I felt like bagging the rest of the trip, and I'll never forget what he said to me, "You know kid, a lot of these guys on the trail are out here because they don't have a family to go home to. Sounds like you do."

One of my buddies from high school (not the same guy who accompanied me on my AT hike) and I grew up hiking, camping and road tripping together out West, picking up hitchhikers in Tucson, pitching a tent in White Sands, and sleeping in our borrowed Explorer in the Gila wilderness. Ivan's* (name changed for privacy) parents were divorced, and his mom was remarried to a guy he regarded as a kind of ogre whom he had no love or regard for. Ivan was a very good looking guy with rugged features, who had done some modeling. While he always seemed to be the kind of guy who would be featured in a *Men's Health* or *GQ* magazine, I always felt there was a deep insecurity about not knowing how or what it meant to be a man that lived beneath the surface. His father didn't really raise him, and his stepfather was a kind of stranger in his home.

As we went to college and even after college, we stayed in touch. I settled down in my late twenties and got married, but Ivan never did. He continued to live a nomadic life that I lived vicariously through. I would send him texts, "Where in the world is Ivan today?" and he would text me back from a sailboat in Iceland or some remote village in a far-off country. He was a talented photographer, who had gone to grad school to learn it. "Man, he is living the life," I thought.

At some point, he became a Mormon and did a two year mission in Russia. I believe the Mormon religion was attractive to him because it offered the prospect of the family he never had and always wanted. The community he joined seemed to take him in, though he found it difficult to meet a girl to settle down with given that he was now in his late thirties and never had a steady job or way to provide. He eventually left the Church of LDS; I assume he just became disillusioned, possibly with the theology, but also that perhaps he never ultimately found what he was looking for: a family and a home.

The last time I texted Ivan he had converted a van while crashing on a friend's couch in L.A. and was living on BLM (Bureau of Land Management) land somewhere in California. He was the definition of a conquistador adventurer, but we were now in our forties and I got the sense in corresponding with my friend that all he really wanted was a family, and by this time it was too late. Whether he was suited for that, or was running from something that haunted him deep down, I'll never know, as we fell out of touch.

Behind the perceived Instagram glory of adventure and the nomadic life, I tend to think a lot of people living "on the road" are not doing it for "kicks" as the Beats would say, but because many don't have a place to go home to or a family to open the door for them. Somewhere along the way the adventures of one's twenties becomes the loneliness of one's forties, running from something, the way a trilobite gets ensconced in amber.

I used to think I was "selling out" in leaving this fledgling life of a wanderer and settling down to get married and start a family in the suburbs. But now that I am in it, I realize it was where I was called to be. I'm grateful to have found my vocation and can devote myself to the business of living it out. I know many who want to but haven't yet met the person to do it with. On days like today, it's a good opportunity to open your home to these friends and strangers if you are able. One of the gifts many of us have been blessed with that makes for the envy of many is, simply, a family and a home, something we can often take for granted.

Happy Thanksgiving, Christian pilgrims. May you always have a door to be opened to you when the road gets weary.

SAINT JOSEPH'S PAIN

Fr. Calloway has done a great service to the Church in promoting devotion to Saint Joseph during this year of the great saint. As he mentions in his book, Saint Joseph lived much of his life in the shadows. Sometimes, though, the greatest witnesses are those hidden from view.

Many pious women have lauded Fr. Calloway's book and devotion to the saint, and laudably so. A man by his nature will never know the discomfort of carrying a child in their body the way a woman can, or the pain that gives way to joy in birth but can only admire it from afar. But for the man carrying his burden, trying to do the right thing, protect and provide for children, and do what the Lord is calling him to, Saint Joseph reserves a place to enter into his hidden life in a way which, I suspect, may be hard for a woman to fully experience.

As I reflect on St. Matthew's gospel account of the Annunciation, I imagine Saint Joseph being in the Divine shadow from the beginning. Bestowed with special graces, and an essential figure in the Holy Family, he was nonetheless a regular human being—unlike Mary, in that he was not spared from original sin; and unlike Jesus, his foster son, not Divine. And yet his quiet obedience was unparalleled. His *fiat* was expressed wordlessly and in deed, "being aroused from sleep, he did as the angel of the Lord commanded him and took him his wife" (Mt 1:24).

WISDOM AND FOLLY

Just prior to his dream and the angel's proclamation, however, he must contend with (if I can speculate) the pain of misunderstanding. Perhaps he didn't care what people thought, or how they talked. But that his wife "was found with child," a child not his own, he is faced with the decision of what to do according to the law, which called for Mary to be "put away." Again, in obedience, he sets off to do so, though "secretly" so as not to exposure her to public example. What was in his heart? A mere man, could he not have felt what he could only have perceived as betrayal, at least initially and if only for an instant? And when it was revealed that Mary was with child "by the Holy Spirit," how to explain such a thing?

We can see that what others think and any preoccupation with it is not mentioned in scripture; he does only what he is called to do. But his burden (which is, in fact, great privilege) is to not only endure the whispers and the pain of such misunderstanding among his own people and kin, but to bring up and provide for a child not his own.

The dangers magnify when the holy family takes flight into Egypt to escape King Herod, as he is charged with protecting not only the child Jesus, but his holy mother as well. What provisions could they have had? Where might they have had to sleep? How many sleepless nights did he endure in living out his role as foster father of the Redeemer in a foreign land not his own? Not long after, the wails of the mothers for their dead children echoed through the land—massacred, every last one (Jer 31:15). The literal future of the human race hinged on the protection afforded the child by grace and deed in St. Joseph's obedience.

We do see in Matthew 2:22 that Joseph was "afraid" to go to Judea under the reign of Archelaus, and again heeds the guidance of the angel to turn aside into Galilee to Nazareth. It is here, as we see in Luke's gospel, that the boy Jesus "grew and became strong." It is fathers who raise their sons in such a way, and while Jesus "increased in wisdom and stature" it is no doubt Saint Joseph formed him as he was called to do, and as if he were his own flesh and blood. Though his son was the God made man whom Joseph served, Joseph was the spiritual head of his household as scripture says, "he was subject to them" (Lk 2:40).

What does it mean to be the spiritual head? The responsibility cannot be overstated. Were St. Joseph to trust his own judgment, rather than listen to God; were he to doubt or falter to the point of saying, "This is too much; I can't do this," we may not have the inheritance of the son. It is not easy to follow God's will when we do not understand.

Let me repeat that: *it is not easy to follow God's will when we do not understand.* As any father knows, there is a burden we shoulder, often alone, even when willingly undertaken, that is the birthing ground for faith. Because we know what is at stake in raising a family, in heading a household. How many targets we have on our back, the value of the cargo we are charged in protecting. If we rely on our own power and intellect to make decisions which affect our family's well-being, we are vulnerable to error. This is what we often fall back on in times of fear and doubt.

And yet Saint Joseph by his silent witness and deep well of trust in being led paved a way for us as fathers today to do what is right by God first, for the benefit of our family, *even when we do not understand what is going on.* We need to tell ourselves this, remind ourselves of it, for Saint Joseph even in these scant passages in scripture, gives us the example of what it means to truly be led by God when you can't see two feet in front of you; when you only have faith to guide you.

We all go through this, as fathers—doubting our abilities, facing our failures and imperfections, second guessing our calling. Tonight was one of those nights for me, when I needed (and obtained) the comfort of Saint Joseph's silent standing by my bedside when I lamented, "I don't know what I'm doing. Saint Joseph, help!"

Thankfully, he always comes to our aid. This is why consecration to Saint Joseph is a medium of grace one would be foolish to leave on the nightstand. He leaves us breadcrumbs in the desert to follow when we are leading our own family in the dead of night. He affords us powerful protection against our enemies, both human and spiritual, as the Terror of Demons. When we trust him and enter into his long night watch, we enter into a place where we learn what it means to walk by faith, what it means to be a father of the family, and what it means to hold safe the precious cargo entrusted to us in Christ.

HAVE ALL THE BABIES

I don't give advice very often, but if anyone in their twenties or thirties was anxious about having kids and wanted my opinion, I would tell them at this point, just have all the babies.

The concerns are always understandable. For me early in my career, when I wasn't making much money and we were juggling a lot and at our wits end with our two, it can be tempting to not be so open minded (and open-ended). This is the faulty promise of contraception: that you can "be done" and just get on with your life without the constant worry and anxiety that comes with being open to life. But where does this anxiety come from in the first place? The contraceptive mentality is so prevalent in our culture it's like the air you breathe or the water you drink. New life is a barrier to autonomy; it throws things off, wrecks best laid plans, causes financial hardship, and generally makes life harder.

Is that such a bad thing? Satan wanted to be autonomous, loosed from the bonds of the Divine. Yes, new kids throw things off, and sometimes upend our best laid plans. But when I think of the "best laid plans" I have laid for myself and what God has put in their place, I'm constantly reminded that I don't always know what's best for me. Do kids cause financial hardship? Sometimes they do. Life is hard to begin with, but sometimes the hardest things bring out something good in us that wouldn't otherwise if we weren't pushed to trust that it's worth it.

Babies are not a threat; they are pure gift, and the reason we all exist in the first place. We seem to have forgotten this. We certainly don't live to procreate but take having babies out of the picture and it wouldn't be long before we all die out, like in the dystopian science fiction film *Children of Men*. Underpopulation, not overpopulation, seems to be more a threat today in many countries thanks to the scar of contraception and may lead many countries to a demographic winter where there is no easy turning course on.

But no one has babies purely because they want to save the planet. Some people do, however, choose not to have them because they "don't want to bring children into this world" or are fear-mongered into thinking they are being "irresponsible" by doing so or consuming too many resources.

I was talking to a mom at our fellowship get together on Wednesday at our house where we are studying St. Alphonsus' *Uniformity With God's Will*. This mother told me that she felt like the text was kind of over her head. I told her that's okay, in scripture St. Paul says that women are saved through childbirth. "I've never read that," she said, a bit incredulously. "Yep. First Timothy 2:15," I told her, and we looked it up. "Well, I'll be," she replied. "So take heart," I said, "You're doing great!"

The fact is, we are all saved through childbirth. Abortion and contraception introduce nothing but disorder, throwing a monkey-wrench into God's divine plan for happiness and salvation for mankind. This is not to speak of those who want children and cannot have them (by way of infertility, for instance), but the decision to delay or prevent children for the sake of the things of this world and our short-sighted plans is, in my opinion, regrettable. I can say without doubt that as a father, "the children have made the man." The notion of sacrifice and protection is wired into us as men, but becoming a father organically taps into those primal characteristics and brings them to fruition.

ON FAMILY

The Catholic plan for life is to be generous in regards to life. Some people do in fact have grave reasons to abstain through the use of NFP, but one should dig deep to look starkly at those reasons and discern their gravity. God is not trying to shortchange us—He wants to fill our cups to overflowing with the choicest wine. I think that children are that wine. Can they be overwhelming, taxing, hard to deal with? Sure. Are they worth it? You bet.

I wish we would have been more open to life earlier in our marriage. Who knows how much more we would have been blessed. We changed course a little late, but God is good all the time, and we still pray that He might use us as His instruments to bring saints into the world. They can't do the work if they are not born. Who knows? You might be the soul they save in the end.

So have all the babies. It's my one regret in life that we haven't had more. But we trust Him still. Listen to our Lord, "Fear not, for I have overcome the world" (Jn 16:33). Some of the richest people in the world are the most alone and unhappy. But for those rich in children, who may not have much but you trust that God wants them here—"You are already filled, you have already become rich, you have become kings without us" (1 Cor 4:8).

SECOND GENERATION CATHOLICISM

My father-in-law is a first generation American. About ten years ago I read his life story in a self-published book written for the extended family in which he describes growing up dirt poor in the Philippines under the harsh tutelage of his father, as his mother had died when he was young. He would gather snails and coconuts and prawns, but also managed to obtain a scholarship to attend UP to study medicine. He came to the United States with my mother-in-law in the early 1960's, where he began his residency in New York in the field of gastroenterology. They bought a house in the suburbs and raised a family. His was a laudable but also relatively commonplace story of those immigrated for a better life and future.

Like many immigrants, my in-laws did not want their kids going through the same hardships they themselves experienced and provided admirably for their needs, including Catholic education K-12. Despite twelve years of Catholic schooling, my wife never really had an encounter with the living Christ until her thirties, right before her and I met. All the formal schooling and religion classes, in the end, only amounted to head knowledge. It was through a lifelong Protestant Christian friend's prayers and encouragement that she began to really have a personal relationship with Jesus Christ, whom she encountered in prayer and reading the holy scriptures. In fact, just prior to us meeting, my wife was "dating Jesus" for a year after a long-term relationship ended. She did have a sense, however, that she wanted to remain Catholic rather than attend a non-denominational church.

I think my wife and I really connected on our first date at a coffee shop because we had both had those life-changing personal encounters with the living God and recounted them to one another. It was alive and well in our collective memory, and we drew from those past encounters with the Holy Spirit. In essence, we knew God was real because we both had experienced Him.

Whereas my wife's parents sent her to Catholic school to more or less transmit the faith (it was never really talked about or taught at home), my faith generated from the latent roots of my infant baptism in an Episcopal church—and by proxy to my father's attendance at the Divine Liturgy, but without teaching and without ever having been confirmed or having received the Eucharist. It was an authentic and real encounter in the wilderness at age sixteen that I recognized, by grace, the fundamentals of my condition: a sinner aware of his inability to save himself and his need for redemption and meaning. I was lost and was found. I formally became a Catholic a couple years later at the age of eighteen.

As a convert not raised in the Faith, I feel like I am a "first generation" Catholic in practice. Like my father-in-law who knew the stakes and what it took to get to America for a better life despite the odds, I recognized that I was saved by grace but had to search out its confirmation, learning the faith by my own volition and continuing to believe because I knew, empirically, that it was true.

The other night I was lying in bed talking with my son, who wanted to join me. He had been having doubts about God—How do I know He really exists? What if when we die there's nothing there? My wife and I have been very intentional about teaching and passing on the faith to our kids, while recognizing they have not had those same adult experiences we have of coming to know the Truth first-hand. They are more or less taking our word for the fact that God exists and that we should live lives of virtue, that our citizenship is in Heaven, and that this life in the world is not our final home. Which, it occurred to me, is maybe why my son was struggling with doubt. Something I know innately, he only knows by way of word-of-mouth. His is a second-generation Catholicism.

Like the wise virgins with their oil, you want so badly to give your children the lived experience you have had so that they "know the truth that sets one free," but by its very nature, it is not something that can be transferred. Like character, you can only live it out yourself, not transfer it to someone else to put on like a borrowed suit.

We can and should pray fervently and often for our children, that they may receive that grace that was so lavishly poured upon us and which we know the Lord desires to give to all those who ask for it, and that they might have a real encounter with the Living God. We should desire the consistent "both/and" so fitting for our Catholic faith of a personal relationship with Jesus Christ as well as our religion with all its rich teaching and doctrine which allows us to live sacramentally and gives us a compass to navigate by.

It's difficult for me to navigate as a parent. If I put too much pressure on my son and panic at his reasonable doubts, there is the possibility of pushing him farther from faith. If I don't use it as a teaching moment and let him drift away on his own, who knows what kind of teaching he will find downstream in the culture. Knowing our children belong to God (and are consecrated to Mary and St. Joseph as well), I don't fear, but I don't always know how to direct things. As a first generation Catholic, I'm learning as I go!

I also realize there are no guarantees that our children will persist in the faith. We pray and hope that they do and do everything we can to teach and prepare them while living it out ourselves with joy. But our children do not ultimately belong to us, but to God. We can only control them so much when they are younger, and they have free will of their own, the double-edged gift from God Himself, exercising it more and more as they get older. Life is not so easily controlled.

I do, however, pray they will encounter the Holy Spirit of God, which cut through me like a wind for the first time at a punk-rock show in a Church basement as a preacher prayed over the crowd on stage. It was an unlikely and unscripted place to have such a genuine and razing encounter. Maybe that's why the Holy Spirit is sometimes referred to as the "wild goose." I followed Him where He led, and He led me to the doors of the Church. I can only pray my own children encounter this God who saves in a real way, so that it's not just second-hand head knowledge we are passing down. I experienced every one of their births for the first time; but I hope to see them "born again" in the Spirit so that they know, beyond a shadow of a doubt, that He exists, that He is Truth, and that He is as real as the air we breathe.

A WALLET FULL OF MEMORIES

As parents of three kids, my wife and I try to be intentional about carving out one on one time with our kids. Some wise Christian friends told us not to waste those little moments of running errands or being out and about—take a kid with you.

I decided to do this with my oldest this past Monday. I had stayed home from work because my wife was sick and was going a little stir crazy near the end of the day. I decided to take my son to return some pants, stop by Lowes, and make a visit to the Adoration chapel to pray. He's been wanting to do everything dad does lately: wearing aftershave, hammering nails into wood, and asking about girls. If she could handle the other two kids for an hour, I would take the oldest out.

Everything was going great. We made an impromptu stop for ice cream. There were two other dads with their sons, which he noticed. It was "our place" and we shared a cone and spun around on the bar stools. When we finished up, we headed to return the pants, but in the store things started to get derailed when he saw a toy he wanted, and I said we couldn't get it. He got huffy, and then when we also emerged empty handed from Lowes, he started feeling like it was a wasted trip.

When we got to the Adoration Chapel, he was upset and sulky. We both kneeled down to pray, him reluctantly at first. He started to blame God for things—He's not really there, He never answers my prayers, etc. I don't pray enough for my kids, but I prayed for him there, very intentionally, that he should never fall away from the Lord.

When we left the chapel, the waterworks began. He was upset because the memories we were making in the beginning of the afternoon, he loved them. "And then you had to RUIN EVERYTHING!" It wasn't what he expected. I knelt down to his level and tried to console him, but he wasn't having it.

"You know D, we can make memories from anything. That's what's great about having an imagination. Anything can be a memory!"

He stopped crying for a moment and looked up, curious.

"Listen, I have an idea. Let's make a memory, something to remember between me and you, right now. Do you want to be my race car co-pilot? Yeah? Well, let's go."

I strapped him in and started the car. "Okay, now listen, there's going to be a lot of drivers chasing us, so you have to have the smoke bombs ready. I'll try to lose them, but I'll need your help."

He was listening, getting excited. "Okay."

We pulled out of the church parking lot and made a left to the highway. Soon enough, a car with headlights emerged in my rearview mirror. "Oh boy, D. Here we go."

"What?"

"Get the smoke bombs ready. I'll try to lose him."

I sped up. "We're losing him!" he cried. "Yeah, but there's a red light ahead. Get the smoke bomb ready!"

He was bouncing in his seat, excited. "Okay, bombs away!" He turned in his seat and threw an imaginary distraction at the guy behind us.

"We lost him!" I yelled, when the driver turned right and we turned and sped away to the left.

We continued to race and lose cars, throwing bombs all the way home. It was a silly game that boys love, that I loved growing up on vacation. I remembered it today, even with my lousy memory. By the time we got home, he was all smiles and told his mom and sister excitedly about everything we did. We managed to salvage a potential disaster with the power of imagination glued together with a few hours of borrowed time. It didn't cost us anything and wasn't scheduled.

When we lose people we love, their memories sustain us. Memories are bonded to time, and they take place in real life, cached in the mind. They can also sear the heart, because we can never repeat them, only replay them. It's a kind of metaphysical currency we deal in. For a boy who has lost his dad, all he has of him are memories and mementos. If my kids ever lose me, I want them to have good ones that are worth their weight in gold.

ON MANHOOD

DO THE HARD THING

"Suffering ceases to be suffering at the moment it finds a meaning."

—Victor Frankl (neurologist, psychiatrist, philosopher, author, Holocaust survivor)

Wim Hof, colloquially known as "The Iceman," has climbed Mount Everest in shorts and sandals, run a half marathon barefoot in the Artic Circle, and been submerged in ice for almost two hours. But for the sixty-two year old Dutchman, these cold weather endurance feats are the least painful of what he has endured. "I can do it all," he notes "because compared to a grieving heart, it is nothing."

His wife (who suffered from schizophrenia) took her life in 1995 by throwing herself from an eight story building, leaving Hof—a young father of four at the time—to pick up the pieces. Between the grief of losing the love of his life and being forced to continue living and providing for his children, Hof had no consolation, no answers to deal with the pain and no recourse to relief. He was paralyzed with fear, gripped by anxiety, and swallowed up in emotional agony...and nothing alleviated it.

Until he disrobed and slipped into a freezing lake one Sunday morning.

While his body was gripped and paralyzed by the cold, his fear, grief, and anxiety melted away.

"Instead of being guided by my broken emotions, the cold water led me to stillness and gave my broken heart a chance to rest, restore, rehabilitate," he recalls. "The only thing that gave me peace was the cold."

While I am not a devoted follower of the so-called "Hof method" of cold water bathing as a mean of mental and physical regeneration, I have been employing the relatively simple habit of turning my thermostat down in my house to 55 degrees and taking cold showers every morning for the past few months. It is both the worst part of my day...and the best. The worst, because the shooting pain of ice water stinging your frigid body with no place to hide from it is akin to a mild form of torture. The best, because it did not kill me, and I live to see another day.

The author Natalie Goldberg, when she was going through a divorce, approached her roshi (Zen master) and asked him, "Roshi, will I get used to loneliness?"

"No, you don't get used to it," he said, "I take a cold shower every morning and every morning it shocks me, but I continue to stand up in the shower. Loneliness always has a bite, but learn to stand up in it and not be tossed away."

The jury is still out in the scientific community as to the verifiable health benefits of cold therapy and ice baths. Anecdotally, I feel more alert, more alive, and suspect that there are more endorphins flowing through my body after emerging from the shower.

But there is something else, though, beyond the positive physiological effects. I know the emotional agony and sense of darkness Hof experienced when he lost his wife. But in my case, I was the one standing on the proverbial ledge eight stories up, unable to find a way to escape. The moral guardrail of my religious faith luckily restrained my desire to meet the same fate as Hof's wife, to escape a jet-black depression that seemed like it would never end. In the darkest clutches of depression, the things that would most benefit mental wellbeing—exercise, friends and family, prayer—are the most aversive.

But what if we could will our bodies away from atrophy, doing the exact hard thing we have no desire to do?

If we are convinced we can't survive two minutes in an icy lake, and we jump in anyway, what do we have to lose if we want to die in that moment anyway? If we die, we obtain the wish of our distorted mind. But if we come out of the experience, panting and shivering but very much alive and with a new lease on life...what if that was the spark needed to ignite the will to live again?

Indeed, in the city of Yukutsk, Siberia—the coldest city in the world—men routinely remove their clothes when it is minus 50 degrees Fahrenheit to take ice baths outside. Their bodies are acclimated to the cold, and they rarely get sick. And in Russia and Ukraine, the Orthodox faithful celebrate the Feast of Epiphany in January by plunging into icy lakes. "Epiphany is purification," one congregant of the ritual observes, "My soul is cleansed, and I'm charged with a good mood for the whole year ahead."

There is no denying that Hof has attained a level of physical transcendence of the limitations of the body by the power of the mind that is remarkable. But he maintains that he is not unique, and that anyone can push themselves farther than they thought possible and gain mental clarity and emotional control, simply by doing the harder thing.

"As humanity has evolved and developed ways to make our lives more and more comfortable, we have lost our ability not only to survive but to thrive in extreme environments," the Iceman notes. "The things we have built to make our lives easier have actually made us weaker."

Though I'm still soft in a lot of ways, I've grown to love my morning cold shower. I mean, I hate it. But I love it. Every time I step into the stall, I know what is waiting for me: cold, hard pain. And every time I turn the shower handle as far to the right as it will go and pull it back, there is a part of me that feels like I am going to die as soon as those thousands of icy needles fly the wall and strike my naked torso.

WISDOM AND FOLLY

But then, I don't. I yelp, and curse, and cry a little. But I don't die. A few minutes, and it's over. I'm still here. I continue to stand up. And I will not be tossed away.[5]

---

[5] This essay appeared in Catholic Stand (catholicstand.com) on December 27, 2022

SEX IS THE SNARE

A Commentary on Proverbs 7, on My Twelfth Wedding Anniversary.

[1] My son, keep my words, and lay up my precepts with thee. Son, [2] Keep my commandments, and thou shalt live: and my law as the apple of thy eye: [3] Bind it upon thy fingers, write it upon the tables of thy heart. [4] Say to wisdom: Thou art my sister: and call prudence thy friend, [5] That she may keep thee from the woman that is not thine, and from the stranger who sweeteneth her words.

Notice the "who" and the "what" in v 1-5. An elder is giving exhortation to a younger. He has traveled longer, farther, and seen the end and where it leads. Like a seasoned scout, he admonishes the younger to "keep my words." Notice the "what" as well. What should be the "apple of one's eye?" This is typically a moniker for one's beloved. But what should be the apple of one's eye? Their spouse? No, "my law." It is *wisdom* which should be one's first love, the captivator—not as a lover here, but as a sister. Of the wife: "may her breasts satisfy you always, may you ever be intoxicated with her love" (Prov 5:19). But like a sister, "wisdom is sweet to the soul" (Prov 24:14).

[6] For I look out of the window of my house through the lattice, [7] And I see little ones, I behold a foolish young man, [8] Who passeth through the street by the corner, and goeth nigh the way of her house. [9] In the dark, when it grows late, in the darkness and obscurity of the night, [10] And behold a woman meeteth him in harlot's attire prepared to deceive souls; talkative and wandering,

Married lovers can communicate, after a number of years, with wordless words. They speak with deft gestures, looks, and the silence of what is not said. A fool, on the other hand, multiplies words (Ecc 10:14). The woman here, provocatively dressing her line as a fisherman ties his lure to bait ignorant fish, is "talkative," multiplying her words. She has "her [own] house," and yet is out looking to "deceive" by being out and about, "wandering." The young man's first mistake was "going nigh the way of her house." And not during the day, when there is accountability and witnesses in bystanders, but under cloak of night, "when it grows late."

The foolish harlot uses her many words to capture the hearts and loins of the young men, because she cannot stand silence, or staying put. The dutiful wife speaks to her beloved's heart in silence, as the years go on in their marriage, because words become extraneous and unnecessary in this communion. In contrast, the harlot hasn't the peace of silence, and is instead agitated by it. She is like a gyrovague, "who spend their entire lives drifting from region to region, staying as guests for three or four days in different monasteries. Always on the move, they never settle down, and are slaves to their own wills and gross appetites." (*Rule of St. Benedict*, Ch 1:10-11).

[11] Not bearing to be quiet, not able to abide still at home, [12] Now abroad, now in the streets, now lying in wait near the corners. [13] And catching the young man, she kisseth him, and with an impudent face, flattereth, saying: [14] I vowed victims for prosperity, this day I have

paid my vows. [15] Therefore I am come out to meet thee, desirous to see thee, and I have found thee.

The trap of adultery is the bait set in the jaws of narcissism. For even for young lovers, their love is full of ego—they love to be loved. As married couples age, they realize this intoxication of "falling in love" is a lure of the Lord, for were they to know the difficulties of the road and years ahead, they may never have married. "Lord, you tricked me, and I was tricked. You overpowered me and won" (Jer 20:7).

And so the wayward woman sharpens and weaponizes the irons of her words, nougat covered barbs, but not before "catching" the young man and making him drunk with the tantalizing kiss which promises more where that came from. She disarms his reason with a flaming arrow of what would normally be reserved for the altar. She even entices with a play on words, "vowing victims for prosperity...paying my vows." Were he not disarmed by a kiss, he may have remembered his own vows, but she has gone on the cunning offensive before he has a chance.

See, too, the bait of narcissism. "You have come out to meet *me?* Desirous to see *me?* Found *me?*" The young man is suddenly a willful object of desire, in his mind. Flattery baits the trap, for "pleasant words are a honeycomb" (Prov 16:24).

[16] I have woven my bed with cords, I have covered it with painted tapestry, brought from Egypt. [17] I have perfumed my bed with myrrh, aloes, and cinnamon. [18] Come, let us be inebriated with the breasts, and let us enjoy the desired embraces, till the day appear. [19] For my husband is not at home, he is gone a very long journey. [20] He took with him a bag of money: he will return home the day of the full moon.

The words continue, now painting pictures of enticement in the mind of the brute. His mind is enthralled with the details of fantasy: "a woven bed, painted tapestry, perfumed." In his body, he is enraptured by her arms and mired in her kiss, but in his mind, he is transported beyond the streets to an exotic country, an intimate foreign chamber devoid of witnesses. For "even her husband is not home," and even the day of his return is set, "the day of the full moon" to allay the anxiety of an unexpected discovery. He is given a set window of opportunity, and he can't believe his fortune. A marathon of night-long inebriated passion. At this point, not only his mind swells with the opportunistic prospect.

[21] She entangled him with many words, and drew him away with the flattery of her lips. [22] Immediately he followeth her as an ox led to be a victim, and as a lamb playing the wanton, and not knowing that he is drawn like a fool to bonds, [23] Till the arrow pierce his liver: as if a bird should make haste to the snare, and knoweth not that his life is in danger. [24] Now therefore, my son, hear me, and attend to the words of my mouth. [25] Let not thy mind be drawn away in her ways: neither be thou deceived with her paths.

Many words. Flattery. "Deceived by the flattery of fools" (Ecc 7:5). "Immediately" he follows her, his reason bludgeoned, any potential protest muzzled. He begins to be led like an ox to slaughter, captivated as Peter, Andrew, James, John, and Matthew were captivated and as in a trance, followed Christ to their ultimate death. "Immediately, they left the ship with their father, and followed him" (Mt 4:22). And yet it is not wisdom, or grace, or the precepts of the Lord that draw the young man away as his father's words recede in the background of his mind, but desire, impropriety...the flesh.

[26] For she hath cast down many wounded, and the strongest have been slain by her. [27] Her house is the way to hell, reaching even to the inner chambers of death.

But unlike the disciples—the followers of Christ who were led from their earthly ties and died for gain—the young victim is led to his spiritual deathbed by the earthly, the temporal, the honey-soaked poison, never to rise again. "The mighty are cast from their thrones" (Lk 1:52). And here the harlot, the tempter casts down the wounded—wounded reason, wounded conviction, wounded temperance. She has wounded virtue and sound mind with her arrows, "piercing his liver" like a bird. He joins the army of corpses, among them even "the strongest." For strength is impotent before desire, for desire disarms and dethrones a man from within. In the post-coital bed, the sheer drapes of fantasy dissolve and the "house, the inner chamber" which brought him here has become his prison, his hell, his death.

"For as wisdom is a defense, so money is a defense : but learning and wisdom excel in this, that they give life to him that possesseth them"
(Ecc 7:12)

SPIRITUAL DIRECTION: MEN NEED NOT APPLY

I realized something very unusual today: I don't know a single guy—meaning, a lay Catholic man (not a priest or religious)—who has a spiritual director or is in spiritual direction. Not a single one. Spiritual direction seems almost entirely geared towards, and utilized by, women.

This is curious in some ways, and not surprising in others. After all, isn't it important, essential even, for growing in one's spiritual life, and advancing in holiness? To have a guide or coach even who can push you to put aside vice, pursue virtue, identify threats and temptations to avoid, and deepen one's prayer life?

And yet, the pervasive language of contemporary spiritual direction is couched in "developing a relationship with the Lord"; not a problem to be solved, but something to be discovered and deepened and celebrated. There is nothing wrong with this per se, but it one hundred percent appeals to female sensitivities. In many ways, if reflects the expression of the feminized liturgy common in so many Catholic churches today: *Sharing. Celebrating. Expressing. Cultivating.* Excuse me, I, uh, forgot something outside.

I've had a number of therapists over the years, and almost all were useless because, frankly, their expectation of improvement came from the expectation of one simply talking and sharing feelings. One therapist I had early on, however, who was working pro-bono, was effective, because she gave me work to do, she had a framework to work within (CBT, or cognitive behavioral therapy), and she meant business. She pushed me to train my brain to think differently in the way a spotter on the bench might yell at you to pump out one more rep.

Women, for the most part, love to talk, to share, to express themselves, to get feedback. They do this ad nauseum online, interacting with one another, asking questions, commenting on every little thing. Communication is key for many women. Maybe they are attracted to spiritual direction for this reason because they get the chance to do all this in a spiritual context with a priest or religious.

Men are another thing altogether. Most straight men don't think or relate this way. Relating to the quote above, most do things as "problems to be solved." Discovering, deepening, celebrating—these thing are important, but the language is just so...gay. I don't know any (straight) man whose sensibilities would be perked by this kind of talk.

So, what then for the men? Is spiritual direction just a thing for women or religious, primarily? Admittedly, it is hard enough to find a spiritual director at all, let alone a good one. Even if you find one, asking them to take you on is a big commitment, and often the good priests and religious are too busy to do so. And then, if it's just a matter of listening to you talk, but not having any objective training in the interior life himself, it may be the blind leading the blind. For this reason I, like most Catholic men my age, are just doing the best we can with what we have—scripture, the lives of the saints, the Catechism, Mass, Confession, and fellowship with one another.

But it's weird, right? We're called to be saints. God gives us the grace we need, even the simplest among us, to reach this state. And yet, there's a place for graduate schools and PhD programs and professors trained in their respective field to teach those who wish to master a subject. We could say "well, you could also just go to the public library and read eight hours a day on the subject." But there's a recognition that we need teachers, guides, to reach our fullest potential.

Of course, the Holy Spirit can accomplish this task through other channels. As a man, I get my spiritual direction these days piecemeal from various trusted friends and sources. Having had such awful spiritual direction in the past, I have a leeriness I have to overcome, and that's assuming I could even find a spiritual director I connect with who also would have the bandwidth to take me on.

I also think there's this deference sometimes that can happen should you be privileged enough to have a spiritual director, like, "My spiritual director told me to do x, y, z," or "My spiritual director advised _____" so that we can kind of shirk some of the responsibility for our own lives and put it on their shoulders. For some people this may not be an issue, but I'm sure some see it as an opportunity to not do the work they need to do or take responsibility for hard decisions.

But I think there's a hole, a vacuum there somewhere. We can see the Jordan Peterson phenomenon with his Rules for Life shtick attracting so many young men; he is essentially filling that void, albeit in a secular capacity. And we see Fr. Ripperger kind of doing that too on *Sensus Fidelium* speaking to both men and women, but it's not effete at all, but attractive to male sensibilities. But these are recordings, not a personal coaching/mentorship/tutelage type of relationship and little accountability as well.

One thing I do think we need to admit, though, is if you are not solid in your prayer life already, and putting in the work and time, you probably aren't ready for spiritual direction anyway. That should be a litmus test, and I think it's a good one, especially for the sake of the priest or religious willing to take you on.

Why do I say priest or religious? Can't laypeople be spiritual directors? I suppose they can, but nine times out of ten they will be a woman (or a gay man), and that comes with it the aforementioned sensibilities that might not be appropriate for a man to grow in his faith or speak to him in a way another man can.

What are Catholic lay men supposed to do? Are the heights of spiritual perfection not for us, but only for male religious, priests, monks, hermits who have teachers to guide them? What do we do when we are faced with temptations, spiritual landmines, confusion, misappropriation, dejection, imbalance? If other men are like me, we just kind of have to figure it out on our own, making mistakes and recalibrating as we go, and utilizing the sacrament of Penance often.

THE STAY AT HOME DAD DILEMMA REVISITED

One of my first posts on my old blog was titled *Fred The Fireman and the SAHD Dilemma.* It was an admittedly confessional piece I wrote five years ago when we were a two-income family with my wife as the main breadwinner, and our kids were in daycare. Though I wasn't a stay at home dad, whenever I was home with my young kids for extended periods of times, I felt like I got a taste of it...and hated it

Now, I love my kids, and I love spending time with them, especially now that they are older. We have made a lot of changes over the years: my wife leaving full time employment and being a stay at home mom, ditching daycare, and homeschooling. Everyone is happier. We have less money but a sense that we are not going against our inner currents. During those years, things just didn't feel right, but we didn't know why. I was always open minded about gender roles, but sometimes nature wants a say too when it comes to the order of things

I remember years ago actually spending an afternoon at a playground with an actual stay at home dad at a local church. He was a young guy, maybe early thirties like me, wife had a good job and he didn't, and confessed to me how hard it was—not the taking care of the kids or cutting the crusts off sandwiches, but having any kind of relationships with other men and being able to relate to them (and vice versa). He seemed so...isolated and lonely. I confess, I couldn't really relate either. I did get his phone number out of a sense of empathy, but never called him to hang out.

My kids were watching a movie a few weeks ago called *Alexander and the Terrible, Horrible, No Good, Very Bad Day*. Jennifer Garner is the mom working in a high-level position at a publishing house in L.A., and Steve Carell, the dad, is recently unemployed and has been looking for work for seven months. It appears to be a temporary situation, as he is actively looking for employment. While doing so, he attends play groups with the baby; when his son speaks his first word, "He called me FOMMY!" (father-mommy), Carell beams with delight, as the other moms applaud.

There's something about progressivism that tries to erase—erase our nature, erase established social norms, erase biology, erase fertility, erase shame, erase God and His precepts. After it has finished erasing, it tries to reinvent—that things don't always have to be this way, that we can write our own destiny script, that traditional values are outdated and based in ignorance. It takes down a fence without knowing or bothering to find out what it was erected for, to paraphrase Chesterton.

Here's the thing: There's nothing inherently wrong in a wife bringing home the bacon and a husband raising the children. Sometimes it makes the most sense on a surface level, and sometimes it is due to survival and necessity. I say "inherently" because it's the exception not the norm for a reason. And I think it's safe to say that the aquifer from which this family dynamic draws its water is feminism, a truly carcinogenic ideology.

In my *SAHD Dilemma* post, "Fred," a fireman, responds with frustrated honesty to a Dear-Abbey type column revolving around a woman having issues in her marriage and the women commenters saying, "He needs to see a doctor," "He's depressed," etc. I think it shows what most men in these situations think and feel deep down inside—that this kind of household setup goes against their very nature as men. Fred explained:

WISDOM AND FOLLY

I disagree with pretty much all the advice given in this article and with the armchair psychologists replying. I am a full-time firefighter as well as the primary caregiver for my two little girls. I can tell you that I found this article by googling "being a stay at home dad sucks." Due to my work shifts, I am able to be home, on average, four days during the week with the kids while my wife works her 9-5. I work with several men who do the same thing I do while their wives work (although a vast majority chose to work a second job instead of being home).

After 4 years of this I can tell you that very few men are cut out for the stay-at-home-dad role. This has been my own experience as well as the experience of every other guy I work with that does the same thing I do. The same issues that stay-at-home-moms face (isolation, lack of stimulating activity) are even worse for men because there are just fewer dads out there than moms and really no other adults around to hang out with. Dad's don't go on "play dates" with their kids during the day because, let's face it, the other husbands in the neighborhood aren't going to want some other guy hanging out with their wife while the kids play together. I wouldn't want that either. The husband in this letter is probably depressed but he doesn't need medication, a professional, or anything else suggested. HE NEEDS TO GET THE HELL OUT OF THE HOUSE AND GO BACK TO WORK. End of story. The guy feels completely trapped in his situation with no end in sight. Put the kids in daycare before this poor man loses his marbles or decides to take a nap in the garage with the doors closed and the car running.

He is not a failure, he doesn't have a mental condition, he's a man who needs to get out and provide for his family for his own sanity. The days I am able to get out and work during the week are the only thing that keep me sane. I get to interact with other adults and solve real problems. I could not imagine having to be home 5 days a week with no way to stimulate my brain for years to come. I don't care what anyone says, (most) men are not cut out to stay home with the kids and I'm not at all ashamed to say that I can't wait until my kids start school so I can work more and do the other things I used to enjoy during the day. Every guy I work with in the same situation says the same exact thing.

Fred hits the nail on the head. At this point in our lives, if we were hard up for money, I would rather take on two extra jobs than be in this situation. My wife was never really happy working full-time in a manager role, and I felt guilty about not providing more. Daycare and everything that goes with it was a kind of trap to justify her high income. I for my part was able to rest on my laurels and wasn't pushed to make more or seek out additional opportunities to support my family. Our kids hated being away from their mom when they were young, and they weren't pining for me either.

I know there are families, even conservative families where the wife has a high-profile career, who maybe could make this kind of arrangement work. I think they are the exception rather than the norm. I think the vast majority of women really want to be home, and the vast majority of men, if given the opportunity, want to work. It just seems to be part of our nature and right order, and when we go against it, we feel the chaffing.

In a two-income setup, you can get pretty used to things how they are. You get used to that extra income, and you build your lives around it—you buy maybe more house than you would otherwise, finance your cars, do more convenience shopping than you would otherwise, take vacations to get away from the stress of work. Elizabeth Warren (of all people) wrote about this in her book, *The Two Income Trap*.

A buddy called me the other day—he's not a stay at home dad but is relatively low on the totem pole in his career. His wife works part time to help supplement their income and makes decent money doing so (they have six kids) but has been starting to feel like she doesn't want to anymore. He confessed how he didn't see how it would work financially if that income went away, and the pressure and unlikelihood of making more money in his current position.

I really, really sympathized with his situation. It was very familiar. I try to avoid, "This worked for us, so it will work for you too" advice. And I think what's scary is that there really is a stepping out in faith that one has to make in trusting that God will provide, even when you don't see a way, when we seek to honor Him and put things in right order. Again, there is nothing wrong with a woman working part-time or trying to be a Proverbs 31 wife for her family; it can even be laudable. But to the extent that it is causing marital and family stress and discord, one may want to take a deeper dive and reassess the causes of the malaise.

These kinds of difficult situations can also require some belt-tightening and sacrifices, careful budgeting, and an honest assessment of priorities and what is most important. Many times the "We can't..." doesn't actually mean one can't, but that one is making choices that wouldn't make a new situation work. There is also the trust issue: do we trust God to make a way when we don't see one and when the numbers don't add up? Do we go all in on (not recklessly, but with confidence) or are we a "man of two minds," as St. James says? These are questions for personal discernment, not external judgement. I have always been a proponent of "do what works," but if something is not working as a result of not being in the current of God's plan for us, it may be worth re-examining in prayer.

One note—men who experience unemployment, especially prolonged, inevitably experience depression riding its coattails. Men were made to work, and when men (especially young men) can't or don't, it comes out in some not-to-good ways, both individually and in society. A wife who can help during these times are a source of grace; this is not what this post is about. Sometimes you have to do what you have to in order to survive. But when the roles and dynamics are switched and push against our nature—as much as a progressive might tell you there's no difference between male and female, that a dad can substitute for a mom (or two two dads or two moms), that the fruit of feminism is progress—well, you may want to examine the fruit of their claims by digging down a few layers to see how it's all playing out.

A final observation: This year of St. Joseph has been pivotal for us. He has been a true patron for our family, and after our family consecration, we experienced great grace (especially in my role with work). So if you haven't undertaken it, I would highly suggest it. St. Joseph is the model par excellence for men and fathers—a worker, a provider, a protector. He was no "Fommy." He was a husband, father, and man, through and through—a true model for men both then and now.

DON'T FEAR THE HEART

I think there is a tendency for men to eschew the heart in favor of the mind, because the heart has feminine connotations. "The heart of the home," "I feel in my heart," etc. Men hold aloft great intellects, great minds, but the heart makes us...squirmy. We're afraid if we talk about it too much we might end up like a Henri Nouwen or something.

The heart goes beyond feelings and intuitions, though. The Dominican Fr. Thomas Joseph White said that the "heart and intelligence go together. The mind is reason's instrument, but the heart its seat." We know that to love is to will the good of another. We don't simply send "positive thoughts and prayers," but exercise love concretely in acts. "Love the Lord your God with all your heart and with all your soul and with all your mind" our Lord exhorts us in Mt 22:37. Love him with all your heart. Love him with all your soul. Love him with all your mind.

Being human is an exercise in synthesis. We are not all heart, or all mind, or all soul, but all things through the one who created us. We have a skeleton to hold up the body and give us form (right doctrine); we have blood to carry oxygen to our organs (prayer); we have muscles (the will); we have organs themselves that all serve a function for the body (gifts of the Holy Spirit); we have a brain, but beyond the physical organ, the metaphysical—the mind; we have a soul. To be human is one of the most remarkable things, the crowning achievement of God's creation.

One should have a lifetime of contemplations in the Incarnation of Christ, and never run dry. For the God of the Universe to take on flesh, to be given a human heart, a mind, and to debase himself to function as we do: eating food, using the latrine, needing sleep. To have infinite love for man constrained by skin. When his heart was pierced by a lance, it could not help but gush forth the life within it.

"I will give them a new heart," says the Lord God. (Ezk. 36:26). On this Feast of the Sacred Heart, we must learn how to love as our Savior loved. He died for all men and all women. He lived as a man but embodied the tenderness of a mother (Mt 23:37) and the strong protection of a father (Jn 2:13-16). He was both strong and tender, unafraid to weep when moved by emotion (Jn 11:35) but stoic in the face of temptation (Mt 4:1-11).

It is not effeminate to feel, to be bruised, to make oneself vulnerable, any more than it is not too masculine to use logic and reason to temper emotionalism. It is a healthy, whole human being who can embody heart, mind, and soul and direct it to love of God and neighbor.

The Sacred Heart teaches us to temper a cold, removed intellectualism—of doing "all the right things" like the older brother—with the love of a father rejoicing over his lost son who has been found. It sheds its cloak and runs undignified out to meet him in order to forget all things. It embraces and slaughters with abandon, it cloaks and hides faults in itself. This heart burns with love, in order that all men be drawn to himself (Jn 12:32). It sears everything it touches.

When we learn to love as Jesus loved, when we conform our heart and model it on the Sacred Heart, we find soon that such love cannot be contained. It must go out from itself, be pierced, and drench the ones who foist the lance with the blood and water of redemptive love. It must love. It can do no other.

WISDOM AND FOLLY

LED LIKE AN OX: THE EFFEMINACY OF CARNAL CAPITULATION

My wife gets annoyed with my somewhat stoic tendencies. I like to go camping not because I especially like camping, but because I appreciate things like a hot shower and a steak dinner even more after doing so. I hate exercise, but I love the feeling of being tired and having earned the right to a good night's sleep after having gone for a long run. Satisfaction is dependent on concordant deprivation.

Stoics, both the ancients and the modern-day, would hold virtue and mastery of the passions as an end in themselves to achieve "a happy life;" that is, a happy life in this world, as they were not interested in the afterlife (Augustine accused them of a "stupid pride" in *City of God*). Dr. Jordan Peterson has taken note of this "vacuum of virtue" in the culture among men, especially, and has gained popularity by putting forth his own "rules for life" based on cultivating universal goods like strength, courage, responsibility, and, to an extent, suffering.

But as Christians, we don't pursue virtue for its own sake, or to achieve maximum pleasure in this life. Virtue in the Christian life is, according to St. Augustine, "a good habit consonant with our nature." It is from the Latin *virtus* which means manliness or courage, and is defined as the excellence or perfection of a thing. By extension, virtue is consonant with right reason, and of course, Catholicism is a religion of both faith *and* reason.

Augustine struggled with the short-circuiting of reason that comes with the sexual act, especially as it pertains to orgasm, but also with the sin of lust—in his personal life, and also theologically—because of lust's disobedience to the will as a kind of moral "intruder."

If virtue is the excellence or perfection of a thing and denotes manliness or courage, vice—the counterpart of virtue—is the absence of perfection. A lack of virtue is a lack of manliness or courage. Vice fills the vacuum when virtue is absent.

The lack of virtue is probably nowhere more evident today than in the rampant vice of effeminacy. St. Thomas includes effeminacy under the vices opposed to perseverance. It is from the Latin *mollities*, which literally means "softness." *Mollities* is the verb used in the Vulgate translation of 1 Corinthians 6:9 which deals with the sexual sin of sodomy. It involves being inordinately passive or receptive. St Thomas in the Summa writes of perseverance and effeminacy as follows:

> Perseverance is deserving of praise because thereby a man does not forsake a good on account of long endurance of difficulties and toils: and it is directly opposed to this, seemingly, for a man to be ready to forsake a good on account of difficulties which he cannot endure. This is what we understand by effeminacy, because a thing is said to be "soft" if it readily yields to the touch.

> Now it is evident that fear of danger is more impelling than the desire of pleasure: wherefore Tully says under the heading "True magnanimity consists of two things: It is inconsistent for one who is not cast down by fear, to be defeated by lust, or who has proved himself unbeaten by toil, to yield to pleasure." Moreover, pleasure itself is a stronger motive of attraction than sorrow, for the lack of pleasure is a motive of withdrawal, since lack of pleasure is a pure privation. Wherefore, according to the Philosopher, properly speaking an effeminate man is one

who withdraws from good on account of sorrow caused by lack of pleasure, yielding as it were to a weak motion (*STh*, II-II, Q. 138, Art. 1).

When we are led by the passions like a dumb ox—whether it be the attraction to fine food and drink, inordinate lust and sexual proclivities, or some habit that rules us—we make ourselves effeminate men. I didn't quit smoking because it was bad for my health or because it was expensive or made my breath smell. Those were all ancillary reasons, but the main thrust was because being led by something, sneaking around, being idolatrous and willing to sacrifice for something not worth sacrificing for, and having my will compromised introduced a kind of effeminacy into my life that disgusted me. If I didn't have my nicotine I was like a baby without his bottle. You can substitute whatever addiction you like. Maybe it's your cell phone, or your morning coffee, that you might be moved to tears were it to break or not be available. Chances are this is an inordinate attachment, and for men at least, bringing such passions and desires in line is an exercising in building up virtue as part of one's character.

See in Scripture what is written about the young man, who is led by the honey traps set out by the adulterous woman. It is a more or less straight path to Hell by way of the bedroom and promised pleasure, a pleasure that seems irresistible to the youth with no sense.

> For at the window of my house, through my lattice I looked out
> And I saw among the naive,
> I observed among the young men, a youth with no sense,
> Crossing the street near the corner,
> then walking toward her house,
> In the twilight, at dusk of day, in the very dark of night.
> Then the woman comes to meet him,
> dressed like a harlot, with secret designs.
> She is raucous and unruly, her feet cannot stay at home;
> Now she is in the streets, now in the open squares,
> lurking in ambush at every corner.

ON MANHOOD

> Then she grabs him, kisses him,
> and with an impudent look says to him:
> "I owed peace offerings, and today I have fulfilled my vows;
> So I came out to meet you, to look for you, and I have found you!
> With coverlets I have spread my couch,
> with brocaded cloths of Egyptian linen;
> I have sprinkled my bed with myrrh,
> with aloes, and with cinnamon.
> Come, let us drink our fill of love,
> until morning, let us feast on love!
> For my husband is not at home, he has gone on a long journey;
> A bag of money he took with him,
> he will not return home till the full moon."
> She wins him over by repeated urging,
> with her smooth lips she leads him astray.
> He follows her impulsively, like an ox that goes to slaughter;
> Like a stag that bounds toward the net,
> till an arrow pierces its liver;
> Like a bird that rushes into a snare,
> unaware that his life is at stake.
> So now, children, listen to me,
> be attentive to the words of my mouth!
> Do not let your heart turn to her ways, do not go astray in her paths;
> For many are those she has struck down dead,
> numerous, those she has slain.
> Her house is a highway to Sheol,
> leading down into the chambers of death.
> (Prov 7:6-27)

I was that young man. I was the fornicator, the masturbator, the viewer of pornography. I know what it's like to be a slave to pleasure and sinful passion, and I am not unique. There is no peace in this prison. But in Christ there is freedom from such slavery; He comes to ransom men by his blood, to unlock the door, but we have to take the steps to follow him out. He takes us by the hand and gives us the grace to resist this sexual and moral effeminacy if we will it.

St. Jacinta of Fatima was shown a vision of Hell by Our Lady and said that "the sins which cause most souls to go to hell are the sins of the flesh." How many men have been brought down and led to their spiritual deaths by an effeminate pursuit of sexual pleasure—married men falling for the adulterous woman, single men fornicating and masturbating themselves to perdition, those attracted to women and those attracted to men, men in power and men without power, rich men and poor men, men from good families and men who were abused, young men and old men alike.

It is pervasive and pernicious, this vice of effeminacy that keeps men like dumb oxes being led to their graves. But the Lord gives us the grace to live the virtues counter to this softness of will and spirit, but we need to pray for this ultimate grace of final perseverance and the immediate grace to not yield to temptation and embrace the suffering that comes from resisting the devil. We also need to practice mortification by way of prayer and fasting as regular habits to counteract these soft tendencies in ourselves.

It's a funny thing though that the more you subject your body and train your will to bring it into alignment with virtue and right reason, trusting in the Lord to give you what you need for the fight, the more natural it becomes. Virtue is as much a habit as vice. Sin and the habit of sin darkens the intellect so we in fact do become like slaves and dumb oxes being led, and it becomes more comfortable to just stay in that prison of habit. It's easier to pluck out a weed when it first comes up then to try to uproot it when it is fully trenched into the soil. Chastity of mind and heart precludes even thoughts and fantasies and situations of occasions of sin, so that it is not by sheer grit and self-determination that we keep sin from making a home in us, but by the grace of God to exercise the will even when it hurts, and we suffer for it to keep it from making a home in us in the first place.

ON FAITH

TRAD PIETY VS. AN ABASEMENT OF TRUST

Most of traditionalist piety is commendable: dressing the part for Holy Mass, keeping silence, frequent confession, recollection after Communion, etc. But there is one thing that I hear somewhat often, and which I bristle at interiorly, and that is a form of trad humble-bragging about the personal expectation of "doing time" in Purgatory after death.

The mentality goes something like this: emboldened by the words of heavy-hitting saints such as St. John of the Cross, St. Teresa of Avila, St. John Vianney, and others who affirmed how narrow the path to perfection is, the Catholic aligns himself with this traditional view of the fewness of the saved. They are aware, in reactionary fashion, of the presumption rampant in the Novus Ordo churches that "Grandma is in Heaven now," or to the teaching of universal salvation that "Hell is empty" purported by more liberal theologians. There is an inherent tendency to overcompensate as a means of differentiation—if in the NuChurch, everyone is saved, then in the TruChurch, almost no one is. We then expect to be in purgatory when we die as a matter of pious, measured realism.

Now, we know our Lord says in scripture that the way is narrow, and few find it (Mt 7:14). But if you have, in fact, found the Way, and God gives you the grace you need to be saved, and wants to forgive your sins before you even ask, and wants you to trust Him as a loving

Father—why is it that we don't take Him at his word? Is it maybe because we don't, in fact, trust Him?

I think when Our Lady of the Miraculous Medal re-converted my wife and I, she included a "bonus gift": for around the same time I went from not being able to stand the insufferable piety of Jesus' "Little Flower" to suddenly finding refuge in St. Therese's Little Way.

St. Therese was 100% orthodox in belief while appearing unorthodox in praxis. When she found out that her novices talked occasionally that they would probably have to expect to be in Purgatory, she reminded them that we in fact offend God when we don't trust enough that we would (or could) get to heaven right after dying. She corrected them saying: "Oh! How you grieve me! You do a great injury to God in believing you're going to Purgatory. When we love, we can't go there." (*Recollection*, Sr. Marie of the Eucharist Letter to Her Father, Isidore Guérin, 8 July 1897)

While still only a novice, the saint commented about this with one of the sisters, Sr. Maria Philomena, who believed in the near impossibility of going to heaven without passing through purgatory:

> You do not have enough trust. You have too much fear before the good God. I can assure you that He is grieved over this. You should not fear Purgatory because of the suffering there, but should instead ask that you not deserve to go there in order to please God, Who so reluctantly imposes this punishment. As soon as you try to please Him in everything and have an unshakable trust He purifies you every moment in His love and He lets no sin remain. And then you can be sure that you will not have to go to Purgatory.

There has always been this tension in the Church of the emphasis on the humanity of Jesus versus his divinity; the fear of God versus the love of God; God as just Judge versus God as the Good Shepherd. Maybe it is because I know my past, my sin, my weakness and incapacity to anything great which now attracts me to the Little Way of trust; of magnifying my own dependence in recollection, rather than my deficiencies that put all the onus to be saved on my efforts. God is big, capable, willing, and worthy to be trusted. He can do the heavy lifting. Why, then, do we think everything rests on us to accomplish what He can do effortlessly?

I know it sounds harsh, but it's almost akin to a kind of trad humble-bragging to assert this "I'm going straight to Purgatory when I die" mentality. If I had to speculate as to the root of this psychology, it may very well be rooted in pride, which according to many priests is the thorn in the side for trads. If people want to persist in this, that is their prerogative. But they should also not impede those who, like St. Therese, see everyone else taking the stairs to Heaven, and realizing their incapacity to follow given the ardor, resolve to take the elevator instead.

When you think about the constant use of paradox and parables by Christ that turned conventional religious thinking of the time on its head, you start to see that maybe St. Therese's status as a Doctor of the Church is warranted. It is so radical, this abasement to simply trust, love, and surrender, that it flies in the face of conventional piety and rigor.

It is, in effect, another way to find our way home for those of us too weak, too infirmed, or too spiritually simple to go the conventional route. It gives those of us who feel otherwise shut out from the possibility of Heaven...hope. Hope that we can be saved not by our strength, but by our weakness; not by our great personal feats, but in our trust in the One who can do the impossible.

Although it can be trad-fashionable to assume we are all going to end up in Purgatory or worse, Hell, I'd rather abase myself in poverty to trust with the Little Flower, in the spirit of her words, "what pleases Him is that He sees me loving my littleness and my poverty, the blind hope that I have in His mercy...That is my only treasure...why should this treasure not be yours?"

"I NO LONGER FEAR GOD, BUT I LOVE HIM": ON CONTRITION OF CHARITY

The Catholic tradition has a type of prayer known as ejaculatory prayer, consisting of short bursts of piety encapsulated by phrases such as, "My Jesus have mercy," or "Blessed Mary, pray for me." This method of "praying without ceasing" helps to keep the lifeline to God open with short, frequent fiery darts of love shot into the heart of God. It is neither too hard to do, nor too burdensome, nor too time consuming. It is both a grace and a habit of the will to pray in this way, for it disposes us to a habit of gratitude, love, hope, and trust.

"I no longer fear God," said the great Abba Anthony, "but I love Him." For perfect love casts out fear. "If a man loves God with all his heart, all his thoughts, all his will, and all his strength, he will gain the fear of God; the fear will produce tears, tears will produce strength; by the perfection of this the soul will bear all kinds of fruits."

So then, without love for God, we cannot know the fear of God. And without the fear of God, we cannot love Him and be made perfect. Remember, "fear of the Lord" is a gift of the Holy Spirit, which brings to perfection the virtue of hope.

During the month of November, I have been trying to stop by the cemetery every day to pray and gain indulgences for the souls in purgatory. Part of the conditions for this, of course, is to be detached from all sin, which can be intimidating. I have to have confidence, however, that God would not place in us the desire to be made saints and not give us the means to attain this state, nor would he set the bar for gaining such graces (indulgences) so high that we would not be able to merit them. For we tend to fall back on scrupulosity when we do not trust. We tend to doubt when we lack in faith. We overcomplicate what should be simple in this faith. And we tend to fear when we do not love.

So it is with contrition of charity, or perfect contrition. It is a great grace we should ask for frequently, and if we ask in love and trust, He will grant it to us.

And what is perfect contrition? Quite simply, it is the sorrow for sins that arises from pure love of God, rather than fear of punishment or damnation. Like detachment from sin, it is not easy, but it is attainable and within our reach by grace. The Sacrament of Confession is a great grace, but when it is not available in times of distress, the Lord does not abandon us on technicalities. As He granted paradise to the good thief Dismas, so too He fills us with true and honest sorrow so that we are truly forgiven and absolved even before making it to Confession when it becomes available. Of course, we must avail ourselves of the Sacrament as soon as possible.

"No doubt, it is more difficult to make an act of Perfect Contrition than an Imperfect one, which suffices when we go to Confession. But still, there is no one who, if he sincerely wishes it, cannot, with the grace of God, make an act of Perfect Contrition. Sorrow is in the will, not in the senses or feelings. All that is needed is that we repent because we love God above everything else; that is all. It is true that Perfect Contrition has its degrees, but it is none the less perfect because it does not reach the intensity and sublimity of the sorrow of St. Peter, of St. Mary Magdalene, or of St. Aloysius. Such a degree is very desirable but is by no means necessary. A lesser degree, but, provided it proceeds from the love of God, and not through fear of His punishments, is quite sufficient. And it is very consoling to remember that for the 4,000 years before the coming of Christ the only means sinners had of obtaining pardon was this same Perfect Contrition. There was no Sacrament of Penance in those days. Even today for thousands—aye, for millions—of pagans, of non-Catholics, and of Catholics, too, who have no time to call a priest to their bedside, the only means of pardon and salvation is an act of Perfect Contrition."[6]

But during dangerous periods of near-death, the temptation for the man who does not know the Lord intimately yet who fears death and Judgement is to not trust in God's great mercy out of love, but to revert to trepidation and rationalization. He may know he will face the Lord soon but be unable to bring himself to contrition out of love. For how can you love what you do not know? Of course, God can grant these great graces to anyone he chooses; naturally speaking, however, it is similar to deathbed conversions for great sinners: not as common as one may think without great grace. We tend to die as we have lived, as St. Robert Bellarmine wrote.

"Now, if it is true that God does not wish the death of a sinner, it follows that He does not wish to impose on His creatures a contrition or sorrow beyond their powers, but one that is within the reach of everyone. And so, if millions of poor creatures who, through no fault of their own, live and die outside the True Fold, if these can obtain the grace of Perfect Contrition, do you imagine, dear reader, that it will be difficult for you-you who enjoy the happiness of being a Christian and a Catholic, and so are capable of receiving much greater graces than they-you who are far better instructed in things divine than the poor infidels are?"

For one who has done his best to love God, to know Him, to trust Him, to serve Him, should he find himself in the occasion of death without a priest available, he should not fear or doubt. For this is how the Devil will work in these final moments to strip the penitent of his confidence with legalism: "With no priest present to absolve you, how do you expect to be saved? You are damned, you are mine."

But I dare to go even further. Often, very often, without even thinking of it, you have Perfect Contrition for your sins. For example,

---

[6] (Quotes in this chapter from the work *Perfect Contrition: The Golden Key to Paradise*, written in the 1950s by an anonymous Italian priest).

when you hear Mass devoutly or make the Stations of the Cross properly; when you reflect before your crucifix or an image of the Sacred Heart. What is more, every time you say the Our Father, in the first three petitions you make three acts of perfect charity, each of which is sufficient to cancel every sin from your soul.

I have written about the benefit of aspirations elsewhere, but see how they prepare us for this great act of faith in perfect contrition, the contrition of charity. "Very often, a few words suffice to express the most ardent love and the most profound sorrow -for instance, the little ejaculations, 'My Jesus, mercy,' 'My God and my All,' 'My God, I love Thee above all things,' 'My God, have mercy on me, a poor sinner.' Aided by the grace of God (and God has promised to give to all who ask), it is by no means difficult to make an Act of Contrition. Take the case of David, who for one curious look fell into the sin of adultery, and then of murder. Having committed these sins, he lived on quite unconcerned about the state of his soul till the prophet Nathan came to reprove him. And this reproach induced David to make an act of Perfect Contrition in a few words, 'Peccavi Domino' ('I have sinned against the Lord'). So efficacious was his contrition that the prophet, inspired by God, exclaimed, 'The Lord has forgiven you.'"

The reason I do the First Fridays and First Saturday devotions is because I, like all fervent Catholics, recognize my weakness. I need the grace of final perseverance, and to receive the Sacraments in my final hours would be a great grace. So, I liken it to a spiritual insurance policy and last testament of will. Regardless, though, love in this life for—for one's spouse, family, friends, and enemies—is never wasted. And love for the Lord is not either. In it we prepare to meet him, and that He will not cast us out as one of those whom He knows not, but as friends welcomed to the banquet. When we forget, when we sin, we fly back to Him in sorrow, because we love Him and want to make amends by way of contrition and penance. For we know that perfect love casts out fear (1 Jn 4:18).

If we have seen the fruits of fear, we have seen it in the past couple years. It has led to chemical dependencies and overdoses; suicides; anxiety and depression; tribalism which seeks comfort in the absence of control. It is not of God. Even for Catholics, we must learn that even though we know "No priests, no Church," we cannot rely on them for everything. Like God's love, the gift of faith, fear of God, wisdom, and forgiveness, everything is a gift and a grace. So, let us learn to love God more and more in this life—through frequent ejaculations, adoration, and begging for the grace of true sorrow, so that we made perfect by the contrition of charity.

CONSUMMATION

It has always amazed me how sometimes the most miraculous things in life can be the most commonplace. Women have been giving birth and having babies since the beginning of time; there's literally nothing more commonplace. And yet every time I think about all the things that have to come together for a baby to be born into the world, and all the things that can go wrong, I tremble and sigh with awe. God is truly the sovereign Lord of the universe.

What leads to babies being born? Well, ideally, marriage is the ball that gets things rolling first. Again, I kind of marvel when meditating on the mystery of the wedding feast at Cana (yes, I do pray the Luminous Mysteries) that God Himself in the person of Jesus not only stooped down to become one of us in the incarnation, but actually cares about our lives so much he would accept an invitation to a communal wedding celebration as a guest.

Of course, as most Catholics with even a rudimentary understanding of Jewish custom and tradition know, weddings were not a three hour affair at the local country club and then you go home. They were week-long affairs; at Cana, the celebration was replete with 120-180 gallons of wine in large stone vessels to keep everyone supplied and jovial. This is an overwhelmingly human affair, in which Jesus the God who became man enters into that affair to be with us.

Think of how modern men and women plagiarize what is meant to be reserved and holy today: we meet, find a few things in common, hook up, and work backwards essentially. We move in together—there is no communal sanctioning or celebration in such an event, just a pragmatic, sloppy slide into cobbling a tenuous life together. We may or may not get married eventually, but even if we did there is nothing "virgin" about that first night together as husband and wife, nothing mystical—just another day of carnal exchange which now happens to be bound by a legal contract.

In many ways, this sloppy slide plays out in the *ekklesia* in the careless, common shuffle for Communion, and our profane attitude reflected in it. We wear common clothes, and do not prepare our bodies and our hearts for what we are about to receive. "They have put no difference between the holy and profane" (Ez 22:26). If we the church are the bride, and Christ the Bridegroom, each encounter in receiving Communion is a sacred consummation. He gives us his flesh which we take into ourselves. Just as in an earthly marriage and what is requires, this marriage between Christ and his people (the church) is not a valid marriage unless it is consummated. "Unless you eat my flesh and drink my blood, you have no life in you" (Jn 6:53).

This spiritual consummation is not a one-and-done encounter, but weekly, sometimes daily. Just as the sexual act between spouses gives rise to life within us (cf. Jn 6:53) and deepens the love between spouses, so too does frequent reception of the Eucharist leads to spiritual life and a deeper love between man and Christ. Just as in our counterfeit offerings of our bodies to another to whom we are not betrothed we profane the temple of the Holy Spirit, so too do we profane and "eat and drink condemnation upon ourselves" when we enter into this consummation unworthily.

The bridal chamber where the consummation takes place (*chuppah*) is the place of intense and ecstatic intimacy (knowing) between bridegroom and bride. On this climactic night, the bridegroom is escorted by the "sons of the bride chamber" (Greek, *huioi tou nymphonos*)—that is, his closest confidants (the apostles, and those who stand in succession to them)—to the *chuppah*. And it is we, his bride, who are called into the chamber to experience this consummation, in which He gives us His flesh to partake in.

There is a reason Yahweh speaks of Israel as his bride whom He has married (Jer 3:14). There is a reason the Song of Songs paints such a sensual, fleshly portrait of intimacy with the Lover. There is a reason St. Paul speaks of the relationship between Christ and His Church as that of the love and submission between husband and wife (Ephesians 5).

Marriage is more than a contract, more than an agreement which can be broken. It's validity, it's lifeblood, the ratifying of the contract depends upon **consummation**—a *fusion of flesh*, and this is the nature of Eucharistic communion. In it we partake in the mystery of Christ's death and resurrection. It is not for everyone, because it is not profane or common, but exclusive to those disposed towards its worthy reception. In it we become one bread, one body, one spirit. One cannot get any closer to the presence of the Lord than during this moment when we become One Flesh with the Bridegroom Himself. It is a moment of profound privilege and intimacy reserved for those who are called to His chamber. We do not "think and speculate" in this moment about the Lord. We TASTE AND SEE the goodness of the Lord (Ps 34:8).

Satan has his work cut out for him in the perversion and debasement of the sexual act during his reign here on earth. But he does it, why? Because in deforming the meaning and act of sex as properly understood, he can obscure our understanding of true spiritual consummation—what it means to eat the flesh of the Son of Man! If we don't understand what sex is and what it is for, our *telos* is reduced to a temporal, sterile, material act of self-fulfillment rather than an eternal, fruitful, profoundly spiritual act of self-abandonment. And if we don't know what committed, chaste, fruitful, selfless sexual intimacy is, is it any wonder we have adopted such a casual, profane, and presumptuous posture in the Communion line?

Just as I find it a marvel that the most profound miracles in this world—like the birth of a baby or the love between a man and a woman—are so common to human experience, so too that the Son of

WISDOM AND FOLLY

God enters into our existence so sensuously in Holy Communion, that we are commanded to feed (literally, *gnaw* in Greek: trogo, τρώγω) on Him to generate new life in our spirit. Almost profane verbiage, yes? An intimacy that was once otherwise unthinkable and unattainable has become the most profound miracle this side of Heaven. For the man who knows he is not called to fast while the heavenly Bridegroom is with him, who experiences this consummation in Holy Communion, the seemingly revolting and profane has become holy.

WHAT'S OLD IS NEW[7]

I was an early adopter to minimalism. When my wife and I met in 2008 I was sleeping Japanese style on a futon mattress-topped tatami mat on the floor in the bedroom of my apartment. When I moved in after we got married at the age of 30, everything I owned fit in a Honda Civic.

I was only a couple years ahead of the minimalist movement, and of course some of it was due to budget, singledom, and mobile circumstance. It wasn't a bad thing either—I had divested myself of a lot of "stuff" when I moved into a school bus, and it was a cleansing kind of game to see how little I could live with in the way of possessions.

But now I'm going to make a prediction—restoration is going to trump renovation in the near future. The grandparents dying and the Boomers downsizing and trying to foist off things onto their millennial children who don't want their stuff is creating a pennies-on-the-dollar flood of furnishings on Craigslist and thrift shops. The craftsmanship is unparalleled, but the style passe. Young people prefer particleboard to hardwood, white to walnut, sleek to plush, so the demand is not there.

---

[7] This essay appeared in *Catholic Stand* (catholicstand.com) on December 4, 2018.

I'm not so young anymore. Yes, my parents were like many Boomers who cut their square footage in half and had been holding things to grace us with that we didn't particularly want. Thankfully the timing worked well that were moving into a bigger space as my parents were moving into a smaller one. My wife's great aunt gave us a massive Japanese china set. We needed a china cabinet for it, and I found a beautiful one at a thrift store for next to nothing. I'd say 80% of our house is furnished with stuff that was free on Craigslist or given to us by my parents when they downsized, and it all seems to go as well, but the motif is more traditional. Our house was built in the 50's. It's cozy, a little messy, and feels nice and lived in. There are toys everywhere, toys people give us, presents at Christmas and birthdays, hardly anything we bought, it's a kind of organized chaos. As the proverb goes, "Where there are no oxen, the manger is empty, but from the strength of an ox come abundant harvests." (Prov 14:4)

Everything that goes around comes around—what's out today is en vogue next year. My prediction? Mid-century is going to make a comeback. IKEA will still have its place among college students and transients. But somewhere, at some point, people are going to wake up in their white room white couch white bed clean dustless childless quiet modern home and experience a curious longing for the forgotten comfort of grandmother's delicate tea sets, grandfather's tan armchairs, the soft yellow glow of incandescent lightbulbs, and yes, maybe even the extravagant opportune of a mahogany China cabinet. But it won't be there anymore except in the highest end antique shops.

In many ways I fear the Faith I am caring for, trying so carefully to preserve, maintaining its integrity, and instilling the rituals and remembrances in our family life as my children are young, will be rejected when they come of age. "Sorry dad," they will say, "we don't want your *stuff*." An old missal, a rosary polished from years of fingering—they'll become like cherry armoires and cast iron cookware: of no perceived use to them.

Everybody has their preferred style, but there is something to be said for a quality handmade chair, an old stone church, a set of steel hand tools because it carries with it a memory, a legacy, and a history.

Non-denominationalism is the IKEA of worship and architecture today. It is modern, sleek, relevant, and sterile. It's roots do not run deep, it's foundation is like that of a vinyl-clad townhouse.

In the secular arena, modern progressives destroy everything they touch. They tear down with no real cohesive or thought-out plan of how to rebuild. They tear down the family and religion, statues and monuments, traditional sexual mores. They are impatient, and content to slap up temporary shanties until they can figure out what next thing comes next. Social change can't happen fast enough. Out with the old, in with the new, until new becomes old and then off to the dump again.

But things get destroyed in the process. Timeless things, priceless things—immortal souls, traditional families, rituals, and connections to our past and our ancestors and predecessors.

My prediction goes beyond furniture and housewares, beyond trends and tastes and kitchen renovations. When we hit the modern bottom, when the demons start to tip the scales and become too powerful, when the non-denominational particleboard gets wet and warped, when the trans-everything nonsense hits fever pitch...a few will start to pine for an ancient faith. They will go online to order and meetup; they will seek and they will not find (Jn 7:34) except in those pockets in which it has been preserved as the pearl of great price that it is, a soft glow of candles in stained glass windows in the darkness, shards of light reflecting off a gold monstrance in the sanctuary, the quiet ancient chant of plainsong beckoning behind thick solid wood doors. It will be exotic and intimidating, ethereal and forbidden, austere and arduous, foreign and yet completely familiar. The Faith of our fathers, the Faith handed down, the Faith communion that takes place in real time...it will be both old, and new.

THE MAMMON OF INIQUITY

It's strange the way the Holy Spirit speaks to us through Scripture in its timelessness. When I posted yesterday about the Siege of Jerusalem, I had no idea it was actually the Jewish day of mourning and fasting (Tisha B'Av) which believe it or not, marks the destruction of the Temple. For Jews, it is considered the saddest day of the year. There was a feeling of solidarity there, I think, between traditional Catholics that I hadn't even realized when writing it. I was only made aware of the significance by a friend after she read it.

While everyone was talking about the Novus Ordo readings for this Sunday (which were especially timely and somewhat uncanny in their exactitude), it was actually the Gospel during the TLM this morning that caught my eye.

Again, I had meant to write about this very passage from Luke 16:1-9 the day before as it seemed apt to the current situation that I had been mulling over, and then there it was being proclaimed at Mass. For those who missed it:

> And he said also to his disciples: There was a certain rich man who had a steward: and the same was accused unto him, that he had wasted his goods. And he called him, and said to him: How is it that I hear this of thee? give an account of thy stewardship: for now thou canst be steward no longer. And the

steward said within himself: What shall I do, because my lord taketh away from me the stewardship? To dig I am not able; to beg I am ashamed. I know what I will do, that when I shall be removed from the stewardship, they may receive me into their houses. Therefore calling together every one of his lord's debtors, he said to the first: How much dost thou owe my lord?

But he said: An hundred barrels of oil. And he said to him: Take thy bill and sit down quickly, and write fifty. Then he said to another: And how much dost thou owe? Who said: An hundred quarters of wheat. He said to him: Take thy bill, and write eighty. And the lord commended the unjust steward, forasmuch as he had done wisely: for the children of this world are wiser in their generation than the children of light. And I say to you: Make unto you friends of the mammon of iniquity; that when you shall fail, they may receive you into everlasting dwellings."

I don't know why I was thinking about this passage this week prior to hearing it. Biblical exegesis is not my thing, and it can be a confusing one to expound on, so I'm not going to do it justice. It may very well be a teaching on usury, but what struck me was this: "The children of this world are wiser in their generation than the children of light." Another passage from Scripture came to mind yesterday from Matthew in parallel with Luke's Gospel: "Behold I send you as sheep in the midst of wolves. Be ye therefore wise as serpents and simple as doves." (Mt 10:16).

We could learn something from this. When it come to our enemies, we pray for those who persecute us—yet they are still our enemies. And what do you want to do with your enemies? Beat them at their own game, as St. Paul writes, "But if your enemy is hungry, feed him, and if he is thirsty, give him a drink; for in so doing you will heap burning coals on his head" (Rom 12:20).

As we navigate the coming days and years, we truly do have to adopt the adage to be wise as serpents and simple as doves. You have to be smart and keep your lower faculties (emotionalism) in check. It's okay to mourn, be upset, angry, etc. But this is not the level at which wars are won. It takes prudence to keep them in check, so that you can advance with a clear mind and unfettered from poor decision making. As Fr. Z wrote the other day, "Don't do anything stupid."

Second, as our Lord says, "your righteousness must surpass those of the Pharisees" (Mt 5:20). Your cheerful fasting and prayer, living the virtues in charity, and not giving the enemy ammunition will serve as an indictment against them. They may rage internally in response, but you also need to learn how to take a beating and take it with fortitude. Don't be a complainer, avoid being too self-focused, and play the long game.

Thirdly, do you not believe that God is in control of everything? That anything proceeds from His hand by chance? Get yourself in proper spiritual perspective. All things proceedeth from the hand of God. Nothing happens apart from His will. Do you trust God? Get your eyes off the ground, and do not lose your focus. Peter sank walking on the sea when he took his eyes for one moment off Christ. Let that serve as a good reminder. Keep your focus. Put your blinders on if needed to stave off the ancillary distractions. First things first.

I went to Adoration a little before midnight last night and was reading the scriptures and happened upon the wisdom of Ecclesiasticus (Sirach) which again spoke to me (Chapter 2):

> Son, when thou comest to the service of God, stand in justice and in fear, and prepare thy soul for temptation. [2] Humble thy heart, and endure: incline thy ear, and receive the words of understanding: and make not haste in the time of clouds. [3] Wait on God with patience: join thyself to God, and endure, that thy life may be increased in the latter end. [4] Take all that shall be brought upon thee: and in thy sorrow endure, and in thy humiliation keep patience. [5] For gold and silver are tried in the fire, but acceptable men in the furnace of humiliation.

ON FAITH

[6] Believe God, and he will recover thee: and direct thy way, and trust in him. Keep his fear, and grow old therein. [7] Ye that fear the Lord, wait for his mercy: and go not aside from him, lest ye fall. [8] Ye that fear the Lord, believe him: and your reward shall not be made void. [9] Ye that fear the Lord, hope in him: and mercy shall come to you for your delight. [10] Ye that fear the Lord, love him, and your hearts shall be enlightened.

[11] My children behold the generations of men: and know ye that no one hath hoped in the Lord, and hath been confounded. [12] For who hath continued in his commandment, and hath been forsaken? or who hath called upon him, and he despised him? [13] For God is compassionate and merciful, and will forgive sins in the day of tribulation: and he is a protector to all that seek him in truth. [14] Woe to them that are of a double heart and to wicked lips, and to the hands that do evil, and to the sinner that goeth on the earth two ways. [15] Woe to them that are fainthearted, who believe not God: and therefore they shall not be protected by him.

[16] Woe to them that have lost patience, and that have forsaken the right ways, and have gone aside into crooked ways. [17] And what will they do, when the Lord shall begin to examine? [18] They that fear the Lord, will not be incredulous to his word: and they that love him, will keep his way. [19] They that fear the Lord, will seek after the things that are well pleasing to him: and they that love him, shall be filled with his law. [20] They that fear the Lord, will prepare their hearts, and in his sight will sanctify their souls.

[21] They that fear the Lord, keep his Commandments, and will have patience even until his visitation, [22] Saying: If we do not penance, we shall fall into the hands of the Lord, and

not into the hands of men. [23] For according to his greatness, so also is his mercy with him."

Does this speak to you as well? If you're like me, it should. We are in many ways currently in the "furnace of humiliation." We cannot afford to be fainthearted, as those who believe not God (v 15). We cannot lose patience and go aside into crooked ways (v. 16). If you love Him, you shall be filled with His law. Prepare your hearts (v 20). Do penance (v. 22). What can the hands of men strip from the hands of God, from which all things come? Not a sparrow falls without Him knowing it.
Be smart. Don't let your lower faculties (emotions) rule you. Learn from the children of the world; be innocent as doves and wise as serpents. Make friends with the mammon of iniquity. Let your righteousness exceed those of the Pharisees. In the end, you will heap coals on the heads of your enemies.

MAKE ROOM FOR MYSTERY

Because my journey to Christ has come by way of influence from both the East and the West—both inside and outside the Church—I have a bit of what I call a "Tex-Mex" spirituality. My first experience of Catholicism was in the Eastern rite of the Church, attending the Divine Liturgy with my father from time to time when he would go. I experienced liturgical plainsong (chant), sometimes known as *prostopinije*, incense, iconography and iconostasis, and a sense of the sacred. When I came into the Church and received the Sacred Mysteries (Sacraments) of Confirmation, Confession, and Holy Eucharist, it was by way of the Byzantine Rite. On the way to a monastery in New Mexico after a year of being a Catholic I sat next to an Orthodox priest on the plane and he gifted me a prayer rope on which to pray the Jesus Prayer which is a hallmark of Orthodox spirituality. It's simple and meditative: with each breath in, you pray Lord Jesus Christ, Son of the Living God...and with each breath out, "be merciful to me a sinner" on each bead. Whereas rosary beads are generally of a hard, solid material, even the beads of a Orthodox prayer rope themselves are made from cloth, so have a flexible dexterity reflective of Orthodox spirituality. I prayed the Jesus prayer with that prayer rope for many years, and later discovered the classic The Way of the Pilgrim which recounts one Russian peasant's experience of the Jesus prayer in his quest to learn to "pray without ceasing," as St. Paul encourages us to do (cf. 1 Thess. 5:16).

One thing I think the Church of the East is more comfortable with in general is the sense of mystery. Not that this doesn't exist in the Latin Church or in the mystical theology of the Western saints, but the influence of Scholasticism and Neo-Scholasticism in the West was so formative to the Latin Church that this kind of mystical and liturgical fluidity can be a different experience for those who experience a Byzantine (or even Orthodox) liturgy for the first time.

Of course, we have been attending the Tridentine Mass for the past three years now—neither the Divine Liturgy of the East or the Holy Sacrifice of the Mass in the Latin Church is especially foreign or novel to us at this point. When my son serves Mass and I observe his movements and those of the altar servers, I can see they reflect this Scholastic influence in liturgical physicality—movements and transitions are crisp and clearly defined, with sometimes military precision. Contrast this in observation with the way a Byzantine or Orthodox priest and congregants bless themselves (thrice, right to left)—there is a rounded fluidity to the movements from head to navel to shoulders, almost like an oval in motion rather than a perfectly delineated cross. I think in the context of liturgy, this may reflect the greater comfort with which the East "sits in mystery" rather than having to tie up and resolve it and assign it to its appropriate clearly defined box.

For those who have come to Tradition by way of the Latin Mass, there can be a kind of tunnel vision in mindset that liturgical integrity must be invested in this kind of Western Scholastic expression of its physicality in the liturgy. The Latin Mass may sometimes feel like the "article-objection-reply" format of the Summa in liturgical form, leaving no rock of objection unturned or corner rounded.

It can also be reflected in the spiritual practice of those in the Eastern and Western traditions. Mystery is not always a comfortable place to be for the Scholastic mind. We are comfortable with checking the boxes—morning offering, mass, rosary, divine office, etc. The temptation to figure things out and have everything in its preassigned box can sometimes rob us of the experience of the mystical. I don't know enough about traditionalist Catholics to know what defines their spirituality. I try to have some structure to my prayer life but for myself, I have always been comfortable with the idea of mystery and was also never especially drawn to Thomistic Scholasticism as a way to understand and experience God.

Of course this is just general observation and not meant to put one above the other. Certainly the sense of mystery transcends East and West, and no one tradition can hold exclusive claim to it. When we pray the rosary, ideally we enter into the MYSTERIES of the rosary and meditate on them. We pray with our heart as well as our head and lips and fingers. The heart is where mystery roots itself. And the heart can sometimes be messy, not clearly delineated and defined. Mary "keep all these things in her heart" at the Annunciation (Lk 2:19) and "wisdom enters the heart," as scripture says (Prov 2:10)

I like Tex-Mex. I like Asian Fusion. I like the Divine Liturgy and I like the Tridentine Mass. I respect the intellectual formidability of the West and the deep mysticism of the East. And I love Catholicism because it is a "both/and" religion, not an "either/or" religion. If you're a Neo-Scholastic type (or as one of my professors in grad school referred to himself jokingly as, a "filthy Thomist"), don't be afraid to engage the heart and make some room for mystery.

"HE WHO LIVES WELL DIES WELL":
THE JOY OF A HAPPY CHRISTIAN DEATH

My buddy's father died last Thursday. He had suffered a sudden brain aneurysm and by the time he was flown to the hospital, it was too late. We had just seen each other not too long ago at church for a baptism, and at a play that my kids and my buddy's kids were in. He was happily married for 54 years to his wife and best friend, and they had six children together. He was an active parishioner at St. Robert Bellarmine parish for 42 years, serving on the parish council and Pre-Cana team, organizing their parish March for Life bus trip to Washington D.C. with his wife, and as a lector, extraordinary minister, and a weekday altar server.

Strange as it sounds, apart from my mother-in-law's passing five years ago (also from a brain aneurysm, ironically), death is a bit of a foreign thing for me. All my grandparents died either before I was born or when I was too young to remember much. I had a few friends of friends who died suddenly in high school who I heard about through the grapevine. So I haven't experienced the sting of death as acutely as many have. I'm sure my time will come; none of us can escape it.

By circumstance, my buddy had forgotten his wallet back home two states over during all of this (and some other concurrent events they were also dealing with simultaneously), and I offered to shuttle it up to him at his parent's house this evening. You never really know when it comes to death how people will respond or what state of being they are in. It's kind of our default mode to put on our mourning face in solidarity when you walk into a room of family members who have experienced sudden loss and are in the midst of getting affairs in order and planning the funeral. But I had a feeling, knowing the faith of my buddy, his parents, and his siblings, that it might be a different affair. Exiting the turnpike and about fifteen minutes out he texted me a different address to meet him at; it seems he and his brothers and sisters had gone out for a bit to play pickleball.

When I arrived at the courts, my buddy came over to meet me with his usual smile and we embraced. I joked with him about not wanting to get pulled over carrying the wallet of an Islamic terrorist (making reference to his ten inch long Osama Bin Laden beard that we're always razzing him about). He laughed and offered me a paddle. It was a humid summer's evening, and the five of us were the only ones out sweating on the courts. We won a match and lost a match, falling to his sister's wicked backspin.

As we walked back down the path to our respective cars, I made mention to my buddy, "Your dad lived a good life, and we have the assurance of faith in Christ. I don't know how people live without faith, honestly."

"Isn't that the truth," he replied, adding when I asked about his mom that she was doing well and happy the whole family was together.

The naturalness of the evening—knowing that the end is not really the end for those with faith—was a testament in and of itself to the promises of our Savior. I did not have to hide my smiles, and while we offered Masses for my friend's father a few days ago to be welcomed into happy repose, my friend and his family were not subject to the existential crisis that those without faith often are. Ask any priest who has ever presided over a funeral for a family without faith and they will tell you the same. It's never easy of course, but as Christians we aren't left holding the pieces necessarily, trying to make sense of everything apart from God's will and promises.

St. Robert Bellarmine (another irony, perhaps?) wrote with profound simplicity in *The Art of Dying Well*, that "those who live well will die well." My buddy's father lived by faith, and lived well. By whatever mystery of God's will he was called back, that assurance will be a monument to his family in perpetuity, and an example to those who look to see the evidence of faith in the world—that Christians need not fear death when they have lived well and placed their trust in the tender mercy of the Divine Savior. *Deo Gratias.*

WHEREVER TRUTH MAY BE FOUND, IT BELONGS TO HIS MASTER

As parents, my wife and I constantly weigh what we expose our kids to. Do we go full-Amish or full-tech? Who do we allow them to play with? What movies do we watch? Oftentimes we try to take a middle-line approach to maintain their innocence and keep them protected, while not coming across as overly strict so that they are feeling like they are living under a dictatorship. It's something every parent has to weigh for themselves in the culture we live in.

Last night I was weighing whether to watch the 1999 science-fi film *The Matrix* with my 9 year old son. It depicts a dystopian future in which humanity is unknowingly trapped inside a simulated reality, the Matrix, created by intelligent machines to distract humans while using their bodies as an energy source. When computer programmer Thomas Anderson, under the hacker alias "Neo," uncovers the truth, he is drawn into a rebellion against the machines along with other people who have been freed from the Matrix. Getting "red-pilled" on waking up to the truth of something is an expression used in reference to the film. There was some language and non-graphic violence, but overall I found it thought-provoking and worthy of exploration from a Christian perspective when I saw it years ago. We decided to watch it; you can judge me accordingly.

In his *On Christian Doctrines* treatise, Augustine writes, "If those who are called philosophers, and especially the Platonists, have said aught that is true and in harmony with our faith, we are not only not to shrink from it, but to claim it for our own use from those who have unlawful possession of it." As an Augustinian at heart (having first read *Confessions* very early in my conversion), I always appreciated Augustine's pre-Christian background in rhetoric and philosophy and how God used it for the good after his conversion to Christianity. Though he rejected the incompatible heresy of dualistic Manichaeism, he "baptized" his Neo-Platonic philosophy in the waters of Christian theology.

Neo-Platonism as a philosophy sought the One, the Good, extolled virtue, and recognized the soul. But it was a philosophy developed before the Incarnation, the "scandal of the particular" in human history with the One, the Good, the Eternal entering into the human fray. In Christ, the soul was no longer "trapped within the body" to be freed from its degraded cell, but dependent on it for existence. The body was good precisely because God made it good. The soul did not exist apart from the body and the human person. The resurrection means we will be reunited with our human bodies in the coming age. As Augustine came to realize, Christianity "is the religion which possesses the universal way for delivering the soul; for, except by this way, none can be delivered."

Though *The Matrix* drew its themes from a mix of Taoism, Judaism, Gnostic thought, and Christianity, I felt I (and my son) had the Christian foundations necessary to parse out what was of the True Good and what was not enough to have a discussion about it. My son loved the film. But what I loved more was he wanted to talk about the themes and what they meant, and so after we watched it we headed downstairs and I brewed some coffee.

We sat down and I brought over a jar of holy water and we blessed ourselves, lit the Advent candles, and I prayed over him for the gifts of wisdom, understanding, counsel, fortitude, knowledge, piety, and fear of the Lord. What ensued was an hour long discussion at the kitchen table about Christology, soteriology, epistemology, metaphysics,

Heaven, Hell, purgatory, human nature, sin, death, atonement, culture, and calling.

He knows his catechism pretty well, his prayers and the tenets of the Faith. But last night I went through the Scriptures with him, starting with John chapter 1: In the beginning was the Word, and the Word was with God, and the Word was God. We talked about the pre-existence of Jesus as God before time and space, that he was co-eternal with the Father.

We then moved on to Romans chapter 6, in which Paul writes about our bondage to and struggle with sin and concupiscence, but also our redemption in Christ and by baptism. That, like those in the Matrix, humanity is enslaved and asleep in a comfortable reality that is not the whole picture but has the capacity to be set free. But this rests on the need for "the One" to do it (personified by Neo in the film), who is Christ. Seeing things as they are, knowing the Truth, is not easy nor comfortable. In fact, in can be quite painful to come to terms with and live by.

Then we moved to Genesis. Why are we in this state? I read to him chapter 3 relating the Fall and the theology of Original Sin to the state we find ourselves in today—why it is hard to be good, to see things as they really are, and why we are constantly being tempted by the "agents" of the Devil to rest in our present reality rather than seek out and strive for Heaven.

We talked about the Oracle (the prophetess/seer in the movie who foretold Neo's coming), and moved into the prophets in the Old Testament, and how they prefigured the expectation of Christ; they too were "waiting for the One," the Messiah, who would finally free the human race from their bondage.

There was a character in the film who gets tired of living in the Truth and longs for the comfortable life of illusion—steak dinners, wine, wealth, and fame—who ultimately hands over Neo to the Machines. We moved into the synoptic Gospels and the Last Supper, where the Son of Man was betrayed by one of his own—Judas Iscariot, "who would betray him" (Matt. 26:25)

At one point in the film, Neo actually dies, but it is through the faith of Trinity (the female character, who believes Morpheus that Neo truly is the One who will save them from their enslavement) that this death is not final. So, we moved on to the Resurrection—that our belief as Christians is that even when all hope seems lost, Christ will come again to save us. That like the early disciples who saw Christ die a true death, we would see him rise and come again in glory—for them three days later, and for us at our particular or the Last Judgement.

And we talked about the saints, disciples who by merit of faith Christ gives the power to heal the sick, raise the dead, and work miracles. That Neo could stop time and dodge bullets and bend spoons—there is nothing stopping one with faith from working such miracles in the name of Jesus except his own unbelief.

The whole time, my son never blinked. He rested his head on his arm and listened to the scriptures, the Word of God which is a living Word, not a dead text, to put it all into context. We do not study philosophy for its own sake, or theology so we can use big words, I told him. We learn about Christ so we can know what is *really* going on; so that because we *know* what we believe, and *who* we believe in, we can live as people with purpose and an ultimate end that we need neither fear nor eschew. As Christ said, "you will have trouble in the world, but fear not, for I have overcome the world!"

It is a great responsibility and privilege to be a father, but thankfully I have a son who is worthy of that honor, and who I actually enjoy being with and teaching him the truths of our Faith. I have to work with what I have in the times we live in, along with the threats, the technology, the culture. But like Augustine who baptized his platonic thought, and Paul, who adapted his preaching to different audiences and implored the Gentiles to connect the "unknown God" they pray to with the Living Christ, I try at least, when warranted and the opportunity presents itself, to "work all things for the good of those who are called according to purpose" (Romans 8:28).

I WILL SEE YOU THERE [8]

A year or so ago my 7 year old son fell from a not-insignificant height. It was the kind of fall on the playground where all the kids (and adults) turn and hold their breath, when time stands still for a few split seconds.

I was driving home from work when my wife called me. She was on her way to the hospital with our son, who seemed physically okay and not in pain, but who kept repeating the same questions over and over.

Not knowing the full extent of the fall apart from the few brief words my wife shared over the phone, and fearing a brain injury, I hung up, and opened up my mental rolodex of holy men and women I hold "on retainer" when I need them most.

Though I have my more established and well-known entourage of saints who have interceded for us in powerful ways—St. Catherine Labouré, St. Pio of Pietrelcina, St. Jude, to name a new—I have a special place in my life for those holy men and women who have not yet been formally canonized. My hope is that one day, in our time of need, they will work a needed miracle for us and in turn give witness to the mighty power of God.

---

[8] This essay appeared in *Catholic World Report* on May 14, 2021 (catholicworldreport.com)

There is Servant of God Fr. Walter Ciszek, whose grainy portrait from a Siberian gulag hangs in our kitchen with the hard-scrabble caption underneath: "Give God your lousy best." There is Servant of God Fr. John Hardon, whose archives of talks and writings I have bookmarked when I need courage and clarity in the midst my personal (and feeble) "white martyrdoms;" and there is Servant of God Frank Parater, a seminarian from the diocese of Richmond, Virginia who died at the age of 22 in Rome of rheumatic fever and who offered his death for the conversion of non-Catholics in Virginia. His "death wish" was an inspiration to me that nothing be wasted, not even our retirement from this earthly life.

As my mind flipped through these holy figures and more, by the inspiration of the Holy Spirit, one man came to mind whose story I had heard about somewhere. His name was Francis Houle. Irving "Francis" Houle was a father of five and grandfather of seven who lived in Michigan, was a fourth-degree Knight of Columbus...and received the stigmata in 1993 at the age of 67. I remembered reading about him, and that he had fallen from a horse as a child and suffered near fatal injuries but was healed when an army of nuns prayed for him.

Whenever I rely on "friends in high places" for help, I try to call upon those who I feel would understand or have a special affinity for our particular situation based on their life or charism. In this case, I felt Francis Houle, the stigmatist from Michigan who lived in my lifetime, would understand and help my son. The whole drive, I kept saying over and over, simply, "Francis, help!"

When I arrived at the hospital, my son was still confused and stuck in a loop of questioning where he was and how he had gotten there. My greatest fear was short or long-term memory loss, as I had never dealt with head injuries before. The doctor who evaluated him, thankfully, determined he was suffering from a concussion but noted that he was very lucky in that he hit a hard part of his skull; if he would have fallen at just a slightly different angle, the potential for lasting damage would have been much more probable.

My son's memory returned over the next few days, and his concussion subsided. Though this probably would not have counted as a miracle in the formal sense, I felt indebted to someone I at least knew understood and no doubt worked in some way to come to our aid, this married father, grandfather, and great grandfather from Michigan who bore the wounds of Christ and healed countless people who he prayed over. He was humble and unassuming; after all, he had children himself.

Not long after that event, we ended up having Thanksgiving dinner at a family member's house where one of Francis Houle's sons joined us as a guest. We recounted the incident to him, and he shared stories of all the people who would come to see his father. Though we didn't discuss personal faith, I got the impression it was overwhelming at times for him and his mother, Francis' wife. He recounted one particular instance in which his father was getting sick in the bathroom, and it was only realized later that he had, in praying over a cancer patient, taken on the poisonous effects of the chemotherapy himself.

As a husband and father of three, it is my greatest hope that I will see the glory of Heaven one day, and that my wife and family will join me there. It is what I live for, and what I hope to die for, God willing.

But when I thumb through that old mental rolodex of those on the roster in the Church Triumphant, I often wish there were more models I can relate to and emulate in my state of life—that is, as a husband and father. Sure, there are married canonized saints throughout history, some together (like Louis and Zelle Martin, parents of St. Therese of Lisieux), and some canonized separately. But for the most part, those canonized are primarily religious.

There are probably a multiplicity of reasons for this beyond the scope of this article, both religious and political. Not for a second do I doubt my calling to be a husband and father, nor do I question whether this is what God has chosen for me as my path to sanctification, which I am responsible for carrying out. But when I look around, can those "friends in high places" relate to this state when they themselves have chosen "the better part," a higher calling, a renunciation of marriage and family for the sake of the Kingdom?

How does one live out the sacrament of marriage—not just to be healthy and happy, in love and old age, but for the purpose of attaining sainthood, for oneself and for one's spouse? What does it look like? How do we exercise patience, chastity, temperance, when the floor is strewn with Legos, we're tired from work and childrearing, and we lose our temper so easily?

I was always taught that the saints exercised heroic virtue. What is heroic about raising a family? Working a job? Taking vacations? Going to Mass on Sundays and praying the Rosary in the evening? What worthiness is there for others to emulate, were we to be canonized some day? "Oh look, she did the dishes in love," or "he worked hard to provide." Yes, I know there is sanctification in the ordinary, humdrumness of life when done with love. But it is that very ordinariness, that part that is not, in fact, "set apart," that makes me wonder if this is, in fact, why there seem to be so few married canonized saints.

Of course, marriage and family life is a daily "dying to self" when done for Christ's sake, because he set the example for us to follow in washing his disciple's feet and offering his life to save theirs. It may in fact be harder to achieve the same level of sanctity as a religious given the unique burdens of our state in life. It does not make us exempt from the universal call to holiness. It just means we need to adapt our circumstances to make it our sole focus, while still maintaining and setting to the responsibilities of our state.

The hidden life inside the walls of the domestic church is largely just that—hidden. And for good reason. Individual families (though they may be holy and worthy of emulation) do their duties quietly. People may hear about them through the grapevine and want to be near them for their ordinary sanctity and warm charity. But they may not have a diocese or a large public gathering lobbying for a husband or wife's cause to be considered, though they may already be wearing the crown of righteousness in Heaven, official title or not.

The process of canonization is careful and methodical for good reason, and it is also for the benefit of us, the Church Militant because we are the ones who need the saints, not the other way around. Though I do worry if I ever, by some miracle, achieve such a state and have church officials combing through my emails and text messages and interviewing my friends and family what they will find out about me.

We know from St. Paul's words to the church in Corinth that the married man is divided and not free from concern, unlike the unmarried man (1 Cor 7:32, 34). Can a married man be saved? Can he wear the crown of righteousness? We know it can be done, for nothing is impossible with God.

"If ye be perfect," says the Lord. But we are not perfect, and any perfect person in marriage or parenthood is, for all intents and purposes, probably not of the human species. And yet, the call is there. We are called to be perfect, as our Heavenly Father is perfect. But it is not by being a St. Francis or a St. Catherine of Siena or even a Francis Houle. It is by being YOU. God made you like no other, and if you are married and a father or mother, he destined you to live out your life as such.

You may not be doing hard time in a Siberian labor camp but if you are loving and forgiving your spouse when everything in you screams to lord their faults over them, and there is no one around to see you do it, you are not only living the beatitudes, dying to self, and doing so in secret...you are fulfilling the Greatest Commandments.

When you give your wife the bigger pork chop because it's the one you want, and you do it day after day, meal and after meal, decade after decade, until your last supper on earth...are you not acting in the same way as a wise virgin trimming her lamp and holding her oil for the day the bridegroom comes?

When you live the virtues for your children to see, and set a hedge of protection around your hearth and home to keep out the things that harm—are you not setting yourself as a human shield, weaving a fence of thorns which you wrap and mend with your own bloodied hands to protect those little lambs whom Christ himself died for? Is your fatherhood, though temporal, not spiritual in the legacy it builds brick by brick, virtue by virtue, sacrifice by little sacrifice?

Whether or not we are formally recognized on earth among men for our sanctity matters very little when you have run the race and are wearing the crown. Our crosses are custom built for our backs, and the weight of all the family affairs we bear as well make it a unique burden and an unlikely joy as well. We are made whole through sacrifice, through suffering, through the school of charity which is the domestic church in which we learn the hard way how to love, how to forgive, and how to hope. There is no use wishing you were a priest or a nun. You have all you need for your journey. God has made you a mother, a father, a spouse. He has made you, YOU. He has to start somewhere today. He may as well start with you.

WHAT YOU LIVE FOR: DRAFTING YOUR DEATH WISH

At First Friday Mass yesterday evening, our priest gave a brief homily on Servant of God Frank Parater (1897-1920), who was a seminarian from the Diocese of Richmond, Virginia. He died in Rome during his theological studies 100 years ago to the day, at the age of 22 from a rheumatic fever.

I have been doing the First Friday and First Saturday devotion—reparative devotions to the Sacred Heart of Jesus and the Immaculate Heart of Mary, respectively—for the past six months. For those who are unfamiliar with it, Our Lord promises the following graces to those who receive Holy Communion on the first Friday of every month (for nine consecutive months) in honor and reparation to his Sacred Heart, as revealed to St. Margaret Mary Alacoque:

1. I will give them all the graces necessary for their state of life.
2. I will give peace in their families.
3. I will console them in all their troubles.
4. I will be their refuge in life and especially in death.
5. I will abundantly bless all their undertakings.
6. Sinners shall find in my Heart the source and infinite ocean of mercy.
7. Tepid souls shall become fervent.

8. Fervent souls shall rise speedily to great perfection.
9. I will bless those places wherein the image of my Sacred Heart shall be exposed and venerated.
10. I will give to priests the power to touch the most hardened hearts.
11. Persons who propagate this devotion shall have their names eternally written in my Heart.
12. In the excess of the mercy of my heart, I promise you that my all powerful love will grant to all those who will receive Communion on the First Fridays, for nine consecutive months, the grace of final repentance: they will not die in my displeasure, nor without receiving the sacraments; and my Heart will be their secure refuge in that last hour.

Frank Parater, as a young man, composed the following letter prior to going to Rome, to be read in the event of his death should he pass, offering his life to the Sacred Heart of Jesus for the conversion of Virginia:

> I have nothing to leave or give but my life and this I have consecrated to the Sacred Heart to be used as He wills. I have offered my all for the conversion of non-Catholics in Virginia. This is what I live for and in case of death what I die for...Since my childhood, I have wanted to die for God and my neighbor. Shall I have this grace? I do not know, but if I go on living, I live for this same purpose; every action of my life here is offered to God for the spread and success of the Catholic Church in Virginia...I shall be of more service to my diocese in Heaven than I can ever be on earth.

Parater was an excellent student and a model of charity, an Eagle Scout, and top in his class, but from outward appearance his was not a manifestly heroic virtue. I have always been attracted to those holy heroes and "big gun" saints—St. Augustine the major sinner turned saint; St. Francis Xavier; St. Anthony the Great; St. Teresa of Calcutta. But what I appreciated about Parater—who I had not known about prior to last night—was that he did not do anything outwardly extraordinary. His devotion to the Sacred Heart was fitting for a First Friday sermon. It was as if he recognized that his death was more important than anything he could do in life. And he prepared for it, testified to in his writing. Not just for himself, but for the Church universal, as well as the Church local.

If you don't have a devotion to the Sacred Heart, maybe now is the time to start. Remember the graces promised to those who do. And if you don't have a death wish, maybe now is a good time to draft one. You never know when the Lord will take you, or how he will use you, whether in this life or the next.

And I'm grateful to have found a new intercessor to petition a miracle from when I need it.

SCRUPULOSITY:
A THOUSAND FRIGHTENING FANTASIES

My seven year old son has a big personality. He is insightful, tender, and sweet. He can also be a fireball, with a larger-than-life presence that can be commanding at times. My wife and I tend to think his emotional state is very attuned and in many instances his acting out is a result of him not being able to express himself adequately. He also can get "stuck in a rut" where his mind sort-of "loops" in a closed circuit on a particular thought. This has happened on more than one occasion where he had gotten so worked up and upset he couldn't get out of it, mentally. It was all we could do between bear hugs (restraining him) and calmly reassuring him to bring him back down. Those behavioral-type instances have lessened in the past couple years, but he still gets a bit obsessive about things sometimes. He will tell my wife and I that he "just can't get it out of my brain," whether it's a toy or a fear. The apple doesn't fall far from the tree in our family. My father has mild-OCD and I have some tendencies myself, as well as my son. It's not severe, just an inclination towards obsessiveness.

I'm not super Type A though, am more of a generalist than a specificist, so it could have been a lot worse. But being prone to anxiety and having been trained in the art of worrying from a young age (a habit learned from my father), I can say that at the root of such struggles, when you drop down in the well, you find the issue most prevalent revolves around control. Loss of control can be a nauseatingly fearful thing. The Israelites were constantly falling into the trap of not trusting God and preferring the illusion of control that idols and false gods gave them.

Early on in life I fell into the self-reinforcing worry trap: if you worry about something enough, you can change the outcome. When you worry about something and the bad thing doesn't occur, it reinforces the erroneous thinking that your worrying is what prevented it. And so you learn that worrying can change things, when in fact nothing could be farther from the truth.

I tend to believe that worry, anxiety, fear, and scrupulosity are all cousins. Early in my conversion, I struggled with scrupulosity of the religious type. The priest who instructed me in the faith and the catechism was not a particularly healthy (psychologically, emotionally) man. I remember the fear of being hit by a bus before I would make it to Confession and living in the fear of Hell. Religion is a poor antidote to such dispositions when it is not accompanied by a real relationship with the Living God.

Over the years such scrupulosity melted away and was not as much a struggle for me. I think this was in large part due to grace, to a deepening prayer life and friendship with the Lord, and also in meeting my wife, who is as Type B as you can get. Loosening the reigns on feeling I had to control everything was aided by having children. I distinctly remember when my daughter was born and feeling overwhelmed at how to raise two kids. I drove to a Wawa while my wife and newborn baby were asleep at the hospital, sitting outside my car smoking a cigarette and just saying to God, "This is too much. There's too much that can go wrong and if I think about it or worry about it I'm going to go crazy. So you take it. I'm turning it over to you." Because we believe in a loving God and Father, we can do this in full confidence that He WANTS to drive for us, wants us to trust Him. His yoke is easy, and his burden is light.

As my own scrupulosity gave way to trust and confidence in God providing for us, I had a friendship with another guy who suffered from religious scrupulosity as well. He struggled with sin, as I had, but also in feeling forgiven. He felt, erroneously, that God was tired of him and tired of his crap and just didn't want to be bothered anymore and that he wasn't worthy of God's love. I gave him information about Scrupulous Anonymous and encouraged him to reach out to them. Unfortunately this also translated into our friendship, and I felt there became more and more distance between us. When I finally brought it up to him, he confessed he didn't feel "good enough" for me or worthy of our friendship. I tried to reassure him that wasn't the case, and while I felt hurt, I respected whatever distance he wanted to maintain. We eventually fell out of touch.

There is a kind of hellish neuroticism in scrupulosity that wants the lock tight assurance of being saved. It is also a tool of the Devil. I think Martin Luther had these kinds of OCD tendencies and this motivated him to develop his theology of justification. As a Catholic, I trust in the mercy of God. I trust that I have been invited to share in the Heavenly Banquet but that this does not depend on anything I can accomplish on my own. And yet, I cannot just sit back and not cooperate with grace. I trust that I am saved, I am being saved, and I will be saved. That freedom, when it trusts and is based in the confidence of a child for his father, and is motivated by love rather than fear, has the potential to burn away the restricting sterility of scrupulosity when it is the presence of the burning Sacred Heart of Jesus.

Salvation is not a human endeavor but is a gift that rests completely on the goodness of the Giver. Christ as man both human and divine synthesizes this need in our human economy as a counter to the rote Law and the limits of wooden idols. He became fallen man so that we might become divine. Spiritual health requires moving beyond mental obsession or spiritual fixation and invoking the heart, the mind, the body, and the spirit in synthesis. This is what makes us human beings able, in freedom, to fall rather than test-taking robots. The Devil does not want us to trust our Father. He does not want us to live in love, but in fear and servitude. He is a legalistic and will flex the Law if it helps him in his purposes. Don't let him. Relish your humanness, know that

ON FAITH

you can fall but trust that God is greater than your sin and failings. Exercise your will in a way that offers your choices as a gift, an oblation to God, in loving obedience. Trust in the unfathomable Divine Mercy of God in Christ. If you struggle with scrupulosity, I pray you will grow in love, trust, and confidence so that you can leave behind such mental legalism like a cicada's shell, a snake's skin, and just rest. It can be hard to rest in Love. But once you have, you know there is no place better to be as the antidote.

"I no longer fear God, but I love Him. For perfect love casts out fear (Jn 4:18)."
St. Anthony the Great.

WISDOM AND FOLLY

WHEN YOU CAN'T TAKE THE STAIRS

Many days—most days—I'm really not sure I'm going to make it. I know that sounds overly pious and fatalistic. It does not minimize my hope for salvation. I try to keep my eye on the prize, on the cross. But my sins and weaknesses, my pride, my *self*, runs so deep, knocking me down as soon as I get back up from the last beatdown, it is very, very clear that I am too weak for perfection and that I have no hope for salvation in the slightest under anything I could ever accomplish.

That is not a bad thing to realize. We are not meant to save ourselves in the Christian life. "Good people" do not go to Heaven because they are good. The more we realize our dependance on Christ for salvation, the more we will embrace our weakness and (paradoxically, *bien sûr*) it is in weakness that we are made strong (2 Cor 12:9). I am too weak to do great works, to attain great heights of mysticism, contemplation, or prayer. But I have a guide that I look to and lean on *à la place de*.

When I was in Detroit this time last year for a conference and was listening to a talk on the stages of divine ascent of a soul, I realized with some sweat on my brow that I had grossly, grossly underestimated the trials and tribulations of spiritual fortitude. By God's grace, I was introduced to the 33 Days to Morning Glory devotion in preparation for consecration to the Immaculate Heart of Mary. I realized that the words of St. Louis Marie de Montfort about her held a key in my hapless helplessness spiritual life: "Mary is the safest, easiest, shortest and most perfect way of approaching Jesus." There may be hope for me yet.

This idea—total consecration—was a complete paradigm shift for me. Rather than trusting in my own way, I would entrust myself (and my family), turn over my rights, to Mary to show me the right way. My judgment can be suspect, my ideas of what I should be doing, how and for whom I should be praying—I wanted to turn it over to someone closer—indeed, the closest—to our Lord than I to show me. So in October of last year, we did just that.

This idea of turning everything over, as I said, was a spiritual paradigm shift for me, a totally different way of approaching prayer, mortification, salvation. It also renewed in me an interest in a saint I had until a year or two ago had previously dismissed: St. Thérèse of Lisieux.

Ten years ago I regarded St. Thérèse the Little Flower as an insufferable "nervy" saint whose little infractions in the convent were, in my eyes, a nauseating expression of a piety I simply could not relate to. Now I am beholden to her. Her Little Way may be little, but it is not easy by any means. Whenever we accomplish a scrap of virtue in our lives our heel can slip from that spirit of helpless dependency on God's love and mercy to an attitude of self-determination in which we set our sights on Heaven by the sweat of our brow. That's when things quickly fall apart, at least for me. So, to follow this way, it's like a GPS constantly recalculating as you veer off course, trying to bring you back to the road you should be on. I did a "big" thing (fasted for a day, spent a long time in prayer, did a noble work of charity, etc.) and suddenly I feel self-justified. Off course. Recalculating. When we come back to repentance, humility, love, directing the will to good, we are back on course. But that does not come from mighty acts, but a deep trust, one that can meet resistance in being developed.

To remember what it means, how St. Thérèse sought to be united with her Savior, the image of the elevator is what stuck with me. From her autobiography, *The Story of a Soul*, she says:

> We are living now in an age of inventions, and we no longer have to take the trouble of climbing stairs ... I wanted to find an elevator which would raise me to Jesus, for I am too small to climb the rough stairway of perfection. ... The elevator which must raise me to heaven is Your arms, O Jesus! And for this I had no need to grow up, but rather I had to remain little and become this more and more.

There's an expression in the business world: *work smart, not hard.* Of course the teaching of the Church is that we are saved by faith *and* works, not faith alone. But this is not about "working towards Heaven," but a different approach that leads to radical trust, radical dependency, radical love—because it's all one has. Not everyone can fast like St. Antony or hear confessions for as many hours as St. John Vianney or write volumes like St. Augustine. But everyone has the capacity to love, to will, to trust. It can take some real "work" to get there, but it is a different kind of work, an inner work, a work that leads to trust and dependency in one's helplessness. The strength of the Little Flower is in her helplessness, her weakness, and her Little Way should give us great hope that Heaven is not beyond us, but that Christ desires we commune with him there forever.

Even if we have to take the elevator.

ON SECRET FAULTS

In Adoration yesterday I had a vision—nothing dramatic, but it did seem as if it came from the Lord. I saw a man sitting on a couch, kind of a heavyset man. He had folds in his clothes, and folds in his skin, and these folds held things from his life. The couch he was sitting on, too, had crevices and places where the remote had fallen, or crumbs had collected, or coins that had been lost. Like Joseph interpreting the dream of Pharaoh about the seven healthy cows and seven plump ears of grain and the seven gaunt cows and the seven blighted ears of grain in Genesis 41, I felt that the Lord was making the meaning of this vision plain.

The Greek aphorism "Know Thyself" is a spiritually fallacious one for the Christian, for a man will never arrive at the bottom of his own heart in his lifetime, and it is "the things that proceed out of the mouth come from the heart, and those defile the man" (Mt 15:18). We tend to consider ourselves better than we are. But who can see his own eye but in a mirror? It is the work of grace that reveals our faults to us. "Who can discern his errors? Acquit me of hidden faults" (Ps 19:12).

Though it is an effort and a work to acquire self-knowledge of our own accord, it is limited. David in the comfort of his springtime, when he should have been at war, falls into sin with Bathsheba. It is Nathan who is sent to him by the Lord to rebuke him when he could not see. The words of the prophet to David, "You are the man!" are not meant to build up but to break down. He was the man who stole the sheep, who put the innocent to death, and who hid the whole ordeal. This was not an occasion for high-fiving, but castigation for the benefit of saving his soul. "Health of body and mind is a great blessing," writes St. John Henry Newman, "if we can bear it; but unless chastened by watchings and fastings, it will commonly seduce a man into the notion that he is much better than he really is."

Or think of Saul, who was a 99%er in obedience in his charge to completely destroy the Amalekites, and whom the Lord sent Samuel to call him out for it with those iconic words, "what then is this bleating of sheep in my ears?" (1 Sam 15:14). Saul was under the presumption that he had fulfilled the commandment of the Lord with regards to the spoils of war. But he deceived himself and brought offense to the house of Israel. Samuel calls him out, the bleating of the sheep the audio indictment of his disobedience.

Do we watch and fast, and ask in humility for our faults to be revealed to us? Are we comfortable in our springtime in rooftop leisure when we should be at war? Do we have a Nathan in our lives, a spiritual guide or companion who is sent by God to set us straight? We should recognize that we are never free in this life of temptation, never safe from a fall. Again the words of St. John Henry Newman:

> The warning to be deduced from it is this:—Never to think we have a due knowledge of ourselves till we have been exposed to various kinds of temptations, and tried on every side. Integrity on one side of our character is no voucher for integrity on another. We cannot tell how we should act if brought under temptations different from those which we have hitherto experienced. This thought should keep us humble. We are sinners, but we do not know how great. He alone knows who died for our sins.

There is never a reason to avoid Confession. God's mercy extends to all who humble themselves, and confessing regularly, even (and especially) for venial sins on our conscience, disposes us to the grace of greater self-awareness. The farther we walk on the road, the closer we get to the Savior, the more unworthy we recognize ourselves to be.

When we meet wise and seasoned people on the road, the Nathans and the Samuels, who can see things we can't and in charity point them out to us for the benefit of saving us from perdition, we should thank God for them. For our secret faults will be our downfall if they remain unconfessed, trapped in the folds of our skin and our clothes; for we will have the appearance of being clean and put together before others, but when we get up from our leisure to stand before the Lord, we will see just how slovenly and covered in crumbs the unaware man is.

ON PRAYER

THE ART OF LISTENING IS AN ACT OF CHARITY

I've always looked to St. Paul's words in his letter to the Philippians as possessing a kind of secret, a key to freedom, contentment, and inner peace. These things always eluded me growing up. And yet St. Paul's words affirm that he is secure in Christ, and this translates to an inner security that is dependent on no man. For he says,

> I am not saying this because I am in need, for I have learned to be content whatever the circumstances. I know what it is to be in need, and I know what it is to have plenty. I have learned the secret of being content in any and every situation, whether well fed or hungry, whether living in plenty or in want. (Phil 4:11-12)

The Gospel is replete with these various keys and secrets; the more we pray, the more we read scripture, and the more we knock, the closer we come to unlocking the doors that keep us in bondage and unhappiness. The world does not know this peace, because it belongs to the Devil. For as St. John says, "The world and its desires pass away, but whoever does the will of God lives forever" (1 Jn 2:17).

God is no gnostic; He does not reserve secret knowledge for a select few but makes the light of the Gospel available to all in plain view. You may have to sell everything you have in order to buy this pearl of great price. But in doing so, you will have laid claim to an inexhaustible treasure that never corrodes, a well that never runs dry.

Sometimes, though, there are so-called "life skills" that even a godless pagan can plant and thus take advantage of a great harvest; But just as St. Augustine baptized the teachings of Plato in the waters of Christianity, so to can we as Christians lay claim to these more-or-less "natural" skills for the glory of God and the good of our neighbor. One of these skills I would like to posit has great potential for the Christian faithful is learning *the art of active listening*.

This morning in prayer I was meditating on Psalm 19:1-4 which speaks to this ability for God to "speak without speaking":

> The heavens declare the glory of God;
>   the skies proclaim the work of his hands.
> Day after day they pour forth speech;
>   night after night they reveal knowledge.
> They have no speech, they use no words;
>   no sound is heard from them.
> Yet their voice goes out into all the earth,
>   their words to the ends of the world.

Why is listening so important? It is a skill, something we are not necessarily endowed with from birth but one we can acquire and hone over time. But why should we? I've been thinking about this lately, and I'd like to highlight some points and posit a few reasons why we as Christians should devote time to working on this more or less natural skill.

1. It's Okay Not to Speak

"Wherefore, my beloved brethren, let every man be swift to hear, slow to speak, slow to wrath" (Ja 1:19) We have read or heard these words in the letter of St. James year after year. This epistle is only four chapters long but is dense and replete with spiritual wisdom that we can benefit from if we take it to heart. He exhorts Christians in this practical etiquette for their spiritual benefit: be quick to hear, slow to speak, and slow to anger.

Sometimes in a spirit of zeal we get the formula reversed—we are quick to speak, and slow to listen. The words of the prophet Isaiah always made an impression on me when he describes the Suffering Servant (which is Christ): "He opened not his mouth" (Is 53:7) Christ did not feel compelled to justify himself before those who held him in bondage: he knew who he was, who he came from, and to whom he belonged. Which leads to the second point:

2. Confidence and Self-Knowledge

"Most of us are just waiting for our chance to speak," as the saying goes. Why is that? Is what we have to say that profound? Or are we just, at heart, insecure about who we are and what we know?

When that is the case, we often overcompensate with words to try to throw people off the trail to our inner sanctuaries. When someone looks us in the eye, it can be unnerving. But often the people who have the ability to look into the soul of another in this way, (or even just look a person in the eye) it is because they are confident in who they are. Even if they know very little, they know that much, and will not try to pretend otherwise. "Know thyself," as the ancient saying goes. Those who stand justified find silence as their greatest witness; 'Fools multiply words" (Ecc 10:14). "The one who has knowledge uses words with restraint, and whoever has understanding is even-tempered. Even fools are thought wise if they keep silent, and discerning if they hold their tongues" (Prov 17:27-28).

3. Respect

Bad listening signals to the people around you that you don't care about them. How can you claim to love your brother when you don't care enough to hear him? And as St John writes, "Whoever claims to love God yet hates a brother or sister is a liar" (1 Jn 4:20).

Active listening doesn't cost you anything. Besides that, it is an act of charity. "The greatest compliment that was ever paid me," said Henry David Thoreau, "was when one asked me what I thought, and attended to my answer."

4. Patience

Patience is a virtue, and an important (but difficult) one to cultivate. How can we practice it? By listening to others in conversation. Unless we are hermits living in the desert, we will always have opportunities in conversation with others to defer our words to a later date, and instead give a platform to one who may desperately benefit from it. When we hold our tongues, it can feel like bridling a wild horse; it does not come naturally, and we may need to concentrate on intentionally holding back words that press against the inside of our mouths. That is practice, and we will not do it perfectly. But practice makes permanence, as they say.

5. Detachment

When one comes to awareness that they know very little in this life, that is the beginning of wisdom. It also helps one realize that the value of the currency of their words is perhaps not of as much value as we thought. When one furnishes their house with second-hand goods, they don't worry about someone breaking in to steal them. When one realized we don't possess much wisdom, we can let our words lie fallow, and offer our field to someone else to plant in for a season.

6. The Gift of Non-Judgement and Being Present

This can be a tough but fruitful practice—to be present to someone, to give them space to be themselves without judgment. Most of us are wounded, damaged in some way, and at heart feel unlovable. Judgement puts one on the defensive; when we disarm this tendency in practice, it can create a receptivity to what is being spoken judiciously.

Conversation is a two-way street, and there is nothing more off-putting that having someone speak down to you, or dismissively throw out anything you might say.

Let me repeat this: you can give someone the gift of your undivided attention, being present to them *and* listening, without betraying your ideals or morality. The Jews crossed the street when one unclean came in their path (Lk 10:25-37); yet Jesus allows those unclean to touch him (Lk 8:43-48) and lifts up those who have been condemned by the crowds (John 8:1-11). Being present to someone means giving them an invaluable gift—your attention and your time. You would be surprised how far that currency goes.

7. Prayer

"My son, pay attention to what I say; listen closely to my words. for they are life to those who find them and health to a man's whole body" (Prov 4:20). I would wager that the way we speak to and treat others reflects our prayer lives. The more one spends in contemplation, echoing the words of Samuel, Moses, Abraham, Jacob, Isaiah, and Ananias: "Here I am!", the more our interactions with our neighbor reflect this docility.

Do we know how to listen to the quiet whisper of the Lord? In doing so, we learn how to love Him in silence. If we don't, how then can we listen in charity to our brother in the flesh? Just as our Lord ties the two greatest commandments together, so too do listening to God in prayer and learning to defer our ego in conversation with others go hand in hand.

The *art* of listening is the *act* of charity. If we can learn to listen, while being rooted in the moral law of God, the grace of Christ's friendship, and the self-confidence to not be swayed by the wickedness of the world, we may well then be approaching the seat of wisdom.

I WILL CELEBRATE BEFORE THE LORD

One of the great privileges of having a late night slot as an Adorer of the Blessed Sacrament is the possibility for unbridled intimacy. Once a week, from 11pm to midnight, I am alone with the Lord exposed under the guise of bread; there are typically no other visitors to the chapel during this hour.

Even so, my Adoration hour is typically how I would be in the presence of other people. Sometimes I read from Scripture, pray the rosary, or simply kneel or sit in silent meditation with the Lord, speaking from my heart.

But this past week, on the heels of a retreat my wife and I attended earlier that day, I felt lead to take advantage of that alone time by verbalizing my (extemporaneous) prayer, praise, and supplication. That is, praying and speaking not just from the heart, but with my lips verbally.

It's a little strange, honestly. But divine intimacy in this manner—being unabashedly intimate with the Lord, like a child without social awareness, like the blind man calling out to the Son of David or the woman with the flow of blood who had the chutzpah to boldly reach out and touch the Lord of Lords' garment—is really a conduit of grace. I found it was like a bleed valve for a water heater or something, releasing that pent up spiritual pressure of always having to be so 'well-behaved' and composed in the company of others.

ON PRAYER

I do love the passage in 2 Samuel in which David dances half-naked before the Lord in the Ark, and how his love for Yahweh Sabaoth overflows in unbridled praise and passion. Here is the verse, which I will break up and add commentary as it relates to this idea of "shameful dancing":

> David again brought together all the able young men of Israel—thirty thousand. He and all his men went to Baalah in Judah to bring up from there the ark of God, which is called by the Name, the name of the Lord Almighty, who is enthroned between the cherubim on the ark. They set the ark of God on a new cart and brought it from the house of Abinadab, which was on the hill. Uzzah and Ahio, sons of Abinadab, were guiding the new cart with the ark of God on it, and Ahio was walking in front of it. David and all Israel were celebrating with all their might before the Lord, with castanets, harps, lyres, timbrels, sistrums and cymbals.
>
> When they came to the threshing floor of Nakon, Uzzah reached out and took hold of the ark of God, because the oxen stumbled. The Lord's anger burned against Uzzah because of his irreverent act; therefore God struck him down, and he died there beside the ark of God.
>
> Then David was angry because the Lord's wrath had broken out against Uzzah, and to this day that place is called Perez Uzzah. (2 Sam. 6:1-8)

This is interesting. I have not read commentaries on this, and so don't have the context, but the idea that poor Uzzah was struck dead simply for trying to keep the Ark from falling seems harsh, doesn't it? It is sobering, but not out of line with the power of Yahweh, which should fill all men with awesome fear and trembling.

The fact, too, that David becomes angry with the Lord on account of His wrath is interesting as well. David, the lover of the Lord, felt comfortable enough having these emotions directed to Him. And yet, as seen in the next passage, David also has that sober and appropriate fear of what the Lord is capable of, his great power and might. He decides to "park" the ark in the house of this Gittite (maybe as a kind of test, to see the outcome of such a decision?), and Obed-Edom and his household is blessed. So David decides to bring the ark to his city:

> David was afraid of the Lord that day and said, "How can the ark of the Lord ever come to me?" He was not willing to take the ark of the Lord to be with him in the City of David. Instead, he took it to the house of Obed-Edom the Gittite. The ark of the Lord remained in the house of Obed-Edom the Gittite for three months, and the Lord blessed him and his entire household.
>
> Now King David was told, "The Lord has blessed the household of Obed-Edom and everything he has, because of the ark of God." So David went to bring up the ark of God from the house of Obed-Edom to the City of David with rejoicing. When those who were carrying the ark of the Lord had taken six steps, he sacrificed a bull and a fattened calf. Wearing a linen ephod, David was dancing before the Lord with all his might, while he and all Israel were bringing up the ark of the Lord with shouts and the sound of trumpets. (2 Sam. 6:9-15)

David's dancing "with all his might" would be a sight to behold. In the presence of God, one who sincerely loves him can struggle to restrain that love. We see this in the saints (St. Philip Neri's near-exploding heart, and St Teresa of Avila's ecstasies come to mind). And yet, as we see in the next verse, the daughter of Saul is disgusted by his unrestraint.

> As the ark of the Lord was entering the City of David, Michal daughter of Saul watched from a window. And when she saw King David leaping and dancing before the Lord, she despised him in her heart.

> They brought the ark of the Lord and set it in its place inside the tent that David had pitched for it, and David sacrificed burnt offerings and fellowship offerings before the Lord. After he had finished sacrificing the burnt offerings and fellowship offerings, he blessed the people in the name of the Lord Almighty. Then he gave a loaf of bread, a cake of dates and a cake of raisins to each person in the whole crowd of Israelites, both men and women. And all the people went to their homes. (2 Sam. 6:16-19)

When Michal approaches David, pay attention to his response. He maintains that he is God's chosen; his confidence in God extends to his rightful vocation. His love for God *compels* him to celebrate. Not only that, but he promises to stoop even lower in unabashed expression of unrestrained worship to praise the Lord God almighty—his humiliation in his own eyes will be his elevation to those who view him. Amazing! This undignified king is so honest, so enraptured with the Lord of Hosts, that he strips and dances without a thought of his reputation or what is considered socially proper conduct.

> When David returned home to bless his household, Michal daughter of Saul came out to meet him and said, "How the king of Israel has distinguished himself today, going around half-naked in full view of the slave girls of his servants as any vulgar fellow would!"
>
> David said to Michal, "It was before the Lord, who chose me rather than your father or anyone from his house when he appointed me ruler over the Lord's people Israel—I will celebrate before the Lord. I will become even more undignified than this, and I will be humiliated in my own eyes. But by these slave girls you spoke of, I will be held in honor. (2 Sam. 6:20-22)

Finally, we see the virility of David, and the frigid barrenness of Michal, reflected in verse 23 in their physical outcomes:

> And Michal daughter of Saul had no children to the day of her death.

I think unchecked emotionalism when it is manufactured (as can sometimes happen in "praise and worship" congregations) should give us pause. But so should a stodgy formalism that despises those who abandon their masks and costumes in favor of intimacy with the Lord. The Lord honors those who fear him, but also to those who love Him He will not abandon David was not wrong to dance before the Lord. He enjoyed that privileged place by his calling as King to do so.

We also have that ability to be honest, humiliated, and forthright before the Lord of Hosts when we close the door and are alone with Him in prayer. We may not dance half-naked before the Lord in the Tabernacle—but if there were no one around to see at midnight on a weeknight, would it be so bad if we did so?

WE ARE ALL A MESS

I was texting with a buddy tonight and he asked how I was. I responded that I am in a good place but given that I am 60% pessimist and 40% realist, I figure it's just a matter of time before the other shoe drops and everything goes to pot. Let's hope not, but you never know.

There have been times when I've been totally dependent on God and others to get me through just living day to day. It's at these times when you appreciate the Simons that are drawn out of the crowd to help you carry your cross and that you have someone else to ease your burden—if nothing else by just being there with you in the suffering. And there are other times, like now, where I feel like I'm on stable ground and can pay forward some of that mercy that was shown to me.

It's a hard balance to strike at this stage in life to prevent being leveraged too severely with sports, activities, social events, work, and everything else. There is no shortage of "stuff" to keep us busy and our calendars covered with dots. The Devil loves idle hands, it is true. But to the degree we find ourselves so busy—sometimes by circumstance and sometimes by our own hand—that we don't have the bandwidth to absorb unplanned things that come up, enjoy time to take a walk or play, listen to a friend, or simply be unproductive, then maybe it's worth taking a look at what we can cull to make some space for life unscripted.

We all have our preferred way of communicating with the Lord. Some guys I know feel they need their missal, the Office, and formal prayers to do that. Others prefer the rosary, novenas, and devotionals. These are all laudable practices, as long as it is what the Lord is asking of us, and we are giving Him.

But sometimes, we find ourselves a complete mess, and compensating for the chaos and lack of control in our lives by holding ever more tightly to "adult" prayer that is respectable and well-presented. When what we really need to do is let ourselves be a mess, collapsing in the lap of the Lord.

My preferred place to do this above all the rest is at Adoration. Don't let the lack of line and form fool you—it's not easy to just 'be' for an hour with nothing to 'do.' It's not always easy to give up our well-guarded time. And believe it or not, it's not always easy to let yourself be loved as you are.

My dad will occasionally walk from his house at lunch time and sit on the bench outside my office. He'll text me to sit with him. I oblige him, but I'm always checking my watch or trying to think of things to talk about, when really, he's just content to be with me for as long as I will give him. "Easy for him, he's retired. He's got all the time in the world," I think to myself. But that's not it. When I think of all the time I piddle away on the things that don't love me back, and how little I give to the ones (and the One) who do nothing but love me, it's something that doesn't make sense in the Divine Economy. God doesn't ask for much. Just our whole heart, mind, strength, and soul.

I know quite a few people going through some very hard things right now. They find themselves a mess. One friend after Mass just burst into spontaneous tears from how hard life was for her at that moment. Others carry the burden more internally.

But what does our Lord long to communicate to us? "Take my yoke upon you and learn from me, for I am gentle and humble of heart; and you will find rest. For my yoke is easy, and my burden is light." (Mt 11:25-30)

I find the spiritual hot springs to find that rest is Adoration. It is in this space where we can stop pretending for a time; where we can lay down our egos and our defenses, and just allow ourselves to be loved. I don't know if trads have a harder time with this than others, since it's kind of "squishy," but no matter. It is the Lord truly present—body, blood, soul, divinity—what can be more trad than that?

He is on the altar before us, in the humble form of bread. Were He not, it would be like staring at a solar eclipse with the naked eye. Have you ever noticed that as He sits on the altar before us, there is no room on the altar for us to offer our burnt offerings, our oblations, our sacrifices? Not here, because as David recognized,

> You do not delight in sacrifice, or I would bring it;
>   you do not take pleasure in burnt offerings.
> My sacrifice, O God, is a broken spirit;
>   a broken and contrite heart
>   you, God, will not despise. (Ps 51:16-17)

Many of us are carrying around broken hearts, keeping it to (and for) ourselves. But the Lord wants it. And I find the place best to drop it beating and bruised before him is at the foot of that altar in Adoration.

Here's the thing, though...it takes a little time for the engine to warm up. An hour is best, and I find that the first forty minutes of settling gives way to fruit that bears heavily in the remaining twenty minutes, when things have thawed and softened enough to hear Him speak, in the recesses of the heart. Some days you feel like you have to chain yourself to the pew, the chair, to keep from "doing something," anything, to distract you from...well, yourself.

The Devil is well aware of this. He will convince you that you have better things to do, more productive things not "wasted" in this way. That you should get up and leave because, "you know....things gotta get done. We can't sit around all day." It takes discipline and fortitude to just be, without an agenda, without a mask, sitting with your mess of a self before the God of the Universe.

This is what He wants. This is where He has made Himself available to you. And so in those moments, when you find yourself in the dimly lit chapel at 2am, or early in the morning, or after work, just say quietly, "This is where I'm to be. This is where He wants me for the next 60 minutes." If all you have is 30 minutes, give 30. If all you have is 15, give 15. But shoot for an hour. Highway miles are good for an engine.

We think others have it all together. They don't. Everyone is carrying something they'd be better off laying down. But they don't always know how. Adoration teaches you how—without words, without instructions, to lay your burden down. It's a true grace to not have to pretend, to be offered rest and respite from everything we think is so important. We tend to forget from time to time and slip back into our old ways. But the more we can set aside time to let ourselves be loved in this way, *learn* to let ourselves be loved, and trust that it's ok we don't have it all together, the more fertile ground our Lord will have to plant in.

One hour in adoration. No agenda, no words, no self-judgment, or condemnation. Just giving God the gift of time, and a broken mess of a heart. Give it a try. I guarantee we're all a mess. But before the Lord, there's no need to hide it.

LIFE BY A THOUSAND ASPIRATIONS [9]

Years ago I read a small book, *The Way of The Pilgrim*, an Eastern spiritual classic in which a man wanders throughout Russia seeking the answer to the question of how one might "pray without ceasing" (1 Thes 5:17). In discovering the Jesus Prayer, he finds sweetness for his soul, and recites it day and night. On a plane ride to New Mexico when I was 19, I sat next to an Orthodox priest who gifted me with a prayer rope, and he taught me the prayer and the breathing to accompany it: "Lord Jesus Christ, Son of the Living God, have mercy on me, a sinner." I have prayed it often over the years. Like the Pater Noster, it is a "complete protein" of a prayer, efficacious to contemplation.

When I write these days, I often have to do so in spits and spurts, fitting in posts and articles in between work and family responsibilities. I often do not spend more than an hour at most on any one piece. But when I look back at the volumes of what I have written and published, it's not insignificant. This should be a testament to the ability not to waste moments and take to heart the words of St. Teresa of

---

[9] This essay appeared on the website for Catholic Spiritual Direction (Spiritualdirection.com) on December 9, 2021.

Calcutta, "we cannot all do great things. But we can do small things with great love."

We all have heard the expression, "death by a thousand cuts," by which it is meant that seemingly insignificant injurious effects can bring a man down over time. In the spiritual life, we know that venial sin—which is far from insignificant, but nonetheless is not death-dealing (1 Jn 5:17)—can coat the soul with soot over time and weaken the resolve against mortal sin. For this reason it is good that they be confessed in the Sacrament of Penance so that we never predispose ourselves to the sin that leads to death.

If a thousand small cuts can rob a man of his breath, it should follow that the so-called "ejaculations" of praise, petition, adoration, and thanksgiving for a Christian can help lead a man to life. "The great work of our perfection," writes St. Francis de Sales, "is born, grows, and maintains its life by means of two small but precious exercises—aspirations and spiritual retirement." And the 16th century Abbott Bl Louis de Blois wrote,

> The diligent darting forth of aspirations and prayers of ejaculation and fervent desires to God, joined with true mortification and self-denial, is **the most certain as well as the shortest way by which a soul can easily and quickly come to perfection.**

What do we mean by ejaculatory prayer? The Latin *iaculum* ('a dart') connotates arrows being shot from a bow. These are short, concise, uncomplicated prayers to aid us in times of temptation, offer God due praise, and lend themselves to petition. I have often relied on ejaculatory prayers as the brickwork in my spiritual life. Often, I get down on myself for not spending hours in contemplation and so accuse myself (sometimes in Confession) of "not praying." The fact is, though, that these seemingly insignificant prayers are uttered throughout the day on many occasions, such that the "left hand does not know what the right hand is doing" (Mt 6:3). Example of some of my favorite and more common aspirations include:

ON PRAYER

"Jesus! Mercy!"
"My Lord and my God!"(Jn 20:28)
"Come Lord Jesus." (Rev 22:20)
"I love you Jesus."
"Lord, save me!" (Mt 14:30)
"God, be merciful to me a sinner" (Lk 18:13)
"Help me, Lord."
'I believe. Help my unbelief." (Mk 9:24)

These are just a few. They do not take much time at all, they come from the heart, and they can be prayed anywhere throughout the day to help us learn to "pray without ceasing" (1 Thes 5:17).

In my next post, I will be writing about Contrition of Charity, that is, making an act of perfect contrition and how efficacious this practice is. While it is the work of grace ultimately, we can dispose ourselves towards it through learning to love God more so that when we offend him, we are "cut to the heart" (Acts 2:37). We grieve because we have injured our Lord "whom we should love above all things," and not only because of the fear of Hell which we incur by our sins. I believe frequent ejaculations help build this simple love of God and trust in His infinite mercy, and that He will not spurn these fiery darts of love, the "arrows that wound God's heart," as St. Pio said.

THE PET PROJECT OF SPIRITUALITY WITHOUT MORTIFICATION

If we are using the saints as our guides and models for how to get to Heaven in this life, I think you'd be hard pressed to find one that didn't believe penance and mortification of the senses was an essential part of the equation.

There's something about people (largely women) who are attracted to "spiritual things" and treat spirituality as "their thing." Like some people are really into professional baseball, some people are really into politics, some liturgy, some volunteering, etc. These love retreats and talks and quiet and relish reading books about all things "spiritual." There's nothing wrong with this on the surface, but we can sometimes approach the spiritual life as a pet hobby sometimes, and even get satisfaction out of it to the point where we pursue it for its own sake.

My wife often rolls her eyes when she takes the kids to the local library and the librarians there get all flustered by having to check out their books or do something in the children's section and interact with actual people. I'm sure they'd much prefer to be cataloging or stacking shelves somewhere in the quiet amidst the comforting smell of books, but the fact is their idealized version of the job doesn't always line up with the realities of serving the actual clientele (kids included).

ON PRAYER

In the context of the Christian life, love of spiritual things can sometimes be an indication of holiness but can also reflect a kind of immaturity and miss the trees for the forest.

There's also the danger of loving the wrong things. For monastics, learning obedience (which is "better than sacrifice," as scripture notes) can be hard, and they need to be pushed out of their comfort zones from time to time. Those monastery toilets don't scrub themselves.

I always go back to a story I heard about St. Aloysius that has stayed with me over the years. When he entered the Jesuits at the age of 17, Aloysius Gonzaga was appointed a spiritual director, St. Robert Bellarmine. Level-headed and patient, Bellarmine listened to Aloysius describe his extreme schedule of individual religious practice, then ordered him to cease it. He was assigned instead to work at a local hospital tending to the sick and infirmed. Squeamish, he was repulsed by the work, and he disliked people, which is probably why he was initially inclined to his private devotions and mortifications. When the plague hit Rome in January 1591, the sick and dying were everywhere, overwhelming the hospitals, and Aloysius had to dig deep and draw on that Italian stubbornness and bulldog-like willpower to stomach the work. He died caring for them and was canonized in 1726 AD.

What's my point? Well, it's two-fold—

First, we don't attain spiritual perfection by obtaining PhDs or licentiates in spirituality, but by applied application. This can mean the sometimes dirty work of serving the needs of the Church and the poor, or even denying or at least balancing good spiritual things so that we don't neglect the household or service due to our spouses.

Secondly, it's natural to want to "pitch tents" on the mountaintop after the Transfiguration. Like St. Peter, we tell Christ, "It is good that we are here!" But what does Jesus tell Peter to do to show his love for Christ? Three times he tells him, "Feed my sheep."

We must pray, as St. Pio says, "those who do not pray are lost." But we must also *do* the things Christ calls us to even when we don't necessarily want to or are repulsed by it. One man's mortification may be another man's comfort, and vice versa. As our Lord tells St Peter, "Very truly I tell you, when you were younger you dressed yourself and went where you wanted; but when you are old you will stretch out your hands, and someone else will dress you and lead you where you do not want to go" (Jn 21:18).

Chesterton said, "don't be so open minded that your brain falls out." In the same vein I'd say don't be so "spiritual" that you forget what it means to love God. To love God consists in one thing—to do His will. If we're not doing that, no amount of talks or retreats or spiritual reading will amount to anything. Mortification is meant to keep us from getting too comfortable in the things we prefer. Sometimes we just need to do the work, and believe me, there's a lot of work that needs doing.

ALL I HEAR IS SILENCE

I came to Adoration a little late this evening. Whether it's a beige carpeted Novus Ordo parish or an opulent historical church, my posture is always the same—dropping to both knees, bowing my head to the ground, and coming before the Lord of Lords as a beggar before his King. For I know my transgressions and my sin, as David wrote, is ever before me.

I have had moments in my life where the Holy Spirit has cut through me like an electric knife, and what the Lord was asking me in that moment was clear as the sky. I know better than to hesitate or delay, and grace has always followed those little acts of obedience to make the way possible.

Other times, and more often now, it is the silence of the Lord that meets me. This is not Endo's Silence—the non-response of the Almighty in the face of seeming futility and the absurdity of faith in suffering that precipitates a crisis of faith and meaning. Nor is it a silent balm that heals wounds when words cannot do pain justice. It is not the thundering silence of the saints, who like Elijah hear the Lord in the quiet whisper. It is likewise not the uncomfortable silence of simply an absence of noise, wondering if there is anyone on the other end of the receiver or if one is simply talking to oneself in one-way conversation.

True, communicative silence is a rarity. Think about the places you can go to achieve it. Podcasters retreat to the sealed capsule of their car to escape the chaos of their homes. You can get silence in the middle of the night as you lie in bed staring at the ceiling when everyone is asleep. But other than that, we are followed by noise like a lapdog.

When we come before the Lord in Adoration, the silence before—and from—the throne is a respite from the savagery of the outside world. Not all of us have inner silence, which must be cultivated and procured over time, the thing of contemplatives. When the beloved disciple reclined and laid his head in the bosom of our Lord, his posture was as intimate as one could get. And this is often the inner-posture I adopt in adoration—not physically, but in my spirit. When I come before Him, my defenses drop, for I know He sees me as I really am. I have nothing to bring, nothing to show for myself, nothing to brag about. All I have is brokenness and failure. This is the intimacy of a King to His servant; we are not slaves or indentured servants, but friends.

But our words fail. Nor does He waste words on us, lest we die. His silence in the Host, where deep calls to deep, is not maddening, not futile, not absurd except on the surface. His silence is a gift, for nowhere in the savagery of the outside world can we enter into not Emptiness of the Void, but fullness of life. It does not arm us with pep-talks but disarms us of the illusions we have about ourselves and our abilities.

It has been a long time since I have "heard" the Lord speak to my spirit in definitive ways in which I respond, "Yes! This is what I must do, the answer to the unasked question!" Where I have asked, "What should I do, Lord?" and He tells me.

No. Instead, silence is all I hear. I have no clarity, no monk-like inner-peace, but like standing on the shore before an ocean of such magnitude and mass, all I experience is my own nothingness and smallness. In the crashing of wave after wave, waiting for a response, all I hear is silence. Not enough to question "Why am I here? Why do I drop to my knees before this bread?" but in faith I continue to come to Him as if He *could* answer me and maybe one day, will.

I continue to come prostrate before the throne, not even sure what to say or ask, but just to offer myself as a sometimes-barely breathing oblation of sacrifice which I have to trust is pleasing to Him. If He wants my heart, I will give it to Him. But not all of it, for I am not perfect, not made in perfection, but piece by piece, trading parts of myself for these portions of silence in return.

Perhaps I should rage more often. But I have not been subject to real tragedy—not had my children ripped from the land of the living or been subjected to financial or existential ruin or had my back against a wall. Perhaps I should make more demands: "Why won't you speak!?" Perhaps it's a sign of my own lukewarmness and lack of trust, that I do not put Him to the test, as the Lord says, "Test me in this" (Mal 3:10), not having put anything of substance on the line. Perhaps I am too comfortable. The silence feels neutral—not healing, not consoling, not disheartening. Just like putting the time in, waiting, for when something—anything—will come to pass.

At ten till midnight as I type, the house is quiet. I am surrounded by my sleeping family. But the silence of the Lord when I am before Him is different. I know He is there, sitting in His monstrance, judging the nations and waiting to take all men to Himself. As St. John Vianney asked an old farmer what he did before the Lord in the tabernacle, maybe all I can say is to echo his words: "Nothing. I look at him, and he looks at me."

LET'S BE HONEST: YOU'RE JUST NOT THAT INTO HIM

Joe Rogan has a great channel on YouTube I'm really enjoying (aside from the cursing). He interviews interesting semi-famous people and just has conversations with them. I've watched a number of them, one being an interview with a former professional race car driver Danica Patrick titled "What Women Don't Understand About Men."

It got me thinking about that film/book that was popular a few years ago, *He's Just Not That Into You* and how these women in the dating world don't understand why a guy isn't calling them back, and it basically boils down to a few uncomplicated points that is for the most part summed up in the title: "He's just not that into you." Because if he was, he would find a way to be with you.

Though I didn't read the book, I think I saw the movie with my wife at some point, and there were some choice quotes that seemed to hit the nail on the uncomplicated head.

Here's the thing: This doesn't just apply to men and women and the interactions between the sexes. It pertains to the relationship between man and his God. If you think I'm being too soft, maybe I can temper the wine spritzer with a stiff shot of Chesterton: "Let your religion be less of a theory and more of a love affair."

Love affairs are a kind of dance, a courting, a pursuit, and a haunting. We see it in the erotic Hebrew canticles like Song of Songs,

Francis Thompson's *The Hound of Heaven*, and the poetic pursuit of divine intimacy in saints like John of the Cross. We see how God courts us with sweet consolations early in our walk with Him, blinding us with the intoxication of divine love; once He has us, He withdraws Himself when we have moved from milk to meat so as to strengthen and refine us. Our drink may turn from wine and honey to gall and crosses, but if the love one has for the Lord has matured in good soil, it does not wither or uproot easily, and one can pass through these desolations eventually into a love for Him where "deep calls unto deep" (Ps 42:7)

So, it's not unreasonable to think of the relationship one has with the Lord in an intimate manner. But such a relationship is only as deep or intimate as one gives; the Lord's depths are infinite, and His longing for us without bounds, so it is only reasonable to conclude that when we don't "know" the Lord more intimately, it is not because of the Lord being aloof, but because, well, "we're just not that into Him."

I pulled a few quotes from Goodreads for the aforementioned book, and though these quotes are in the context of dating in the secular world, use it to reflect on your relationship with the Lord, which is really the extent of your prayer life (knowing and conversing with the Lord in an intimate manner):

"If you can find him, then he can find you. If he wants to find you, he will."

"If a man is really into you, nothing will stop him from being with you—Including a fear of intimacy."

"Alone also means available for someone outstanding."

"If he's not calling you, it's because you are not on his mind."

"The word "busy" is the relationship Weapon of Mass Destruction. It seems like a good excuse, but in fact in every silo you uncover, all you're going to find is a man who didn't care enough to call. Remember men are never too busy to get what they want."

That last one kind of hit home: "We make time for the things we care about." When we claim to be so busy that we don't have time to pray, or it's an afterthought, what we're really saying is "It's not that important." Prayer is how we get to know the Lord—what His will is for our life, what He wants from us, what He desires and what pleases Him, and how we learn the sound of His voice. It's akin to spending time with your wife as the bare minimum maintenance measure for a marriage. You simply cannot please the Lord without faith (Heb 11:6), and you can't deepen your faith without prayer.

So, what we are saying when we prioritize twenty minutes in the morning of scrolling around on YouTube or watching the news or checking the stock reports instead of closing our door and praying in silence before the Lord isn't that we don't have time, *but that the time we have we don't want to spend with the One we claim to love*. And what is the First and Primary Commandment, lest we forget: "You shall love the Lord with all your heart, soul, and mind" (Mk 12:30).
The Lord uses the word *know* frequently in scripture. "Then I will tell them, 'I never knew you! Depart from me, you lawbreakers!'" (Mt 7:23) to those He casts out into outer darkness. To 'know' someone in the biblical sense is also a kind of physical consummation, such as in when Joseph "knew Mary not" in Mt 1:25.

Let's just be honest about it: It's not that we're "too busy"—it's that spending our time in this way doesn't excite us or please our sensory appetites. When we act this way, we are willfully choosing something else over the something *more*. In the dating world, this would be called *settling*. We are settling for less. And as in a marriage that has the potential to grow stale and subject to the test, when we don't spend time with our love, we "know" them less and less—physically and emotionally. When we wake up years later and feel as if "I don't even feel like I know you anymore," we can ask ourselves, "Well, why is that?"

ON PRAYER

Though it is true that people can drift apart or grow at different speeds that may not always match and align with one another, the thing about prayer and knowing the Lord in an intimate way is the deficiencies always lie with us. God pours out everything He has to those who earnestly seek Him: there is no lack, and no limit or bottom to the depth of His Mind. When we choose this-over-that, we are saying, "I value this thing over that thing." And how often does the One who should be our first love get the short stick, leftovers, and castoffs. If there's a simple maxim in the dating world as to why you're not getting callbacks from that guy you're interested in, it may be that "He's just not that into you." If your spiritual life is coming up short, the answer is probably the least complicated: "You're just not into Him." How can you tell? You're not giving your time, or you're giving it away to other things. You're not speaking, and you're not listening. Instead of asking, "How can I serve you? How can I please you today? What do you want me to do?" you're going your own way, doing your own thing, and consulting the Lord as an afterthought. And all this is not complicated—It happens in prayer, and if you're not praying or making time for prayer, it shouldn't be a surprise that you *know* the Lord less than you would otherwise.

The solution, too, is not complicated: make the time. Trade out the items in your time-budget so that prayer gets first seat and other things fill in around it, rather than the other way around. If all you have is early mornings for uninterrupted time, make the time then. If you're not able to spare fifteen or twenty minutes, perhaps your priorities are out of whack, and you admittedly do not feel that prayer is time well spent. I know if I'm honest with myself, this is really what I'm saying when I choose to piddle opportunities away or give into that inner-resistance (which the devil capitalizes on) that says I'd rather be doing x,y,z—anything really—than praying. And do it in the humility (that foundational virtue) that admits that you have failed to love the Lord your God with all your heart, soul, and mind—that pre-eminent Commandment with which we cannot know—and thus love—either God or our neighbor or even ourselves.

So if you're not praying that much, or you've put it on the back burner as I have, maybe it's worth being honest with the self-admonition that "I'm just not that into Him." That's ok, as long as you don't stay there. As anyone who has been married awhile knows, you can "fall back in love" through a renewal of that first love time and time again throughout the course of a marriage—but it often takes time, work, and a reorientation of the heart.

Do you really want to be one of those foolish virgins to whom the Lord said He "never knew?" Start making the time, shifting your priorities to get them back in line; right order has a way of keeping things from getting out of whack so that we keep first things first, and secondary things second. If you find yourself alone and uncomfortable, ask yourself why. Like the author said above, "Alone also means available for someone outstanding." We know who that "someone outstanding" is—Jesus, our first love, whom we have neglected and shelved so often and on so many occasions when all he really wanted was our time and our heart. But it's never too late to get reacquainted.

YOU HAVE TEN FINGERS

Twenty years ago while I was in Haiti, walking along a dusty road to Hinche, I came across two boys next to a bicycle. I asked them in broken French what was wrong, and they pointed to the snapped chain. Taking a closer look, I told them with an air of confidence, *pas bien*—no good. They would need a chain tool to repair it. I fiddled with it for about ten minutes while they patiently watched, eventually throwing up my hands in exacerbation. One of the boys stepped in, placed the link on a stone, took another stone in his hand, slammed it down on top of the link to set the pin, set it on the chainwheel, and rode off. *Pas mal.* I always remembered that humbling encounter of third-world ingenuity.

In China, where Christians are regularly jailed for worshiping under a Communist regime, not having access to Bibles does not stop them from imbibing the Word of God. When they have no access to the physical bound text, they have small scraps of paper with scripture verses written on them and commit them to memory before they are confiscated, because "they can't take what's hidden in your heart."

I turn 41 next week, and middle-aged malaise has set in. I'm heavier, and groan-ier. I used to eat whole cheesecakes without gaining a pound and biked across the United States in my twenties, averaging eighty miles a day. Now I'm proud of myself when I go to the Y once a week and swim more than 30 laps. I felt good when I went though, because for once I pushed through the myriad of excuses I come up with on a regular basis and *just did it*. Though the motivation may have been disgust with myself and a desire to change, the satisfaction of doing something physical lasted throughout the day. It even lasted into today, when I went for a (albeit, short) bike ride and even pushed it into the big ring for a bit near the end.

Even if I didn't have a pool to go to, or a bike to ride, I could just as easily do push-ups and sit-ups in my bedroom with no equipment needed. Often it's not the equipment we lack, or the tools we don't own, but the drive that's missing. And it seems to scale in direct proportion to what we have, and not what we don't.

When I undertook a brief trial in "mini-retirement" in my late twenties (essentially being in between jobs for a couple months), I thought I would take the time to write a book. I had a whole writing studio set up—and hardly wrote a thing.

Even now, working largely remote for the past year, I realized how much I don't need from my office—file cabinet and papers. Essentially, I can do all my work with a laptop and a kitchen table. Even the mouse I use is ancillary.

When we consecrated our family to the Immaculate Heart a few years ago on the 100th Anniversary of Our Lady of Fatima, my wife and I committed to praying the rosary every day. And for the most part, we have kept that promise. Every now and then I will neglect it—either from tiredness or forgetfulness—but it's not often. When I do let my guard down, chinks in the armor often develop slowly and perniciously.

The rosary is a spiritual tool, a weapon—but it's not just fancy crystal or amber or even humble wood beads strung together. The physical "scripture on a string" can aid us in meditation, but it is not *ipso facto* necessary. If we leave it at home or neglect to carry it with us, there's nothing—except our inner excuses—keeping us from using what we do have—our ten fingers—to pray.

IF THE LOVE OF THE WORLD IS IN YOU

Sometimes you forget the things you take for granted as a Christian. It seems hard to remember a time before the life of faith when I would catch myself at a party or watching Saturday Night Live with my friends thinking, "is this all there is?"

For many converts, the nudging towards the eternal, the curiosity towards "something more" beyond what is in front of us, is that wide part of the funnel that narrows as we move towards the Truth. Just as the Lord Christ used Samaritans and other foreigners to bring about the Kingdom of God, and just as St. Paul writes about Gentiles who have the eternal law written on their hearts (Rom 2:14-15), my own journey to faith began on the impetus of those outside the walls of Christendom.

In high school I had gotten my hands on some lectures of a Hare Krishna devotee. In one of the recorded tracks, an interviewer is asking about his iconic robe and *shikha* (a tuft of hair at the back of head specifically kept by Vaishnavas and Brahmanas to signify renunciation of the world). "Do you ever go to a movie? To a football game?" the reporter asks. "No," the devotee answered. "We experience our pleasure on...a higher realm. The purpose of life is to please God, Krishna."

"A priest," the reporter noted, "would not find it sinful to go to a sporting event."

"It's not so much that it is sinful," the devotee noted. "But if, in watching the event—the configuration of colors on a pasture doing this or that, I forget my eternal purpose, it becomes…quite a serious matter of eternal consequence. After all, Jesus Christ said, "If any man love the world, the charity of the Father is not in him"" (1 Jn 2:15).

The world and its lures are subtle and pernicious. *Horror vacui*—"Nature abhors a vacuum," as the saying in physics goes. The Lord bestows upon us the gift of work and leisure, but both can become an end in themselves rather than a means to an end; that is, our eternal end. This is why work on the Sabbath is such a serious violation of the Law. The great St. John Vianney saw the people of Ars working on Sundays as if it were any other day and it was one of his first spiritual admonitions he made upon his arrival in the small wayward village. We have six days to work, and on the seventh we are commanded—not given a suggestion—to rest. In doing so, we honor the Sabbath and, by extension, God Himself.

Likewise, leisure can become idolatrous when we place the acquisition of goods and pleasures above that which belongs to God and the poor. There is no sin in enjoying the things of God, but we must remember St. Paul's warning, in Romans 1:25: "They exchanged the truth about God for a lie, and worshiped and served created things rather than the Creator—who is forever praised." The consequence of idolatry—that is, prioritizing things outside of right order, putting created things before God, forgetting our eternal purpose and trusting in made-made creations—is that our thinking becomes foolish, and our hearts become darkened (Romans 1:21).

Such descents into idolatry and disruption of the eternal order do not happen overnight. Like unconfessed venial sins, which deposit layers of spiritual soot and silt upon our souls and prevent the light from penetrating, our susceptibility to the temptation to more serious sins increases in proportion to the extent which we forget our eternal purpose, our spiritual raison d'être. "They forgot the God who saved them, who had done great things in Egypt" (Ps 106:21)

When it is written, "If any man love the world, the charity of the Father is not in him" (1 Jn 2:15); and "You cannot serve both God and mammon" (Mt 6:24); and "In the same way, those of you who do not give up everything you have cannot be my disciples" (Lk 14:33), we find a dichotomous inverse relationship—the more you love the world and the things of the world, the more the world claims you for its own. When we forget who it is we serve, who put us here and for what purpose, we start to slip. When we become unbalanced and shelve prayer and due worship in favor of catching up on things we have prioritized instead to get ahead in the world at the expense of what we owe God in justice, we lose our spiritual equilibrium. Our Lord is clear—we cannot serve two masters, for the God of Hosts is a jealous God (Ex 34:14).

And so, we must admit, when we neglect mental prayer and due worship, meditation and recollection of what the Lord has done for us, we have become idolators and blasphemers. We gravitate and expend our energy on what we value; we make time for what matters to us. Like setting off on a spur that takes us farther from our destination the longer we traverse it in a state of forgetfulness, we can wake up and realize we are far from home. We become like fools, lost and without a map or rudder. We realize we have put our faith in perishable things thinking they are of the utmost importance in the moment; things that rot and are temporal. "And the world passeth away, and the concupiscence thereof: but he that doth the will of God, abideth for ever" (1 Jn 2:17).

But thank God when we do "wake up" from our spiritual slumber, finding ourselves like prodigals far from home, even when we have not committed heinous sins but simply drifted too far from shore. We can find our way home again, for the Father stands waiting like a beacon on a hill, a lighthouse on a shoreline. We tune back into the right frequency, the divine wavelength, by rededicating ourselves to prayer, in order to hear the way we must go. We find our map in the pages of Scripture. We recommit our time, dropping it in the basket of eternal reward. And we confess our waywardness in the Sacrament of Confession, which is more powerful than an exorcism.

"Be careful that you do not forget the LORD your God, failing to observe his commands, his laws and his decrees that I am giving you this day. Otherwise, when you eat and are satisfied, when you build fine houses and settle down, and when your herds and flocks grow large and your silver and gold increase and all you have is multiplied, then your heart will become proud and you will forget the LORD your God, who brought you out of Egypt, out of the land of slavery" (Deut. 8:12-14). Whereas the Devil does everything he can to make us forget what we have been ransomed from, the Lord urges us to remember—to set memorials on the ascent that we revisit. When we slip into forgetfulness of our eternal purpose and favor the temporal, God reminds us by grace through any means necessary to wake us up. And when the Devil urges us to remember our sins and failings in light of God's omnipotent perfection, our God forgets them. "As far as the east is from the west, so far has he removed our transgressions from us" (Ps 103:12).

The next time you forget your eternal purpose, what your ransomed life is for, use it as a barometer for your spiritual state. If you are far from home, call out for help in prayer. If you don't know the way, go to Scripture and the tradition of the fathers. If you have sinned, confess your faults and ask for forgiveness. Recommit yourself to the works of penance. Take time to be alone and give the Lord the oblation of a broken spirit (Ps 51:17). In doing so, you will recall your eternal destination, and your status in the world as merely a pilgrim. As St. Catherine of Siena said, "Everything has a purpose, and it is vast beyond our ability to comprehend."

IN DESPERATE NEED OF A FRIEND

Each morning my wife and I have been praying and reading Carmelite meditations on the interior life. Since the Feast of Corpus Christi, the meditations have been focused on the Real Presence and the Eucharist miracle.

It was on Monday early this week that I realized the little chapel near us—a historic mission church, the oldest in our state—had Perpetual Adoration on Mondays. We had just gotten home from the beach that day, where we were blessed with the opportunity to have a similar kind of "mission Mass" at the home of a couple downstate in the country on Sunday not unlike this first mission near our house that was started at a family's home in the 18th century. A priest came to offer Mass and a handful of faithful families attended. It was good to be around our people, and we had a potluck afterwards as the kids ran around teasing the sheep in the adjacent field. The weekend prior I was in St. Louis and got to attend High Mass three days in a row for First Friday, First Saturday, and Trinity Sunday at the magnificent St. Francis de Sales Oratory. I felt spoiled almost, this being the first time since the pandemic I had been able to freely attend Mass. Whether we are in a magnificent cathedral or worshiping with other families on a sheep farm, Jesus is truly present in the most Blessed Sacrament of the Altar.

But it had been months since I was able to go to Adoration, and I wasn't sure what to expect. Would the chapel be overflowing with people who had so desperately missed being near our Lord and able to gaze on His Face that there would be no available pews? Would parking be an issue? Surely the months of being separated from Him physically would have created in people a hunger for spiritual bread with the need to be sated.

I should have laughed at my idealism. When I arrived at the small chapel, it was completely empty save for one woman in a pew. I entered through the back and dropped to both knees at the sight of the Lord in the monstrance on the altar. I took a seat in a pew where I would spend the next hour.

Adoration is my favorite type of prayer because I am not scripted by nature. To be able to be myself, with all my sighing and gesticulations and to be able to collapse and be myself before the Lord of Hosts is a great source of comfort. When I lived in Philly and would visit the Lord in Adoration in my poverty of spirit, I would lie on the pew, though completely undignified, since I would spend sometimes the better half of a day there. I was once taken for a vagrant. "I look at him, He looks at me," as St. John Vianney recalled a peasant telling him. This is the essence of Eucharistic Adoration, distilled.

When the only other person present left after about twenty minutes and I was now alone in the church, I moved to the Prie Dieu near the altar, a few feet from the Lord, to get closer to him. I couldn't believe the privilege—a private audience with the King of Kings, undisturbed before His Majesty, with no one around or waiting even to take my place.

And then I became sad thinking of the Lord left alone were I not there.

For more than three months now into the pandemic, we have hardly had access to the sacraments apart from a few exceptions. Where are all the people? After the French Revolution had gutted the life of faith in France in the 18th and 19th century, the Cure d'Ars upon arriving in his new assignment found the little church "cold and empty as the hearts of the worshipers." Has the pandemic made our hearts cold? Fearful? Has Satan sifted us even now? Even after taking for granted what we have had for so long within our means, there was no line to get in the church, no overflow or standing-room-only. I was alone in a church with the Lord in his poverty.

As a newly assigned parish priest, St. Manuel González García dreamed of how welcoming and communal the experience of being a pastor on his first assignment would be, "of having a Church full of souls eager to listen to his sermons, of people fervently praying the Rosary with him each day, and of organizing a beautiful procession in the streets. He pictured crowds hastening to Sunday Mass."

The reality when he arrived, was a Church poorly attended, where only those getting married or baptizing their children came, and a population that was not a community, but a cluster of human beings who worked side by side, and never invested in the Church or each other. The building itself was dirty, almost abandoned, and the altar cloths torn and burnt. The neglect included the tabernacle covered in dust and cobwebs. He considered begging for a different assignment, fleeing. He wondered how he could fulfil a mission, any mission in such a place, but kneeling before the tabernacle, pondering how impossible the task before him, he felt someone looking at him "in desperate need of a friend."

He writes:

> The Evangelists are the ones who taught me the word "abandonment." I decided to use this word, not to speak of the hatred, envy, or persecution of the enemies of Jesus, but rather in reference to the disloyalty, coldness, ingratitude, inconstancy, insensitivity, indelicacy, and cowardice that Jesus experiences from his friends. This leaving him at the moment when they should all have been with him, this failure to assist him with their presence and their unconditional loyalty when he needed it most is what the Evangelists call abandonment and flight. "And they all forsook him, and fled" (Mark 14:50).
>
> There are two ways in which the tabernacle is abandoned. One, exterior: the habitual and voluntary absence of Catholics

who know Jesus but do not visit him. I am not speaking of unbelievers, or of the irreligious, or of uncatechized Catholics, from whom Jesus in the Blessed Sacrament will feel persecuted, hated, slandered, or unrecognized, rather than abandoned. I am speaking of Catholics who believe and know that Our Lord Jesus Christ, true God and true Man is really present and alive in the Blessed Sacrament. But they do not receive him in Holy Communion, nor visit him, nor have a friendly relationship with him—even though they live close to a Church, and otherwise have time and energy for recreational activities.

The second way is by interior abandonment. It is to go to him but not to really be with him. It is to receive him with the body, but not with the heart. It is to go to him saying words, bowing our heads, kneeling down, but not performing these acts of piety with our hearts. It is when we do not meditate on what we are receiving. It is when we do not prepare ourselves to receive him with a clean heart and with great spiritual hunger. It is when we do not taste and give thanks for the Food we have received. It is when we do not talk to or listen to the Guest who is visiting us. It is when we are not open to receive and keep the graces he brings us, the warnings he gives us, the example he teaches us, the desires he reveals to us, the love he shares with us. How many times will the Master have to repeat to some communicants and visitors to the Blessed Sacrament: "This people honors me with their lips, but their heart is far from me" (Mt 15:8).

Jesus, alone, abandoned in the hearts of his friends! Jesus visits souls and lives in the "homes" of his friends (through Holy Communion) without being understood or listened to or assisted or asked his opinion or even taken into account! This interior abandonment is repeated in alarmingly great proportions.

The empty church, the foot of the cross at his death, the garden in which he sweat drops of blood—these are the places his friends go to meet him. The masses jeer before his trial and drop branches of palms upon his entry into Jerusalem and are nowhere to be found in his hour of need. And yet for these masses He came too, longing to gather them under his wings..."and you were not willing" (Mt 23:37).

Will the many be saved? How few the saved. How empty the churches when men's heart grow cold in those last days. It is these moments when I am alone with the Lord offering this small gift of an hour when I cannot hide anything, that I recognize my own poverty. I have nothing to bring, nothing to give, but a contrite heart and a broken spirit.

We must console the heart of Jesus. Our audience before the Lord is an unspeakable privilege, one that we even now can do at all hours and days. If we cannot, we can make a tabernacle for him in our hearts upon receiving Holy Communion—room at the inn for him to dwell in our impoverishment. We can come to him, see him, whenever we want. And yet we don't. We find something of more importance. But "The time is coming when you will long to see one of the days of the Son of Man, but you will not see it" (Lk 17:22). Go while you can, to sit at his feet, to learn his commands, to listen in the privileged silence of empty churches and neglected tabernacles. Console him while he is still able to be found.

I WILL NOT RISE FROM HERE

I was listening to a man last night on YouTube recount how he came into the Catholic Church. As a young, wayward man, a couple he was acquainted with had prayed the rosary for him every day for a year, unbeknownst to him. He credits that act of persistent charity, in large part, for his conversion.

That snippet from his story resonated with me, because a year ago I had undertaken a similar practice for someone—a kind of "spiritual adoption"—in large part because I believe someone unknown to me had prayed me into the Church, and I was indebted. This was not a family member or even a close friend I was praying for, but someone I got a strong feeling and premonition about—that our Lord wanted this soul, and someone needed to pray for them to bring them home.

For years, I saw the examples of the blind men calling out to Jesus to be given their sight and refusing to be quiet (Lk 18:39); the woman with the flow of blood boldly pushing her way through the crowd just to touch Jesus' cloak (Mk 5:25-34); and the parable of the persistent widow (Lk 18:1-8) as a kind of foreign example of annoying persistence—something I didn't possess. When I was sixteen and struggling on the second day of a multiple day bicycle stage race I was in, I pulled over and my dad gave me a pep talk, "If it's too hard, just quit. You don't have to finish." I took his advice. I always remembered that.

But in the life of faith, this kind of stubborn persistence is really a kind of exercise of faith. It offends the Lord more when we ask so little of Him. Our Blessed Mother told St. Catherine Laboure in the vision in which she appeared to her that "The pearls that don't have rays are the graces of the souls who don't ask." The blind men receive their sight, the woman is healed of her flow of blood, and the persistent widow is granted her request by the judge—all because they refused to give up, had faith that the Lord would grant their request, and were almost annoyingly persistent. The Lord says:

> Will not God bring about justice for his chosen ones, who cry out to him day and night? Will he keep putting them off? I tell you, he will see that they get justice, and quickly. However, when the Son of Man comes, will he find faith on the earth? (Lk 18:7-8)

We often think of St. Monica, the mother of Augustine, as the model of persistent imploring. And it's true. But I came across the story of a young woman tonight, St. Gemma Galgani, who took "not taking no for an answer" to a whole other level. She spiritually adopted sinners and was willing to give the Lord years of her life simply for the conversion of total strangers whom she didn't even know. That blew me away.

Another thing about her story that filled me with a somberness about the reality of the cost Christ paid, and just how narrow the way to salvation is and about how many the Lord will say "I never knew them":

> I will relate another fact in the words of a most reliable witness who told me of it. "I was asked," said this person, by a lady acquaintance to recommend her brother, a great sinner, to Gemma. I did so accordingly and she while in ecstasy began to plead to Jesus for him. But He [no doubt to try her faith] replied that He knew not that sinner. "How do You not know him," she said, "since he is Thy child?" Then she turned to

Mary, but seeing that even she remained silent and wept, she began to pray to Blessed Gabriel of the Dolors [Passionist], and he also was silent. But Gemma, for all that, did not lose courage. She redoubled her prayers. At the same time she said to me: "That man must indeed be a great sinner. Jesus says He knows him not, Mother weeps, and Blessed Gabriel will not answer me.

After a year of this assiduous praying, one day, while returning from church with Gemma, I met the servant of the above-mentioned lady in the greatest consternation. The brother of her mistress, she said, was dying. We were greatly pained, but we had only gone about twenty yards when Gemma exclaimed: "He is saved, he is saved." I asked her who? "The brother of that lady," she answered. I learned afterwards that this man breathed his last pressing the priest's hand precisely when Gemma was going home. That coincided exactly with the moment when she said aloud, "He is saved, he is saved."

Whereas St. Pio often wrestled with the Devil, St. Gemma wrestled with the Divine Justice, the Judge Himself, imploring for mercy on behalf of sinners, especially those she had spiritually adopted:

In spite of all these efforts, Our Lord remained inflexible, and Gemma again relapsed into anguish and discouragement, remaining silent, as if she had abandoned the strife. Then, all of a sudden, another motive flashed to her mind that seemed invincible against all resistance. "Well, I am a sinner. You Yourself have told me so, and that a person worse than me You could not find. Yes, I confess it, I am the worst sinner, and I am unworthy that You should listen to me. But look, I present Thee another advocate for my sinner; it is Thine own Mother who asks You to forgive him. See! Oh, imagine saying no to Thy Mother! Surely You cannot now say no to Her. And now answer me, Jesus, tell me that You will save my sinner." The victory was gained, the whole scene changed aspect, the tenderhearted Saviour had granted the grace, and Gemma, with a look of indescribable joy, exclaimed: "He is saved, he is saved! Thou hast conquered, Jesus; triumph always thus." And then she came out of the ecstasy.

When it was over, having withdrawn to my room, with my mind engrossed by a thousand thoughts, I suddenly heard a tap at my door. "A strange gentleman, Father, has called and wishes to see you." I bade him come in. He threw himself at my feet sobbing and said: "Father, hear my Confession." Good God! I thought my heart would burst. It was Gemma's sinner, converted that same hour.

St. Gemma adopted sinners—not in the general sense, but specific persons—and she did not take no for an answer, even when the Lord Himself refused to budge! And so neither shall we. We should be bold in our petitions, make reparations on their behalf, and lean on the Mother of God to advocate for us and "our sinners," even when our personal holiness falls short compared to that of St. Gemma's. Persistence in the spiritual economy is not uncouth or inappropriate, but laudable, for it displays a faith that refuses to give up, refuses to go away, until it obtains what it came for—the souls of those lost. Don't ever give up.

St. Gemma Galgani, pray for us!

ON THE CHURCH

GETTING ON BASE

I re-watched *MoneyBall* the other night. It's based on a true story of a former ball player-turned-MLB scout and General Manager of the Oakland A's, Billy Beane (played by Brad Pitt), who attempts to rebuild the "runt of the litter" A's on a limited budget. He recognizes major league baseball is an "unfair game" where there are rich teams and poor teams, and they are the poorest of the poor.

Billy knows it's either business as usual of managing the decline and keeping things status quo, or "thinking differently" with an unconventional approach. He takes a chance on Peter Brand (Jonah Hill), a young statistician with a degree in Economics from Yale and pilfers him from the unappreciative Cleveland Indians so he can run numbers for him. "Baseball thinking is medieval," Brand tells Billy, "They are asking all the wrong questions. And if I say it to anyone, I'm ostracized, I'm a leper." It takes a lot of calculated risk on Billy's part, putting his faith in a different way of doing things (statistical analysis) and in Pete himself. If Billy fails, he fails big and can be easily written off with his little experiment. But in reality, he has little to lose…because they are losing already.

You can see this "medieval thinking" in a great scene with Billy in the board room with all the scouts trying to replace three of their top players. As his managers go around the table trading their insights about players and potential, Billy knows nothing is going to change because his old-school colleagues are acting as if it's business as usual. In fact, they don't even see the problem:

"You guys are just talking. Talking. Lalalala. Like this is business as usual. It's not."
"We're trying to solve the problem, Billy."
"Not like this you're not. You're not even looking at the problem."
"Okay, what's the problem?"
"Look Billy, we all understand what the problem is, we..."
"Okay, good. What's the problem?"
"The problem is we have to replace three key players in our lineup..."
"Nope. What's the problem?"
"Same as it's ever been. We've got to replace with what we have existing...."
"Nope. What's the problem?"
"We need 38 home runs, 120 RBIs, and...."
"Wrong. The problem we are trying to solve is there are rich teams and there are poor teams. Then there's 50 feet of crap. And then there's us. It's an unfair game. And now we've been gutted, organ donors for the rich. Boston's taken our kidneys, Yankee's taken our heart, and you guys are sitting around talking the same old good body nonsense like we're selling jeans, like we're looking for Fabio. We've got to think differently."

Billy sees the potential to rebuild in "cheap players;" that is, undervalued players with various defects who have been passed over by everyone else who nevertheless have potential to do one thing: get on base. He doesn't care if they are walked or whatever; their on-base percentage is all that matters to him. Getting on base eventually translates to runs, which means wins...and Billy wants to win, not just manage a mediocre decline to maintain the status quo.

He meets resistance from his managers, scouts, and team at every turn, and for a while their initial losing streak seems to prove the inevitable: that the experiment has failed. But Billy sticks to his plan while he's taking it in the teeth from everyone, and little by little, base by base, things start to turn around. It's a big gamble...but it pays off in the end, and fundamentally changed the game of baseball.

In a way, the Church—from the individual parish to the KOC to the Bishops themselves—is like those old guys in the board room: they might recognize but can't answer the question "what's the problem?," and when they try to, they use the same line of thinking that worked fifty years ago.

The Church today is like the Oakland A's in *MoneyBall*. There have been a few players willing to try something new. One is Church of the Nativity in Timoninum, Maryland, where the pastor there took a playbook from Rick Warren and attempted to overlay what worked with Protestant pastoral initiatives on a Catholic framework. Whether that is appropriate or not to do is certainly up for debate. My family and I were curious about it a number of years ago after reading the book *Rebuilt*, which details the parish's transformation. It was kind of a Protestant-Catholic fusion which was unconventional to say the least. It was a novel "success" in the sense of bringing more people into an otherwise dying parish in an bold manner, and I at least give the pastor and his team credit for at least doing something beyond "business as usual."

We see the Holy Father taking initiatives to "make a mess" of things. We see a Synod on Synodality trying to democratize the Church. We see the Knights re-doing their regalia. All in the hopes of "bringing people in."

And me? I'm just a guy on the ground. But I have to be honest, I think they are not seeing the problem in its entirety, because they are not asking the right questions. And if they are, we must admit, many are not willing to break out of the mold to address it because "business as usual" is not working—but anything else is simply too risky to "how we have always done things." And so it is Band-Aids on a nicked aorta.

So, what is the problem?

Is it that we don't have enough parish programs? That we need more youth ministry?

Nope. What's the problem?

Is it that the laity need more of a voice? More participation of women?

Nope. What's the problem?

Is it culture? That we need to "get with the times" and be more inclusive?

Nope. What's the problem?

Is it that people are leaving Catholicism for Orthodoxy, or their local mega church? Are we not hardcore enough? Not welcoming enough?

Nope. What's the problem?

What's the problem?

What. Is. The. Problem?

We're asking the wrong questions, and I believe the problem is we have *lost faith*. We have lost faith in the Church, Her apostles, and the hierarchy. We have lost faith in the supernatural, in grace, in miracles. We have lost faith in the ability to transform the culture, because we are losing the battle for culture.

But here's the thing—we have everything we need; the solution to "the problem" is right under our noses.

We have the Truth. We have the promises of Christ to never abandon his Church. We know how the story ends, that He conquered death by death. We have the power of the sacraments, and the example of the saints—who were the moneyballers throughout history, who thought differently and were willing to suffer and labor and be ostracized because of their unfailing faith in the promises of the savior (Lk 9:1-25).

Our Lord sent the disciples out one by one to "get on base." He didn't discount Saul because he was persecuting the Church but chose him as His appointed messenger (Acts 9:1-25). We can see Paul opposing Peter's reticence to eat with the uncircumcised (Gal 2:11-14), which was a radical departure from everything Peter ever knew. But the New Covenant does not work while still holding on to the Old, for no one puts new wine in old wineskins (Lk 5:37). For the Lord Christ is "doing a new thing" (Is 43:19).

In order to get base runs, we need to do the hard, risky work of thinking differently. We can't be saying to ourselves, "I'm a good Catholic," or "I go to Mass on Sundays," or "I write checks and volunteer at my local parish." These are all good things, but they are the wrong questions. The question we should be asking is, "Why am I not a saint? Why am I not trusting the Lord when he promises we will work miracles in his name?"(Lk 10:9).

We do not think big because we do not have faith. And even if we have faith, we must be willing to go out into the vineyard and *do the work*. Otherwise we become like the brother who says to the father "I will go" and does not (Mt 21:28-32).

At the end of *MoneyBall*, Billy is recruited to be the new General Manager of the Boston Red Sox, because their owner believes in what Beane is doing and that the "business as usual" dinosaur of MLB thinking needs to change. While tempted, Billy ultimately declines the $12.5M offer (and the chance to become the highest paid GM in history) and stays with the A's. The Sox ultimately go on to win big that season using Billy's "Moneyball" approach, but Billy has no regrets. He has already won the ultimate game. But he didn't get there with a "business as usual" approach.

We can often feel like we're on a losing team remaining in the Church. We are a laughingstock to the world, and the hierarchy is full of hypocrisy and cronyism. We are hemorrhaging believers from the pew, and our priests are aging out. We might be tempted towards Eastern Orthodoxy, or non-denominationalism, or atheism, or something altogether. For those who remain, it can sometimes feel like the band of misfit players on the Oakland A's. But as the story ends, those players know the wins are in them; they just need someone to inspire them to dig deep and find them.

Wars are won battle by battle. And as any general knows, you have to think differently to win. Runs are scored base by base. It doesn't matter if you get on base by a walk or a home run. We need to start thinking differently as Catholics—we need to do the work of becoming saints not to be an all-star, but because by doing so we inspire our teammates to greatness, to be their best selves—who God made them to be. Some are pitchers, some are catchers, some play left-field. Some are lefties, some are righties. But we get to Heaven together as Catholics. Every player matters.

As a Church, we need to get on base. We need to take the risk of looking like fools, of getting out of our comfort zones, of believing with everything we have, and of sacrificing for those who are lost. We get on base, we score runs. We score runs, we win. Maybe not in the eyes of the world, but we're not playing for them. We must think big, not mediocre. We are competing for the crown which never fades. And we must run our race to win (1 Cor 9:24).

THE CHURCH IS HIERARCHICAL FOR A REASON

The other night we watched a movie called *The Whale*, which was historical fiction of the account told by a cabin boy of the Essex in 1820 which Herman Melville based *Moby Dick* on. A theme within the film was that of the order of command—even though there were tense disputes between the captain and his second in command on decisions, the second in command always deferred to the captain. Ultimately, the captain is responsible for the ship and the welfare of the crew. He calls the shots. He carries the burden.

When we think about our institutions—our government, military, law enforcement, and the Catholic Church herself—they are often able to weather crises because of this hierarchy of rank and chain of command. Ultimately, one man is responsible at the top, and those under him exercise their authority and are responsible for others under him.

When I moved to a Catholic Worker to help run a House of Hospitality in my twenties, this model of 'natural hierarchy' was eschewed. No one was really 'in charge,' but a democratization of decisions was adopted by the community. In reality, nothing really got done, and I found myself chaffing at this de-centralized model. It was similar to the commune-type model of the Capital Hill Autonomous Zone in Seattle a few years ago, which was predictably doomed to failure and disbandment when no one is ultimately responsible.

WISDOM AND FOLLY

The natural order here on earth is reflected in the angelic hierarchy in Heaven, which St. Thomas enumerates as follows in rank order, from highest to lowest

Seraphim
Cherubim
Thrones
Dominions
Virtues
Powers
Principalities
Archangels
Angels

The model of the Church—Pope, Cardinals, Bishops, Priests, etc.—lends itself to order (hopefully!) The Church is not a democracy, thank goodness. It has endured for two thousand odd years and will continue to endure—but not because of democratic rule. Maybe that's why the Church in America is a bit at odds and in tension with our Protestant-roots in its founding; democracy (even in a democratic republic) is a different kind of model that the Church was not founded on.

And there was a reason Christ founded His Church with men; men are disposed to this natural order, this hierarchical structuring, which they respect and understand. Women are more disposed to democratic discussion and working things out through conversation and compromise. But women are not permitted to Holy Orders and do not comprise the hierarchy. Like it or not, this is what Christ ordained, and not without reason. We may chaff under bad popes and insolent bishops, but must admit that this chain of command works, and it must be respected. This is why in monasteries, obedience is a virtue to be extoled. Obviously our conscience must be followed and respected, but always in light of maintaining order in our souls and in our corporate environments.

"Order and virtue are synonymous terms," St. Francis de Sales wrote in *The Secret of Sanctity*. "Order," he said, "is the guide of virtue, and virtue is the guide of order. Whatever good you do, if you do it not in order, you do it not well. If your life is marked by order, you will be happy; if your life is one of disorder, you will be miserable." (*Advantages of a Rule*)

THE FAITHFUL BISHOP: A MEDITATION

This afternoon was a little strange, in a hand-of-God kind of way. I had taken a day off from work, as we had a homeschool evaluation scheduled for our kids at 10 o'clock. I also had a call with a priest from the Avila Institute for spiritual direction at noon (which was scheduled back in January—a four month waiting list).

The conversation with the priest was rather ordinary and commonplace. I gave him some of my background, a bit about my prayer life (how I struggle with discipline and consistency) and mentioned my negative experiences in spiritual direction in the past. He was a good listener, measured in his speech, and simply stressed the importance of regular mental prayer (half an hour per day) where we pray in silence and meditation, and converse with God. He discussed a little about the dangers of pride as well, and how we have to be faithful to our vocations (in my situation, to my wife and children).

It was nothing I didn't already know, but that's actually what I found most fruitful about the half hour phone call/session—that the spiritual life for most of us is rather—well, uncomplicated and rather mundane. We may have particular struggles or issues during times of transition, but really the crux of his advice was "mental prayer at least a half hour per day," "be faithful to your vocation," and "be flexible" (meaning, have a plan B if your plan A for prayer is derailed). Most of us will never reach the precarious heights of spiritual perfection and ecstasy and will struggle to advance beyond the first or second castle of the interior life (to use St. Theresa's terminology). But a lot of that largely is on our shoulders. Have I been doing a half hour of mental prayer a day? No. Am I surprised then that I have largely plateaued in my own spiritual life and advancement in virtue?

So, after our session I figured, "Well, no better time to start than now," and asked my four year old if he wanted to go with me to visit Jesus at the Adoration chapel, since my wife was taking the other two to their theater auditions. We left the house around 12:45 and pulled up and entered the chapel right around one o'clock. I saw a woman from our parish who was leaving at the time I came in, who thanked me profusely for a letter I had written to the bishop, which had been making the rounds. I was a little embarrassed with the people who did the same after Mass on Sunday. Maybe it stuck a chord, said what others were thinking. I don't know. In any case my point in writing it was to encourage our bishop and be true to what I would say I would do: pray and fast for him, his intentions, his office, and the particular situation he finds himself currently in with all eyes on him as the bishop overseeing the diocese in which the President of the United States attends Mass and calls home.

Though I had every intention of spending a half hour of personal mental prayer before the Blessed Sacrament, this was somewhat derailed by a handful of retirees starting a vocal devotional. So, it was on to my plan B and I decided to just roll with it and join them, figuring there was a reason we arrived when we did. What's funny is that it was an hour long prayer session specifically for priests. Bishops are priests, right? Hm.

I decided to devote the next hour of prayer to our bishop, specifically. One of the retirees hands me a book, devoted to praying for priests. Odd. We end up praying the Divine Mercy chaplet, reading the message of Fatima and the particular Marian locutions in this book, and other prayers of petition. But we begin with the rosary, praying the Sorrowful Mysteries. As I meditated on each mystery, I called to mind our Lord, but also our bishop and the priests in our diocese standing *in persona Christi*. What would happen were our bishop be moved by prayer and conscience to take a similar stance to that of the Archbishop of San Francisco, on the cusp of a possible overturning of *Roe v. Wade*, and forbid communion to politicians who advocate for abortion (which includes our President)?

He would find himself in the Garden, feeling as if he would sweat blood for fear of the choice before him—to take up his cross in order to be faithful to Christ, his Bride the Church, and his priestly office. Why was he in this position? Why did God put him in this diocese, at this particularly volatile and acrimonious point in history? Was it to maintain the status quo in an objectionable lukewarmness like his predecessor? Or was he being called to follow Christ on the road to Calvary? Couldn't someone take this chalice of decision-making from him, spare him from this fate? Couldn't he just live out his vocation in comfortable anonymity, rather than in the spotlight of public condemnation? "Why, Lord, why?" He would think in agony. "I don't want to do this. I don't want to be here. I don't want to make these decisions. When I followed you until now we enjoyed the palms being laid on the street, the mingling, the working miracles and helping people in service. But this? There is no one here. There is no one else here to make this choice. I am alone, and I am scared. I can feel the mob, the newspapers, the politicians, the angry people breathing down my neck. I can feel the eyes of the faithful on me; I want to be faithful, I want to follow you—but not to this. Please, take this chalice from me."

After rising, he would be turned over and led to the blood soaked pillar in the public square. His hands would shake uncontrollably as they were bound with chains and his clerical garb stripped from his torso. "You want to play dirty, do you? " the politicians in the box seats above think to themselves, "Well, we'll show you who rules this house." With a wave of the executive finger, they signal to the brutes below to commence with the scourging. Tax-Exempt status? Stripped. "How many people were depending on me to not rock the boat?" the bishop winces to himself as the lashes paint stripes on his back. *Who do you think you are?* the Most Powerful Man in The World asks him incredulously. "Don't you know I have the power to grant you your freedom or nail you to a tree? I'm a good Catholic. Just who do you think you are?" The man of God endures lash after lash, scourge after scourge, until he can hardly stand under his own weight. If it weren't for his hands chained to the pillar, he would have slumped over to the ground after the first few blows.

"Every wound needs some salt," his executioners surmise. And so after his public lashing, the pain of humiliation begins. The press, the news outlets, start their digging. They're out for dirt. Who is this Bishop So-and-So. Didn't you ____ ten years ago? Isn't that a little hypocritical of you? Aren't you a Christian? The glaring flashes of the cameras, the microphones shoved in the face. "Anything I say they will twist around," he thinks to himself, and recalls the scripture, "He opened not his mouth." They weave a mocking crown and press it firmly upon his bare head. The blood runs into his eyes, he grimaces while trying not to cry from the pain of humiliation and the piercing. "I just want to do Confirmations and bless the CYO baseball games in my miter," he laments. "But instead here I am, crowned with thorns of shame instead." And for what? For trying to be faithful to Christ. For being faithful to his office, his priestly calling, and the sheep in his care...including the one in office putting him through all this.

Next, he is paraded through the streets. He's not used to this. He spends much of his time in the chancery reading angry letters from parishioners who are upset at parish closures, and those requesting his presence at the KOC golf outing next weekend. Now the weight of the cross made custom for him is being laid on his shoulders and he is commanded: *walk*. He doesn't understand why this is happening. Hasn't he been faithful? Hasn't he been a good priest, a good (albeit, newly ordained) bishop in this new diocese? He puts one foot in front of the other, barely able to hold his head up. He hasn't had any water, his back is lacerated, and he can hardly see from the blood from his head running into his eyes. From the jeering crowd a man steps out, proscripted by one of the agencies, to make sure he makes it to the final destination. "Is he going to hit me too?" the man of God thinks to himself. He recognized him though—one of his sheep. The man is embarrassed—embarrassed to be there, embarrassed to have to help this traitor to the state, this priest who thinks he is Christ incarnate.

But in obedience to his conscriptors, he pushes a shoulder under the cross and takes the weight, if nothing else to get this thing over with. The man of God is relieved to avoid being crushed to death, and to not be alone in this ordeal. As they walk, the man from the crowd shakes his head incredulously, pierced by conscience. He had been a lukewarm Catholic all his life, and here is this priest, this bishop, literally living out the bible stories his mother had read to him as a child. He hadn't been to Mass in years; confession, decades. Step after plodding step, they say nothing, but as they make their way up the hill, his burning shame gives way to courage, to conviction, that what this man of God is enduring is worthy to be followed.

When they arrive at the end of the long, winding road, the man of God can hardly stand. His limp hands are forcefully yanked, his knuckles hit the wood of the cross and his fingers are spread. When he sees the size of the nails, he almost faints...but instead, he begins to pray. "Father, Father..." It dawns on him the words of scripture, "You do not have many fathers." How many times have his flock called on him: "Father! Father!" And now he is calling on the Eternal Father, the one who has given him this privilege to suffer as his son suffered. He looks around from above the ground, in agony, as he is raised up with ropes. There is nothing but vicious hatred towards him, towards his Church, that has all of a sudden decided to take a stand for something. He looks for his friends and finds only his own mother and a few faithful sheep praying their rosaries silently, mouthing prayers on his behalf. He is too weak to speak, to hold his head up, to pray even. "This is not what I signed up for," he thinks in a moment of weakness. "Isn't it?" The words come to him in a haze. Is this not what you were called to—to follow my son wherever he is led, to be his hands, his feet. And now your hands and feet are united with his. The man of God prays only to endure to the end; his fate is sealed in the world, but his soul is still in limbo. The one who has been roaming the earth for the past hundred years, given free reign, is vying for him. "I can make all this go away," he whispers. "Just give him the bread and tell your priests to do the same." It would be easier, wouldn't it? the man of God agonizes. And who am I to judge anyway?

ON THE CHURCH

But in his final hour, he is filled with something, like a wind. He knows he only has a few breaths of life left in him. The wind speaks to him in silence; he is fortified. *"I come to do your will,"* he echoes the words he has read hundreds of times before, but now that will is costing him everything—his good name, his health, his retirement, his Church, and now his very life here on earth. He has made a mess of things, it seems. "Father," he prays, "please take my spirit. But when you do, let the spark of my life fall to the ground below and ignite your Church. Fill them with the fire of your love. Do not let my ecclesial death and my life as a priest be wasted."

"All I ever wanted was to be faithful," the man of God thinks to himself. "All I wanted to be was a good priest." And as he closes his eyes, he is carried off by the quiet words of repose, "Well done, good and faithful servant. You have fulfilled the vocation I have set out for you. Well done, good and faithful servant."

BEAUTY WILL NOT SAVE THE WORLD

Dostoevsky's famous line in *The Idiot*, "Beauty will save the world" has been adopted by traditionalists as a subdued rallying cry to undo the damage of wreckovations, restore the liturgy, and Make Catholicism Great Again. I have been to some beautiful churches and cathedrals (like Sacré-Cœur, for one) and they indeed give testimony to the Psalmist's song, "The heavens declare the glory of God; and the firmament shows his handiwork." (Ps 91:1)

Unfortunately, many of our modern-day churches do not inspire such majestic awe. From the strictly utilitarian to the downright ugly and architecturally banal, one finds themselves having to believe not because of their surroundings in these environments, but in spite of it. I was listening to a convert recount her journey into the Church last night who began her search for the Truth by way of philosophy as an atheist. She recounted her stumbling blocks to the faith, "I couldn't take my (intellectual) friends into the church and say, 'see how beautiful it is', because it wasn't. I couldn't take them to the Mass and say, 'see, isn't this transcendent?' because it wasn't." She mentioned that she was attracted to the Mass but at the same time repulsed because she could see those present at the Mass seemed not to believe any of it, as reflected in their dress, posture, and lack of reverence. It could be up for debate whether the modernist churches and the liturgy in this context failed to inspire faith in those worshipping there, or if they were built to simply reflect the existing faith (or lack of it) in the modern age.

Like my own journey, however, it was in reading St. Augustine (*Confessions*, in this case) that this particular convert was led to pray for the first time and instilled in her the burning desire to be baptized. Perhaps it was because this convert (and I) read ourselves into Augustine's wrestling—that his problems and struggles were our problems and struggles as well—that made *Confessions* such a formidable part of our conversion.

One of those struggles for Augustine was having been exposed to eloquent rhetoric at an early age, he found the Christian scriptures not eloquent or flowery, but crudely written and uninspiring from a literary point of view. And yet it was not Cicero, but the Lord himself that captured the heart of the rhetorician through the living Word in order that he might rend it in two. Augustine reflects on his first encounter with the Bible:

> I resolved, therefore, to direct my mind to the Holy Scriptures, that I might see what they were. And behold, I perceive something not comprehended by the proud, not disclosed to children, but lowly as you approach, sublime as you advance, and veiled in mysteries; and I was not of the number of those who could enter into it, or bend my neck to follow its steps. For not as when now I speak did I feel when I tuned towards those Scriptures, **but they appeared to me to be unworthy to be compared with the dignity of Tully**; for my inflated pride shunned their style, nor could the sharpness of my wit pierce their inner meaning. Yet, truly, were they such as would develop in little ones; but I scorned to be a little one, and, swollen with pride, I looked upon myself as a great one." (*Confessions*, III, 5)

The "Beauty Argument" is one that makes sense intellectually—build it (beautiful), and they will come, to co-opt a line from *Field of Dreams*. Once people see the beauty of Catholicism, they will be unable to resist the allure of Truth. It's a wager being made when many other efforts to "revitalize" the Church (reform the liturgy, YouCat and World Youth Day, Bishop Barron's *Catholicism*) have fallen flat and failed to produce a wave of converts.

So, I'm making another wager in light of the world we live in—*beauty will not save the Church*. It is a worthy thing, and reflective of God's nature, but it's not enough. I think we are entering a new epoch in which our age is so blinded by delusion, so corrupted by modernism, so obstinate and stiff-necked in our pride and sin, that there is not going to be a raising but a *razing*; not a renaissance, but a decimation. Not a comfort, but a severe and unrelenting beating.

Our Lady has over and over again been trying to get our attention. Fatima, Akita, Quito, and others. And her message is direct and consistent: repent and do penance. Not eloquent, not flowery. Direct and crude.

Have we, though? Has she really gotten our attention? Have we taken it to heart and changed, amended our sinful lives? The evidence is to the contrary. Those who take the messages seriously may, but the majority of the world is asleep at the wheel. Men became so wicked that God had to do a "great reset" with the flood in Genesis. He promised to never again send a flood (Gen 9:11).

And yet our Lady's message is consistent with that of her Son's: "Do you think that these Galileans were worse sinners than all the other Galileans because they suffered this way? I tell you, no! But unless you repent, you too will all perish" (Lk 13:2-3).

I think God is getting ready to get a big stick out to bring us home. "I sent you saints, stigmatists, miracles. You did not listen. My Mother tried to warn you, you would not listen. Now you're going to have the ears to hear, but only because everything you have held on to will be taken away from you and you will be unable to do otherwise."

"And when he (the Holy Spirit) is come, he will convince the world of sin, and of justice, and of judgment" (Jn 16:8).

I pray that when the Lord does come, he sears us with fire to burn away the dross of what covers us from seeing ourselves as we truly are—helpless sinners, completely dependent on the mercy of God. I pray that the churches—the ugly ones, the beautiful ones, the humble village churches and the great cathedrals alike—will be so filled not with tourists and admirers, but with sinners crawling there on their knees in tears. I pray that priests have the fortitude to withstand hours upon hours, almost prisoners in the confessionals, because the lines will stretch for miles with no end in sight. I pray that it will not be too late to repent—to see clearly—but that our Lord might give us one last chance to turn away from our sin and turn towards Him.

In my opinion, beauty is the icing on the cake, the cap of perfection of Creation. But when a world is so blinded by sin and degenerate that they call what is beautiful ugly, and what is ugly beautiful, how can they be converted by beauty? Perhaps it is ugliness-the ugliness of seeing their sin not through a glass darkly, but face to face with eyes that cannot be closed—that will sear their conscience and move them not to admiration and swooning, but tears and rending their hearts before Him.

BISHOPS ARE BORN OF FAMILIES

I have never been to Rome. People keep telling me I have to go to see St. Peter's, the Vatican, the plethora of liturgical wonders and beautiful art, and experience the history of our faith. After twenty three years as a Catholic, it is a bit strange that I have never really had the desire or inclination to make the trip.

I don't know if this is a conscious or unconscious dis-inclination. I'm not a history buff, though I am open to learning in order not to be ignorant. I can appreciate fine art but can't say I'm a connoisseur by any means. And most of all, I'm really not a "churchy" guy.

I have to qualify with that, because I have been writing about the Faith for half my life so one would think a love of all-things-church would go hand in hand with trying to live a life of faith. But I've always found myself following the St. Benedict Joseph Labre / St. Francis / St. Juan Diegos of the world in my journey of faith, rather than hanging around gold-gilded ambos or immersing myself with church or diocesan events. It has just never been a draw.

So I was a little out of my element when our family was asked to formally greet and welcome the new bishop of our diocese at his installation Mass this afternoon. I also suffer from severe liturgical stage fright (which is probably why I was never an altar server and bombed out of being a lector at our old parish). Liturgical pomp and circumstance is not my thing.

But this was a big deal. It was the first time in over one hundred years that a priest (a monsignor in this case) would be ordained a bishop in our diocese (His predecessors had all been ordained as bishops prior to being assigned here). In addition to every single priest in the diocese being present at the Mass and ceremony, there was a large cadre of bishops, two cardinals, and a Vatican nuncio present. It was as close to a pontifical-type ceremony as I would probably experience apart from being in the Eternal City itself.

Complicating things a little was the fact that this was only the third *Novus Ordo Missae* I had been to in almost three years; though I had retained the muscle memory of it over the years, my children were largely unfamiliar with the New Liturgy, having been raised up in the TLM exclusively. We didn't play a large role in the ceremony, obviously, but we were still a part of it, and my kids were on the same knowledge level of the NOM as 5th graders in a CCD class.

Complicating things a little more was the fact that this is the President's home diocese, and while it was not the focus of the appointment and ceremony (and rightfully so), it has to be in the back of people in the larger Catholic world's mind—just what is his intention in addressing the "issue at hand" that the USSCB is discussing? Just what (if anything) will he *do* as bishop? Will he be "one of the good ones?" Etc.

People are savagely critical concerning the bishops, and not always without good reason always either. But this is our home diocese, and we have a new shepherd who is new in the role, in a new part of the country, in a politically-sensitive situation that is the envy of no one. As more traditionally minded Catholics who have come to love and cherish the traditional liturgy, we have a stake in the game on the local level, especially as talk of the *motu proprio* against the Latin Mass looms large. We want to see Tradition thrive and grow. And so, I reasoned, the least we can do is extend a warm welcome on a basic human level to this successor to the apostles as members of his flock, and be the best representatives of joyful traditional Catholics we can be, to let him know we are here—not as a "force to be reckoned with" but simply as sheep in his care among a diverse flock.

WISDOM AND FOLLY

Though I don't know much about him, after meeting and talking with him briefly, the new bishop seemed to have a genuine, pastoral spirit, was approachable, and seemed to be an overall good man. Again, this is just first impressions base on limited knowledge. It's okay to say such things though, I think—to extend a degree of courtesy on a basic human level and not immediately cut a man of the cloth at the knees just because you don't think he's doing enough or is "spineless" or what have you. At least give the man a chance to get settled for a day or two and get his bearings before unloading on Catholic Twitter if you feel the need to do so. Ha!

My wife and daughter veiled as they usually do, though they were pretty much the only ones I noticed who did so, and we all received Communion by dropping to our knees on the marble and receiving on the tongue (which was not an issue, though most received in the hand). The Mass and ceremony were almost four hours long. I was running on two hours sleep, and our kids were champs but were beginning to melt near the end due to churchy overload, not to mention hunger and tiredness. My three young kids were three of....four. In the entire church. There were some older teenagers, but largely it was middle age and older (sometimes much older) Catholics in attendance. I was thinking, "Where are all the families?" only to realize a four hour ceremony in the middle of the day on a Tuesday may preclude fathers who are working or young mothers with young children who may not have survived it.

As the bishop addressed and thanked all the dignitaries and ecclesial members that came before him and who formed him as a priest, and spoke to the religious communities and laity of the diocese that he is to serve, and as I looked at row after row of priests, bishops, cardinals, etc. (whom I am grateful answered God's call to Holy Orders), it occurred to me that every last one of them came not from some spontaneous ecclesial progenerating, but from a *family*—a mom and a dad who were called to the married state. They not only gave these men life but formed them in the faith so that they might respond to the call from Our Lord to be shepherds of, well, *other families*. From Our Lord Himself to St. Peter, the first pope, to the Apostles on down, it was the same story—they came from families. Families are the building blocks of societies.

I'm fond of the saying, "No Priests, No Church." But another saying also holds: "No Families, No Priests!" Families are the stock from which our Lord calls his priests out, to leave father and mother and forsake marriage and families (in most cases) to respond to his call and follow him.

When looking around the church at all these ecclesial V.I.P.s, I caught myself from time to time during the ceremony thinking, "I'm just a husband and father, a layman." Of the hundreds of other people in the church among the laity, it was just me and another dad there with small kids (in his case, one son). Our priests are aging—so many elderly priests! Most Catholics parishes are aging as well, and not being infused with new life. But the hallmark of a traditional parish is just that—lots of lots of families, young families, with kids (sometimes lots of them!) Sometimes, often, they are also shepherded by young priests, with young seminarians stepping on deck. It's not a demographic cliff, but a sign of hope and rebirth. And at the root of it is, you guessed it: the family.

Bishops don't exist in vacuums. They aren't formed in test tubes. They are born of families, they are formed by their fathers and mothers, and they also have to learn their jobs and how to pastor as well from their brother priests. There can be a symbiotic relationship I think between our celibate clergy and the families they serve when the families themselves live out their vocation as witnesses to the faith proper to their vocation, and the priests see it and are fortified in their own vocation when they know who it is they are serving and shepherding.

It's not an easy job to shepherd. Sheep are constantly straying, and you have to keep them in line with the firmness of a father who disciplines those he loves without being so heavy-handed that it borders on abuse. In a culture of relativism and lukewarmness and religious ignorance, it becomes even harder. I realize there are lousy bishops out there who do damage to the Church and her witness by their ecclesial malfeasance. But I also think there are good men just trying to do a hard job, and to do it for the Lord when there's often no instruction manual.

We don't expect them to be supermen, or solve all the local diocese's problems, or simply serve as the whipping boy or target for our angry letters (although that's how we treat them sometimes). We just want them to shepherd us as a spiritual father so that biological fathers like me can raise our own kids in the faith and live our vocation in marriage in a way that pleases God and serves the Church. That may mean more faithful families as offshoots of the family root (grandkids! great grandkids!), or it may mean supplying the Church with the men who go on to become seminarians, priests, bishops, cardinals, and even popes. To the degree we do that well, as fathers of our families, is the degree to which we re-infuse the Church with the faith, and supply the clergy from healthy spiritual stock for future generations. Let's be sure to remember to pray for our bishops, both the good ones and the bad ones.

No families, no priests. No priests, no bishops. No bishops, no Church. No Church, no hope!

HEALING THE CHURCH FROM THE GROUND UP

There's a economic philosophy in Catholic social thought called Distributism; some of you may be familiar with it, with Chesterton and Belloc being it's chief proponents. Although I haven't studied it in-depth, my main takeaway it's based in the concept of subsidiarity—that "a community of a higher order should not interfere in the internal life of a community of a lower order, depriving the latter of its functions, but rather should support it in case of need and help to co-ordinate its activity with the activities of the rest of society, always with a view to the common good."

I've thought about this economic philosophy as it applies to the "lower orders" of the Church—that is, the domestic Church, i.e., the family. From the head on down, we see nothing but dysfunction in the institutional Church. Any "top-down" solutions are fraught with bureaucratic oversight and inefficiencies, not to mention not being in touch with the nature of the lower orders.

But by nature, the Church is hierarchical, so we are working within the confines of this chain of command. If you are an American conservative, you are already familiar with the view (counter to our current administration) that the purpose of government is not to solve every societal problem through over-regulation and control, but through ensuring the rights of the populace by way of the Constitution. That is, the principals on which this nation was founded supported "we the people" to self-govern and gave them the means to do so by ensuring those rights. But this requires virtue, as John Adams famously noted, "Our Constitution was made only for a moral and religious people. It is wholly inadequate to the government of any other."

Likewise in the Church, her raison d'etre is to lead men to Heaven, not carry them there. She does this by way of the Mass, the Sacraments, doctrine, holy scripture, and giving us tools for our toolbox (sacramentals). The saints are our guides in the varying ways one may attain to this goal, those building blocks which form the foundation of the Church Militant. When the Church is ensuring those things are in order, even fallen man is given the resources and hope, in cooperation with grace, to attain to virtue and save his soul. But note the important caveat in Distributist thought—the higher order should not interfere in the internal life of the community, thereby depriving the latter of its functions.

Friends have been sending me news of the possible revocation of *Summorum Pontificum* and the return to the *motu proprio;* I'd be lying if I said I wasn't filled with a low-level dread at the prospect of this happening under Pope Francis' pontificate. *Summorum Pontificum* allowed greater freedom for priests to celebrate the Traditional Latin Mass (though, arguably by many traditionalists, this should be the standard, not the allowed exception). If the indult is revoked...well, I'm not exactly sure what that would look like, but I think it's safe to say there would be less access and greater restrictions for traditional worship. From where I'm standing on the ground as a layman, father, and husband trying to lead his family to Heaven, this seems to qualify as "depriving the latter of its functions," and is an intentional "interference in the internal life of the community."

As I've written before, our family has benefited from great grace by way of the traditional Mass and have appreciated the ability to take part in traditional worship. I don't know why it ever went away in the first place, but that's a post for another day.

There are some in the Church who feel they have been psychologically or spiritually harmed by "traditionalists" who act without charity. This may be so, but it is not a 'top-down' but a 'bottom

-up' problem. No amount of reform in taking away the Traditional Latin Mass and attempting to scatter traditionalist faithful will stamp out those who want to worship in this way. And so the solution lies in healing at the root (*sanatio in radice*) through the building of virtue and healthy spirituality that expresses itself in charity and self-giving. The onus is on the families—not to be responsible for other people's hurt feelings, but to ensure they are doing everything they can to live out their faith and do their part well, with the tools to do so.

I've pondered how to live this out in my own life and the life of my family as a way of healing the Church from the bottom up. One thing my wife and I came up with, however, trivial, is to host a once a month gathering of disconnected Catholics in our area for food, fellowship, and spiritual study, which we will be starting next month. Our hope is to fortify one another and draw on that human capital present in other Catholics "on the ground" so that if and when "the sheep are scattered," we will at least have made contact with one another and can reach out for support here in the "lower orders." Living the virtues ourselves, praying the family rosary, attending Mass, inviting others in and outside the faith to explore Her claims, tithing and sacrificing for intentional causes—these are all ways we are trying to heal the Church and build her up. I've also been trying to invest more in our men's scripture study, which I lead once a week, so that the men might have fraternity and be able to lead their families well.

Honestly, I'm not sure what else to do. We are focusing on the local level with the hopes it will fan out and in a whisper-down-the-lane way, give people the perhaps soon to be restricted access to the tools they need to live holy lives should things go dark. What I do know, is that help is not coming 'from the top.' If we weren't on our own already, we may soon well be.

SPARE NOT THE ROD: A LETTER TO OUR BISHOP CONCERNING CANON 915

Your Excellency, it was a pleasure having the opportunity to meet you at your installation Mass last summer, as well as at the Diocesan synod meeting this Fall. My wife and I include you in our intentions in prayer every morning, and our local men's group does as well. We hope you are acclimating to the area and are getting the chance to "smell the sheep" under your care through various pastoral visits and events.

I write to you today as a lay Catholic father and husband after reading the news of Archbishop Cordileone's recent instruction to House Speaker Pelosi that she is not to present herself to Holy Communion due to her persistent and long-standing advocacy for abortion. If I'm being quite honest, it was a glimmer of hope for me as someone who came into the Church 24 years ago who had been convicted that the Catholic Church possesses the fullness of Truth. That integrity (of the Church) has at times been tested by those who claim to live the faith and yet act in opposition to what She teaches. I couldn't understand it as an 18 year old, newly minted Catholic and I still struggle to believe it today.

Nowhere is this more blatant and scandalous as it is with Catholic politicians baptized into the faith who advocate in direct contradiction to Church teaching. While this could encompass a myriad of issues, the clearest offense against the sanctity of human life, the Natural Law, and our future existence is abortion.

For a new Catholic entering the Church today, they may wonder "Why has it taken this long?" to simply enforce, in spiritual charity, Canon 915 which states, "Those who have been excommunicated or interdicted after the imposition or declaration of the penalty and others obstinately persevering in manifest grave sin are not to be admitted to holy communion." This canon is punitive but for the purpose of repentance and conversion of heart, which is a spiritual good. I don't know the interior motivation for Archbishop Cordileone's recent action, but I want to give him the benefit of the doubt that it was made not as a political statement but for the good of Mrs. Pelosi's soul, and the benefit of the faithful at large. It shows, for us on the ground, that maybe there is hope that we were not sold a bill of goods in coming into the Church or persisting in believing in the wake of scandal after scandal. And it is truly a scandal that pro-abortion politicians (among others) present themselves so presumptuously to receive our Lord, eating and drinking condemnation upon themselves.

As a father of three, I know that if I "spare the rod" (to speak proverbially) for my children because of the blowback I know I will get from them, it shows on my part a lack of love, as scripture says. As a father, I discipline because I love my children. I also know better than they do what is good for them at this young age.

My vocation is not holy orders, but matrimony. But for those ordained, you also are fathers. And many like myself (lay Catholics trying to be faithful, trying to be good, fasting and praying) have often felt bereft, like wayward children without a spiritual father because we were not pushed and instructed sufficiently to live the faith in this godless age. We kind of learned on our own, many of us, and with the help of grace.

But what the Archbishop has done is set a jarring precedent that the Church actually stands for something, and that he will not "spare the rod," so to speak, in this particular circumstance. This will have an undoubted ripple effect not only for the faithful, but the hierarchy and Church as a whole. And, your Excellency, as I'm sure you are well aware, you are at the epicenter of this political and spiritual storm, at an unprecedented moment in history.

Our President—arguably the most politically powerful figure in the Western world—along with many other Catholics like Ms. Pelosi who advocate for that which is contrary to the faith, present themselves (in this diocese) in the same sacrilegious manner, scandalizing the faithful, undermining the credibility of the Church, and damning their own souls. I am, of course, not unaware of the implications which such actions (the enforcement of Canon 915) would have. It would fill me with trepidation. But to the degree to which I fear men more than I fear God, I would have to question myself. "Who shall we fear?" King David writes, "The Lord is my light and my salvation."

I am, of course, not in your shoes. It is not easy shoes to be in, to be quite honest. I may not envy you in this role, but I most certainly pray for you. Because with prayer, all things are possible, as it says in scripture. And certain demons are not driven out without prayer AND fasting.

For that reason, I, my wife, and a contingent of those in our local men's group, will be doing so much more intentionally during this political firestorm that is certain to touch us all at some point or another. We often feel like "lambs led to slaughter" as faithful Catholics in this diocese and in the secular world at large. But we have faith, hope and charity! We can do all things in Christ who strengthen us. Whom should we fear?

I can see you are a man of faith and prayer. I would, in closing, ask you to pray for your fellow bishop, Archbishop Cordileone, and consider his example which gives courage to the lay faithful to live out the faith in an acrimonious culture. The Church will not be renewed without witness, and witness will not come without suffering. What better witness than to live out in each of our respective vocations, the teachings of Christ and his Church? What more honorable way to enter Heaven than covered in the stripes our Savior himself displayed out of love for his sheep? The enforcement of Canon 915 in this diocese will give you those lashes, undoubtedly. That is for your discernment, of course. Courage must be seen to be lived out by those in the pews.

ON THE CHURCH

Thank you for taking the time to read this letter; I hope it will be received with the charity in which is was written. You will most certainly be in our prayers.

THE CHURCH WILL HURT YOU

If there's any specter that haunts me to my core, that fills me with a putrid horror and an unspeakable sadness, it is the act of apostasy. Lucifer fell from Heaven, and he is working overtime to bring down as many people from the ladder of divine ascent with him as possible. In a previous essay titled "Apostasy And The Casualties Of War," I wrote:

> I was thinking about apostasy, the specter that seems to hide in every closet, every corner, under every lampstand I encounter these days. The smell is nauseating and unnerving; it gets in your clothes like cigarette smoke. Faith in this age is under siege, and I'm not even talking about the collective faith of Catholics or Christians in America; in the heart of each and every man, his faith is under fire. Someone or something is seeking to wrench it from his being, cause him to lose heart or strip him of faith or consolation, hope and fortitude. My buddies and people I know are lying all around me, getting picked off by snipers, getting legs blown off, getting mowed down by machine guns, losing their souls one skipped prayer, one missed Mass, one self-justifying excuse, one innocent click at a time.

Why do people abandon the Faith? Who will endure to the end? Is it just a matter of time before I join their ranks? Will I lose my children to the age? A friend of mine, a once faithful Catholic and family man, stopped going to Mass. Family members too. People experiencing loss and suffering, instead of doubling down and tying themselves to the mast, gradually stop praying altogether and simply drift away or run aground. For some it's a sin they can't let go of, or a past, or a trauma, or a hurt, or a betrayal, or seeing too much of how the sausage is made. For some it's the old question of why bad things happen to 'good people,' or why God would allow someone they love to suffer, or some earnest but unanswered prayers. I feel like the guys to my left and to my right and in front of me and behind me are just being shredded by machine gun fire, and who's to say I'm not next, my family, my children."

This evening I stumbled across a public post of a couple leaving the Catholic Church. As I read it, I picked up on a similar theme and common thread to the public posts of other Christian apostates. Joshua Harris—who wrote the best-seller *I Kissed Dating Goodbye* (which I read in college)—made a public announcement on his Instagram account:

> My heart is full of gratitude. I wish you could see all the messages people sent me after the announcement of my divorce. They are expressions of love though they are saddened or even strongly disapprove of the decision.
>
> I am learning that no group has the market cornered on grace. This week I've received grace from Christians, atheists, evangelicals, exvangelicals, straight people, LGBTQ people, and everyone in-between. Of course there have also been strong words of rebuke from religious people. While not always pleasant, I know they are seeking to love me. (There

have also been spiteful, hateful comments that angered and hurt me.)

The information that was left out of our announcement is that I have undergone a massive shift in regard to my faith in Jesus. The popular phrase for this is "deconstruction," the biblical phrase is "falling away." By all the measurements that I have for defining a Christian, I am not a Christian. Many people tell me that there is a different way to practice faith and I want to remain open to this, but I'm not there now.

Martin Luther said that the entire life of believers should be repentance. There's beauty in that sentiment regardless of your view of God. I have lived in repentance for the past several years—repenting of my self-righteousness, my fear-based approach to life, the teaching of my books, my views of women in the church, and my approach to parenting to name a few. But I specifically want to add to this list now: to the LGBTQ+ community, I want to say that I am sorry for the views that I taught in my books and as a pastor regarding sexuality. I regret standing against marriage equality, for not affirming you and your place in the church, and for any ways that my writing and speaking contributed to a culture of exclusion and bigotry. I hope you can forgive me.

To my Christians friends, I am grateful for your prayers. Don't take it personally if I don't immediately return calls. I can't join in your mourning. I don't view this moment negatively. I feel very much alive, and awake, and surprisingly hopeful. I believe with my sister Julian that, "All shall be well, and all manner of thing shall be well."

Another popular Christian band singer:

I've been terrified to post this for a while—but it feels like it's time for me to be honest. After growing up in a Christian home, being a pastor's kid, playing and singing in a Christian band, and having the word 'Christian' in front of most of the things in my life—I am now finding that I no longer believe in God.

And a long time listener of a Christian radio ministry:

> Over many years I have been blessed to receive free tapes, CDs, and books from your ministry. Thank you. At those times, I really appreciated them. Now I no longer believe in the God of the Bible or in Jesus Christ. Ten years of full-time ministry proved to me that there is no God, and that the God of the Bible does not care. I now reject Christianity and have come to peace.
>
> What was at first a great loss has now turned to joy, peace, and freedom. I did not leave the faith because of some extreme sin. I left because the God of the Bible, Jesus Christ, and the Holy Spirit are all a fantasy. I'm happy I now live in the real world. I only feel guilt about the many people whom I led to Christ and exposed them to the lies of Christianity. I'm not mad at Christians; I'm not mad at you. However, I am mad at myself for not being a more critical thinker. I won't make this mistake again.
>
> Again, thank you for the many years of help and teaching you all shared with me. I do appreciate what you all are trying to do with the knowledge you have. Please remove me from your mailing list. Save the money, don't waste it on an apostate like me. I was just giving your CDs away. But now my conscience no longer can tolerate the further spread of a false hope and disappointment.

As someone who has had periods of having to fight tooth and nail to stay alive by my own hand during periods in which death seemed a welcome respite, I see a few things worth noting in the loss of faith (spiritual suicide) and the loss of life by one's own hand (actual suicide).

There comes a point when one considers leaving this world; when the pain, darkness, and tumult reach fever pitch—where everything becomes quiet and calm, like the eye of a hurricane. When the salesman of death shows up at the door with his offer, the fog kind of clears and a lucidity sets in. "I could really do this. All this could go away." *Yes,* he affirms, and hands you a razor blade. When the end is near, the light at the end of the tunnel comes into view, there's a kind of false peace and enchantment as one considers the possibilities of a world in which hurt no longer exists.

Of course it is all a lie. The Devil sells lemons. As soon as the check is cashed he is nowhere to be found. Until it's time to collect the collateral, which is your soul. But here's what happens and what it looks like, from a reference guide on how to recognize suicidal persons:

> Stage 3 (the final stage) begins when the suicidal person makes the decision to suicide. The moment the decision is made, it goes "unconscious" and the person goes on what we call "auto-pilot." People in Stage 3 are imminently lethal; however, they seem more "normal" than they have seemed in a long time. At this point, the depression seems to suddenly lift because the person has made the decision to die and is no longer wrestling with the decision. Unfortunately, most mental health professionals and family members are not trained to recognize "auto-pilot," and they breathe a sigh of relief because their patient seems so much better, not realizing that he/she is on a collision course with suicide. People on "auto-pilot" typically attempt suicide within the next 48 hours. Be alert when a depressed patient who doesn't seem to improve after months of intervention suddenly seems to get better. Instead of relaxing, we should become more vigilant when we see a sudden, overnight improvement. We should listen closely to any indication that the individual has decided to end their life and mobilize support among family, friends, and medical/behavioral health providers.

Like those in the wake of suicide—those badly shaken family and friends—the desire to know "Why?" is both overpowering and natural. We want a reason, to make sense of things, since we were robbed of that sense by a senseless act. The most unnerving thing, the existential doubt, though, comes when we realize that sometimes, there is no reason, nothing to pin the tail on. This shakes us to our core. We build houses, take shelter, because we were not meant to live out of doors as civilized people. And suddenly we are in the great plains under expansive skies, with nary a blanket to shield us from Nature herself in all her terrible glory.

Whether or not one can point to this or that, one thing is undeniable: the Devil has gotten what he came for, what he exists for. He exists to draw men from the Way, the Truth, the Light. He throws a blanket of darkness over our shoulders and wraps us tightly. And he often disguises himself as an angel of light to do it so that we don't smell the sulfur.

Like divorce, or a metastasized cancer, the warning signs often come too late. Those "perfect couples" that seem to have it all together and then the next thing you know they are sharing their little "announcement" of parting ways. What the hell is going on behind closed doors? Sometimes, it is true—it's not a heinous sin, or a betrayal; it could be boredom, or a desire for something new, or just an unwillingness to try (to fight even!) anymore.

For anyone who gets news like this from close friends—of suicide, of divorce, of apostasy—it can shake you pretty good. Because, if them...why not you?

After all, they may have gone to church every Sunday, prayed together as a family, did all the right things and still find themselves as newly minted apostates (by their own admission) outside the Ark. But there is that false lucidity: "My heart is full of gratitude," "I'm waking up to reality," "We've found peace," Etc. I could understand if one was leaving a cult, the sense of relief. But the Church—the Bride of Christ—is not a cult.

In reading this particular public profession of leaving the Church that I had stumbled upon, someone made a comment and mentioned that the best piece of advice he had gotten as a new convert was a jarring, almost cryptic statement from a priest: *"The Church will hurt you."* As a new convert, I remember going to Mass in spite of those around me, not because of them. Not that I had anything against my fellow men, my fellow Catholics, but they weren't the *raison d'etre*. I think that perspective has helped shield me in some ways from disappointment and betrayal, because I always just kind of expected it.

Something else I think the Lord, in His Providence, shielded me from by slamming doors in my face, is never having worked for the Church. It wasn't for lack of trying. I got a Masters in Theology so I could serve the Church in some capacity. I applied for jobs in Youth Ministry—nada. Campus Ministry—"we've gone with someone else." Director of Faith Formation—thank you for your interest. I didn't even realize at the time what He was preserving me from, by grace. But it may have just saved my faith, by grace. I like sausage—then again, I don't work in a sausage factory.

The Church will hurt you. Whether you live in an intentional community, whether you're a Trad or a Charismatic, a Catholic or a Christian, a homeschooling parent of many and a picture perfect believer—you will at some point get disillusioned. "Do not put your trust in princes, in human beings, who cannot save." (Ps 146:3). You have to believe and fight for your belief with tooth and nail, you have to be a stubborn S.O.B., a dumb ox almost, a Rottweiler with a stick that refuses to let go. "It is better to take refuge in the LORD than to trust in humans." (Ps 118:8)

It may very well be a mystery why people defect from the Ark while claiming they are so much happier and more at peace with their new lives and newly-affirming host of non-judgers. But there is no lasting peace apart from Christ. Divorce from the Bride—the Church—is a tragedy of eternal consequence. It shakes believers—the ones who have also been betrayed by such flagrant, self-assured apostasy—to the core, as much as good friends getting divorced after thirty years of marriage do. Satan is having his field day. He has been given the reins. The only thing you can do is tie yourself to that mast, and don't let go.

A REVOLUTION OF SAINTS

I've been reading a lot—a *lot*—the past few weeks about the McCarrick scandal in the Church. Of course it goes deeper than this one incident with this one prelate, to a much deeper and darker network within the Church. The abuse and betrayal is both sickening and saddening. But I don't want to pile on to what has already been written and said much more comprehensively by others than I could write. Instead, I just want to bring one thing to light, one thing that is both unnerving and, for me, as distressing as all the hurt and betrayal caused by this scandal.

And that one thing is this: I think many of those in authority—priests, bishops, cardinals—are playing the game, talking the talk, being good administrators, saying the right things.

My fear is that there are many who don't actually believe what they are professing.

I know this shouldn't be surprising to me. After all, Paul calls the followers of Christ "fools" in the best sense of the word (1 Cor 4:10)—those who are completely committed and willing to lose face for the Kingdom. But because we are worldly, feeling like a fool in the eyes of the world can sting a little. It reminds us we have not truly left behind everything to follow Christ but retain our friendship with the world. Who wants to be a fool anyway?

I learned quickly after becoming Catholic that there were "qualifiers" to the mandates of our faith. We are called to feed the hungry and clothe the naked—but not, like, literally. It is hard for the rich to enter the Kingdom, but, you know. We are called to enter into death with Christ. But let's not get carried away now.

When I read the Rod Dreher piece in the *American Conservative* about the "conservative" prelate who headed up the Napa Institute and the ensuing "call to holiness" to attendees, I could see myself as one of the gullible idiots who "actually believes this stuff." It may be a wakeup call that renewal may not necessarily be coming from the Church hierarchy or from more parish programs, and that we would be holding our breath in thinking that. In these situations, anger and impatience is palpable. But if we are going to start a revolution, it will need to be a revolution of the spirit. And it will have to start from the inside out.

That's why I feel such love and affinity for disciples like the supreme dodo, Mother Angelica. I do hope she is canonized, because we need more witnesses to a faith that puts in on the line. We're past the point of cultural Catholicism for sure. But we're even past the point of doing what's safe and comfortable and expecting a return on our dollar-fifty investment. We need more Mother Angelica's to show us what a "theology of risk" looks like.

> You want to do something for the Lord...do it. Whatever you feel needs to be done, even though you're shaking in your boots, you're scared to death—take the first step forward. The grace comes with that one step and you get the grace as you step. Being afraid is not a problem; it's doing nothing when you're afraid.

You might say, "well, not everyone is called to be saints." I don't understand you. I mean, I understand what you've been told, and I've heard the words before, but they do not compute. I was raised very conservatively—not with regards to politics or socially, but to eschew risk, to play it safe, to be careful. Such things have no place in the life of a disciple. We are called to be innocent as doves and wise as serpents, yes. But faith is a great gamble. You gamble with your life. You only have one life. It is a big gamble, but it's not reckless when you trust and have a relationship with the One you are willing to look like a fool for.

> I am convinced God is looking for dodoes. He found one: me! There are a lot of smart people out there who know it can't be done, so they don't do it. But a dodo doesn't know it can't be done. God uses dodoes: people who are willing to look ridiculous so God can do the miraculous.

What made Mother Angelica a "dodo?" I think it consisted of two things: she was herself, and she believed. Why would anyone profess this religion of ours without believing it? Prayer, mortification, self-sacrifice, poverty—none of it makes sense without belief, and is useless without it. Mother Angelica believed it, believed the words of our Savior, "ask and you will receive," (Mt 7:7) and "I will do anything you ask of me," (Jn 14:13). She BELIEVED! Hers is a high-stakes faith.

> He expects me to operate on a faith level, not a knowledge level. He expects me to operate—if I don't have the money, if I don't have the brains, if I don't have the talent—in faith. You know what faith is? Faith is one foot on the ground, one foot in the air, and a queasy feeling in the stomach.

Have our prelates forgotten their calling? Do they believe what they preach? I'm not sure. But I wonder how much of that underlies the current mess. If you don't really believe what you're pitching, how can you expect anyone else to? If you don't have faith, what is your career-oriented religion worth?

It can feel paralyzing as a member of the laity to exact any institutional change in something so insulated and far removed. I wouldn't know the first thing about "reforming the Curia." But I do know that all throughout history, reform came from bottom up, not top down. It started with an uneducated rabble of twelve. God sent the holy fool, St. Francis of Assisi to rebuild what had fallen into disrepair. During the upheaval of the Reformation, God drew up great saints to renew the Church: St Francis de Sales, St. Philip Neri, St. Thomas More, St. Teresa of Avila, St. Ignatius of Loyola.

You don't get anywhere without risking something. And we don't get anywhere without an army. The power doesn't rest in mighty ability or smarts or talent—it rests in FAITH in the ONE TRUE GOD who has the POWER to accomplish EVERYTHING! I have literally never made a convert in my entire life, and I may never. To devote my life, everything I have and am, to something that may never be accomplished in my lifetime—that is the mark of a pitiable fool.

No matter. We are fools for Christ, are we not? We may not be able to make converts or exact reform, but we can reform ourselves, can we not? And not just me, and not just you, but *anyone*, by the power of Christ, who gives the grace to those who ask to accomplish the work. It is so simple, so uncomplicated.

Even if our parish priests do not believe that sainthood is possible for your 'average Joe'—we will believe. Even if our bishops do not risk or suffer indignation for the Faith—we will risk, and suffer indignation for the Faith, for our Christ. Even if we live out a "revolution of one" in our own homes, having no examples around us to follow except the Jesus of the Gospels and the saints we read about in books, and never see the fruit, we can die with the assurance that we did not go comfortably or quietly to our graves.

That's a theology worth learning, a risk worth taking. That's belief in action, the ember of which will spark the revolution of saints, the renewal in the Church, and the fortification of final perseverance in the Last Days. One foot on the ground One foot in the air. A queasy feeling in the stomach. That's faith...for those who believe "these sorts of things."

CONVERTS ARE MADE BY WITNESS, NOT PASTORAL LETTERS

Last night as I was doing the tedious work of painting the floor grout in the kitchen, after everyone had gone to bed, I was listening to a talk on Sensus Fidelium by Fr. John Echert on confronting the great Catholic crisis of our time. The talk—on the pernicious heresy of modernism, the homosexual factions in the seminaries in the seventies, and the marginalization of orthodox priests—was given three years ago and is even more true today. He even makes a somewhat prophetic statement in the last minute of the talk about the upcoming synod that was spot on. As I went to the fridge to get something to eat I noticed a slight but off-smell; some black beans in the back had gone bad, making the fridge smell.

There is something rotten in the church. Those who stand up for Catholic teaching are thrown under the bus and left to fend for themselves. No one from above is coming to their rescue. Our bishops talk a good talk with their letters and their "strong statements" but would they take a beating, lay their life down for their sheep? In some countries they are outright subversive of orthodox teaching. There is something rotting in the church, and people are starting to notice the smell.

Today's Old Testament reading from the book of Daniel is one of my favorites. In it we see the firm witnesses of the youth—Shadrach,

Meshach, and Abednego—who refuse to bow down to worship the idol of Nebuchadnezzar, the King of Babylon. At first the King was pleased with them as government administrators, but when they refused to bow down and worship false gods he became enraged and ordered their death by fire. They reply "King Nebuchadnezzar, we do not need to defend ourselves before you in this matter. If we are thrown into the blazing furnace, the God we serve is able to deliver us from it, and he will deliver us from Your Majesty's hand. But even if he does not, we want you to know, Your Majesty, that we will not serve your gods or worship the image of gold you have set up." They are thrown into the furnace, but the Lord saves them; they do not die.

These are young men who know the God they serve. They politely and firmly take a stand against a king and refuse to bow down. Like young St. Jose Sanchez del Rio, who boldly broke the necks of the cocks fighting in the Lord's house and who stood firm against those blasphemers without fear, we need to trust the Lord to deliver us when we are called to be such witnesses. Do not get too comfortable, do not get too cozy.

You want to bring people to Christ? Take a stand. Be bold. Honor God, even with your very life. Refuse to bow. Something is rotten in the Church, and appeals to the top are not worth holding your breath for. It may take your life on line, and even then people may scroll past your story and you die in obscurity. No matter. The Lord sees.

Be faithful with what you have. Don't bow, don't cower. Answer the call in the way the Lord has called you. Converts are made by witness, not pastoral letters.

ON WRITING

WHY DO I WRITE?

There was a song in *Good Will Hunting* by Luscious Jackson titled "Why Do I Lie?" It's catchy, I like it, and I liked the movie when I saw it twenty years ago. It also reminds me of one of my favorite and meaty passages of scripture, Romans 7, where Paul asks, "Why do I do that which I hate?" So apropos.

It's good to take stock of why we do the things we do from time to time. A smoker might ask themselves "why do I smoke?" Or an overeater why they overeat. Because I'm anti-social? Because I lack confidence? Because I need a bit of pleasure here and there through vice? Because I'm anxious? It helps us get to the root of our motivations, why we do the things we do. Most people go through life with little self-reflection, and so find themselves trapped in cycles of self-perpetuating habits.

Writing is no different. I was thinking about it this morning and came up with a few reasons as I reflected on them.

Charity

I try to write as an act of charity, first and foremost. My hope has always been to do the work of an evangelist, but my writing has shifted over the years to also trying to fortify the people of God in their own walks. Not by prescribing anything, but as an act of solidarity from one sinner to another. To give witness to the love of God, and grace. As St. Paul says, "in preaching the gospel I may offer it free of charge, and so not make use of my rights in preaching it" (1 Cor 9:18). This is because I have been forgiven a debt, and the debt I must work to repay.

Penance

Writing is less a penance than something I just do—neither pleasurable nor painful. But as above, God has entrusted some kind of talent in me, that I'm apt to bury, but just can't. So, the goal is to multiply it for His glory. That means if any of it is about me, it is only as a subject, not a focus. Defer, deflect—all glory to God and the Gospel. I could think of worse penances.

Compulsion

There could also be worse activities of compulsion: gambling, drug use, etc. Compulsion is a strong force; even when we want to stop, we can't sometimes except by a monumental act of the will. As Jeremiah lamented, "If I say I will not mention his word or speak anymore in his name, his word is in my heart like a fire, a fire shut up in my bones" (Jer 20:9). This is what writing is for me. A shame and a glory. A fire and a scarring. A hot potato that needs to be passed to someone else, lest it burn your hands. Paul said he was "compelled" to preach the Gospel (1 Cor 9:16). He fears if he does not. Maybe that is what I mean by compulsion.

Encouragement

I am not a good friend. But sometimes I can be a cheerleader for the faithful of Jesus Christ, even though I get burdened myself. That's when it gets tough, and doubt creeps in. "What you have heard from me through many witnesses entrust to faithful people who will be able to teach others as well" (2 Tim 2:2). I don't sleep a whole lot, and think, chew cud, process, discern, and spit out. What's there is, I figure, maybe of use to others who may not have the time to digest the weightier matters of faith.

Vanity

This is becoming less of an issue the older I get, but I did want my name out there for a while. This has faded, as Ecclesiastes notes, "All is vanity." So much vanity out there, a vice we're not often aware of. It goes back to that self-reflection: why do we do the things we do? Jesus says to not let our left hand know what our right is doing. This is good, because as I've said on more than one occasion: you're not that important. People can live without your insights. It keeps me in my place. Deo Gratias. But affirmation is my love language, so it's an ongoing struggle.

Connection and Community

I also like to connect people together by way of degree. Maybe my writing can serve that purpose, string disparate people in different isolated circles together. Seven degrees of Kevin Bacon and all that. Again, all for the sake of the Gospel. There is solace in knowing you are not alone—especially if you've felt the acute pain of loneliness, as I have, even in the midst of others. Feel free to use the blog as a well of sorts to meet and discuss. Comments are always open.

Education

I'm not an especially educated person, but I used to read (a lot!) and think about things, and there is so much to learn in the Church you will never plumb the depths. That is a great gift to have such a bottomless well of grace and tradition and history. I'm just scratching the surface and offering the flakes for others.

WISDOM AND FOLLY

Legacy and Remembering

I write to remember. For better or worse. I want to leave a legacy for my children. My wife has already threatened to print and compile all 600 of my blog posts from the past few years for them. I do it for me. For the Lord. But also for them. Lord, just let it be after I pass, though. It's too embarrassing otherwise. Let it be a kind of knit-blanket from their father they can keep to remember me.

Working Out My Demons

I write to process. I talk things out with my wife and friends, too, but writing is where I do it alone. It goes back to that question of "why do I do that which I do?" I have time to think and digest and throw it up on a page for later. To go back to, maybe, to learn and more forward. Breadcrumbs for my family, and my own consciousness. I struggle sometimes, a lot. It's for me, not anyone else. But I'd rather it be used than sit rotting in a diary somewhere. I've benefitted greatly from the honest humanity of others. Maybe I can pay it back someday in the same way.

Glory to God

All glory belongs to God. I didn't ask for this. I don't know why I do it. But He does and he knows what He is about. Just use me Lord, as embarrassing as it is. Just don't let it be about me. Take it all and make it new.

THE WITCHING HOUR

I don't write about writing much, probably because I don't think of myself as a real writer. I try to keep this blog focused on issues of faith and Christian living. But that always intersects with the ramparts that hold up the theme, and that is the act of writing itself. So it may deserve a little *in memoriam* post of its own.

Despite the fact that I have been writing without pause for over twenty years, I will usually refer to myself as 'a guy who writes,' and not a writer. Anyone who wants to be a writer sees it as a blessing endowed which holds the key to unlocking their dreams. Anyone who knows what it means to be a writer (i.e., one who writes) knows that it is really a curse which has you under compulsion, a compulsion you often beg in earnest to be taken from you. If you find yourself in bed at 3am, consider yourself blessed.

I don't know any other way to be, any other way to live, but I will tell you this: writing is a shameful exercise. We rightfully recoil and seek to cover up someone who disrobes in the public square. And yet those who write, who are urged forward by silent muses, do it all the time, for the public and in the public square, for all to see. It's almost like a koan: if a writer writes his words, and there is no one to read it, does it make a sound? I'm not a journaler. I have no use in writing secret words for my eyes only. I write to be read. The depths of my pride and exhibitionism know no bounds.

WISDOM AND FOLLY

Every writer knows they are at heart a kind of fraud, or at least that is the fear. Aren't we all, in some way or another? Don't we all curse the day we were born, at some point? But here's the rub, and the honest truth: I don't like who I am. It took a searing private message from a virtual stranger taking me to task to remind me of this. It was something I was grateful to receive, but man did it sting, and in the best most humiliating way possible. Social media is both a blessing and a curse. I want to do the work God has set before me and honor Him in that, but that public exhibitionism so inherent in writing—about everything—often bleeds into this work, and it shows up there. It's not enough to do something for the greater glory of God in obscurity—I need to make it known to the world. Because everything in life you see as a story, because you see opportunities to write and exhibit and make sense of your life as narrative in everything you do, when you end up doing the work God calls you to, you write about it shamelessly. You hope it is for the benefit of others, you want your light to shine before others, but pride is pernicious, and the capacity for self-deception runs deep. When you are filled with doubt in the dead of night, there's no one to turn to. The people you love most are asleep upstairs, the friends you rely on for building up and support have retired to their respective beds, and the God you serve is silent in the vigil hours. My wife has heard me lament *ad nauseum*: why can't I be normal? What is wrong with me, and how can you stand to be married to me?

In reading the words of the prophet Jeremiah tonight, I found some solace—not because of anything prophetic on my part, but because his lament is one I have uttered myself.

> O Lord, You have deceived me and I was deceived;
> You have overcome me and prevailed.
> I have become a laughingstock all day long;
> Everyone mocks me. For each time I speak, I cry aloud;
> I proclaim violence and destruction, because
> For me the word of the Lord has resulted in reproach
> And derision all day long. But if I say, "I will not
> Remember Him Or speak anymore in His name,"

ON WRITING

Then in my heart it becomes like a burning fire
Shut up in my bones;
And I am weary of holding it in,
And I cannot endure it.
For I have heard the whispering of many,
"Terror on every side! Denounce him; yes, let us denounce him!"
All my trusted friends,
Watching for my fall, say:
"Perhaps he will be deceived, so that we may prevail against him
And take our revenge on him."

But the Lord is with me like a dread champion;
Therefore my persecutors will stumble and not prevail.
They will be utterly ashamed, because they have failed,
With an everlasting disgrace that will not be forgotten.
Yet, O Lord of hosts, You who test the righteous,
Who see the mind and the heart;
Let me see Your vengeance on them;
For to You I have set forth my cause.
Sing to the Lord, praise the Lord!
For He has delivered the soul of the needy oneFrom the hand of evildoers.
 Cursed be the day when I was born;
Let the day not be blessed when my mother bore me!
Cursed be the man who brought the news
To my father, saying, "A baby boy has been born to you!"
And made him very happy.
But let that man be like the cities
Which the Lord overthrew without relenting,
And let him hear an outcry in the morning
And a shout of alarm at noon;
Because he did not kill me before birth,
So that my mother would have been my grave,
And her womb ever pregnant.
Why did I ever come forth from the womb

To look on trouble and sorrow,
So that my days have been spent in shame?"
(Jer 20:1-18)

As Monsignor Charles Pope said of Jeremiah, the best kind of prophets are the reluctant ones. Nobody should want to be a spiritual director, or a prophet, or a writer, or a guider of souls, or a person of influence. As Msgr Pope writes:

> Prophets suffer because they love and care for the ultimate well-being of God's people, not merely their present comfort. They suffer because they do not fit into tidy political or tribal categories. They speak for God, who transcends such groups. Yes, although the prophet is *totaliter aliter* (totally other), the human cost is high, and he comes to resemble Christ on the cross. The prophet's own notions of grandeur must be crucified. The idea that most people will ultimately accept the truth must be crucified.

This is not my issue, because I am not a prophet or called to that task. But my struggle to simply avoid sin, as well as self-recognition and affirmation, is burdensome. It's the 3 A.M. dawns, when you've been up most of the night wrestling and then the embarrassing compulsion of being driven to write about it, as you do with everything, drives home an even deeper truth of how tied you are to the world, how amateur in the spiritual realm, how sensitive to criticism, how unable to sit with tension, how unsure, how weak, how prideful, how effeminate in the need to express and how far from the strong and silent type you are, how unwilling to do what is arduous and uncomfortable, how quick to complain and seek out consolation.

And yet...

And yet despite all that, I do not doubt God's love for me at 3 A.M. steeped in sin and pride and worldliness. As much as I lament with Jeremiah the day of my birth, I also read the words of David and share the quiet acknowledgement of His wonderful deeds, His incomprehensible providence, and the marvel of His intricate creations:

> O Lord, You have searched me and known me. You know when I sit down and when I rise up; You understand my thought from afar. You scrutinize my path and my lying down, And are intimately acquainted with all my ways. Even before there is a word on my tongue, Behold, O Lord, You know it all. You have enclosed me behind and before, And laid Your hand upon me. Such knowledge is too wonderful for me; It is too high, I cannot attain to it.
>
> Where can I go from Your Spirit? Or where can I flee from Your presence? If I ascend to heaven, You are there; If I make my bed in Sheol, behold, You are there. If I take the wings of the dawn, If I dwell in the remotest part of the sea, Even there Your hand will lead me, And Your right hand will lay hold of me. If I say, "Surely the darkness will overwhelm me, And the light around me will be night," Even the darkness is not dark to You, And the night is as bright as the day. Darkness and light are alike to You.
>
> For You formed my inward parts; You wove me in my mother's womb. I will give thanks to You, for I am fearfully and wonderfully made; Wonderful are Your works, And my soul knows it very well. My frame was not hidden from You, When I was made in secret, And skillfully wrought in the depths of the earth; Your eyes have seen my unformed substance; And in Your book were all written The days that were ordained for me, When as yet there was not one of them.
>
> How precious also are Your thoughts to me, O God! How vast is the sum of them! If I should count them, they would outnumber the sand. When I awake, I am still with You.
>
> O that You would slay the wicked, O God; Depart from me, therefore, men of bloodshed. For they speak against You wickedly, And Your enemies take Your name in vain. Do I not hate those who hate You, O Lord? And do I not loathe those

who rise up against You? I hate them with the utmost hatred;
They have become my enemies.

Search me, O God, and know my heart; Try me and know my anxious thoughts; And see if there be any hurtful way in me, And lead me in the everlasting way. (Ps 139)

He knows my anxious thoughts. He searches me and knows my heart, even when I don't know it, or am caught off guard by it. He knows everything about me, and has a plan for me—yes, that grand narrative lens I see the world through as a writer, as a Christian, as a sojourner. When I try to keep it in, keep the screen clean, the page blank, my bones groan. Please leave the thorns in my ribs, if they be for Your purposes, since your grace is sufficient (2 Cor 12:9). See in me, Lord, if there be any hurtful way in me. And don't leave my side, even in the dead of night. My sin is ever before me. When I am awake, let me still be with You.

Please pray for me.

LETTER TO AN ASPIRING WRITER

Someone reached out to me today via LinkedIn seeking advice and constructive feedback on getting started as a writer, specifically as a Catholic writer. I imagine they came across one of my published articles on-line and were wondering where to get published, where to connect with other writers, and how to obtain feedback on their own work. This is not the first time someone has reached out in this way.

I haven't responded, though I thought it would be a good opportunity to kill a few birds with one stone with a blog post on the topic in the form of a letter to said inquirer.

Dear _____,

Thank you for reaching out. No need for academic salutations; I am not a Professor, and am not an instructor. To be honest, I don't even consider myself a proper writer. I've never learned the discipline in a formal sense, aside from high school English and a couple of Creative Writing classes in college. As I find myself saying often, I'm just a guy who writes some things every now and then.

I may or may not be of any help to you when it comes to your inquiry. Though I have a few published articles, essays, and poetry floating out there on-line, it is for the most part incidental that they exist. I have been writing for as long as I can remember, try as I might to hang it up for good. Every attempt to do so invokes the deep, resigned sighs of Jeremiah the Prophet, "But if I say, 'I will not mention his word or speak anymore in his name,' his word is in my heart like a fire, a fire shut up in my bones. I am weary of holding it in; indeed, I cannot" (Jer 20:9)

For novice writers (as you describe yourself), having your work published (whether in periodicals, books, or other mediums) seems at first to be the pen-ultimate validation. No one says, "I want to wander in the desert for forty years." They say, "I want to reach the Promised Land."

But wandering in the desert in search of something for years, decades on end, even, is more in line with the vocation of a writer. There is no Promised Land, no resting ground where one can say, "I've made it." There is only the mirage of oasis after pit-stop oasis. The Israelites would frequently erect altars of remembrance to remember what Yahweh had done for them as a people (see Genesis 28, 33, 35; Exodus 17, 24; Joshua 4). Writing is not unlike this. Because my short and long-term memory is so poor, writing is a way for me (and anyone really) to *remember*. It is also a way to find out *who we were, who we are,* and *who we are to become*. People often journal for this reason.

But journaling is not what you are seeking advice on, if I can speculate. A person who journals writes for themselves and themselves alone; a writer is, alas, burdened with the compulsive need to have his words read by someone other than himself. Whereas a journaler would be aghast were someone sneak into their room and read their diary, a writer would not put it past himself to leave such written accounts out in the plain sight of day in the hopes that someone, somewhere, will discover it.

It's curious, isn't it. Is this vain-glory, exhibitionism? I have wrestled with this over the years, the need to be acknowledged. I have even prayed novenas to Our Lady petitioning for the grace to be untethered from "the praise and adulation of men." My blog is a diary of sorts, but if I were the only one able to view it, I would have shut it down years ago. It's an outlet of sorts, yes. But the burning need for it to be given over to someone (anyone) somewhere (anywhere!) accompanies it.

I gave up coffee for Lent. In a sense, being published is like that first sip of coffee after a month and a half of tea. You'd been anticipating the day when you can have it. And then you do. And then it's done. You are still yourself; it's now just a little harder to hide.

I joke with my wife (half joking, quarter joking, not really joking) that our kids can be whatever they want when they grow up. They just can't be writers. In thirty years of writing, I could probably pay for a month's worth of groceries from Aldi with what I've been paid for my "labor." And that's ok; I'm not a writer anyway. But if I were, as I say to my wife, "it's a cruel fate indeed."

I like to garden; but I wouldn't want to be a landscaper. I like to monkey on bikes in my garage, but I would never want to be a professional mechanic. I love my Catholic faith, but the day I pay my mortgage with YouTube apologetic videos or podcast musings would be the death knell of zeal.

Writing is like this. My father, pragmatic as he was and is, was right: hobbies are good, and writing for me really is a hobby, and maybe a little more. It's a way to live—to make sense of life—but it's no way to make a living. I'm not sure if that is/was your intention in reaching out (I'm speculating), to see about how to make a living or side-income from writing and/or publishing. Forgive me for assumptions. But I can think of no other endeavor that bleeds so much out of you for so little given in restitution.

Which brings me to my next point. In meditating on Christ writhing in agony on the Cross, it can sometimes cross one's mind to ask, "Why would anyone endure such a thing?" Why would anyone literally bleed out, crushed by the weight of unrequited love, poured out as an unbibed drink offering, abandoned and alone in his final hour with the echoes of "Hosanna!" ringing in his ear? Only a fool would give himself over to such a fate. Only a fool would die for love.

And yet we are fools following Christ, the God of redeemed folly. "God was pleased through the foolishness of what was preached to save those who believe" (1 Cor 1:21).

Think of publishing as your Palm Sunday, while remitting your true opus as a writer to the cross. Because if you want to be a Catholic writer with anything to offer the world, this is where you nail up your work. Naked and uncovered, on full frontal display, with only your mother and a close friend as your final faithful audience. Those palm-laying masses? They are retiring in their home. Your disciples and friends? Denying they even knew you. You're not even sure your own Father is there to acknowledge your offering.

But here's the difference: when you give freely of what you've been given, the gift multiplies. When charity has been perfected, it is no longer self-seeking (1 Cor 13:5). It gives, and it gives. If I can say anything truthfully, this is what I have always tried to do as a "writer." Sure it starts out like a freshman nursing student who enters into the profession because she wants to "help people." Over time, that naivete becomes calloused over with the scars of rejection after rejection, the seeming pointlessness of tapping away on a keyboard at 3am ("for what?"), the slight-of-hand critical remarks on your syntax that you take to heart and die over. But it becomes a burning ember, not a flickering flame. If you can retain the heat of pure intention—to write in order that you might *give*—you can continue in your vocation.

Speaking of vocation, I have tried not to curse what God has given me, though not always successfully. "Do not call unclean what God has called clean" (Acts 11:9). It's not easy. Writers are minor prophets—warning, admonishing, lamenting, praising. To be good you have to know your place and your calling, where it is you fill in the cracks with the mortar of your spilled ink.

Do you want to write for yourself? Buy a diary. Do you want to be recognized? Start a TikTok channel. Do you want to coax depressives off a ledge, inspire the young, give fortitude to the weak, console the heartbroken, speak the Truth, fill the hopeless with hope, the faithless with faith? Then do that, with the tools God has entrusted you with—the pen (or keyboard, as it were). You may never get paid for it and may never be recognized on the street. But consider those the upsides rather than drawbacks. If God has given you a gift, He expects it to be used, not buried (Mt 25:14-30). The safest place for your talents is with the banker, not in the ground.

Do I have any closing advice for you with regards to writing? I'll give you the advice that was given to me: just write. And I'll add my own: make yourself and your words a gift to the world, given freely and without charge. If you do that, I suspect you'll never be disappointed. Because in the end, you may die a fool...but you'll die hanging on a tree with the best of them.

WHAT MAKES AN ARTIST AN ARTIST?

It's a hard-knocks lesson in juxtaposition being a Catholic artist. Orthodox Catholicism, by definition and nature, is "conservative" in that it seeks to conserve the *depositum fidei* in its original form, and preserve it for generations to come. Change is often made slowly, thoughtfully, deliberately; "A U-boat doesn't turn on a dime," as they say. Creative license is somewhat frowned upon, and often for good reason. Order, syntax, tradition—these are the qualities that make for predictability and creating an establishment to last. And the Catholic Church is very much establishment.

But there is also in the life of faith the unpredictable "wild goose" of the Holy Spirit and His work of grace. The Holy Spirit is the mystical, the wind [which] blows wherever it pleases. "You hear its sound, but you cannot tell where it comes from or where it is going. So it is with everyone born of the Spirit." (Jn 3:8). There are also the diverse body of the saints, who have perfected the art of being. They are always depicted with a halo because they know who they are, and from whom they come. They *see* with eyes that see; that is, they see reality for what it is, where others would rather not go. Their lives are not formulaic quid-pro-quo arrangements with the Divine, but the creative living out of their vocations as they are particularly called to do. They constrain themselves—by mortification, doctrine, and material reductionism, so that they might be truly free. And if "conservatism" has one great core value, it is freedom.

Conservatives, in general, though, tend to be suspicious and reticent about art. When I use the word 'artist' I mean it in the big-bucket sense to encompass all those who seek to create: musicians, writers, visual artists, film makers, poets, etc. The difficult thing about creating anything is that it tends not to want to be constrained. "Life finds a way" as Dr. Ian Malcolm said in *Jurassic Park*. In the novel, the good doctor elaborates,

> Physics has had great success at describing certain kinds of behavior: planets in orbit, spacecraft going to the moon, pendulums and springs and rolling balls, that sort of thing. The regular movement of objects. These are described by what are called linear equations, and mathematicians can solve those equations easily. We've been doing it for hundreds of years.
>
> But there is another kind of behavior, which physics handles badly. For example, anything to do with turbulence. Water coming out of a spout. Air moving over an airplane wing. Weather. Blood flowing through the heart. Turbulent events are described by nonlinear equations. They're hard to solve—in fact, they're usually impossible to solve. So physics has never understood this whole class of events. Until about ten years ago. The new theory that describes them is called chaos theory.
>
> Chaos theory originally grew out of attempts to make computer models of weather in the 1960s. Weather is a big complicated system, namely the earth's atmosphere as it interacts with the land and the sun. The behavior of this big complicated system always defied understanding. So naturally we couldn't predict weather. But what the early researchers learned from computer models was that, even if you could understand it, you still couldn't predict it. Weather prediction is absolutely impossible. The reason is that the behavior of the system is sensitively dependent on initial conditions.

Use a cannon to fire a shell of a certain weight, at a certain speed, and a certain angle of inclination—and if I then fire a second shell with almost the same weight, speed, and angle, what will happen? The two shells will land at almost the same spot. That's linear dynamics. But if I have a weather system that I start up with a certain temperature and a certain wind speed and a certain humidity—and if I then repeat it with almost the same temperature, wind, and humidity-the second system will not behave almost the same. It'll wander off and rapidly will become very different from the first. Thunderstorms instead of sunshine. That's nonlinear dynamics. They are sensitive to initial conditions: tiny differences become amplified.

The shorthand is the "butterfly effect." A butterfly flaps its wings in Beijing, and weather in New York is different.

Chaos is not just random and unpredictable. We actually find hidden regularities within the complex variety of a system's behavior. That's why chaos has now become a very broad theory that's used to study everything from the stock market, to rioting crowds, to brain waves during epilepsy. Any sort of complex system where there is confusion and unpredictability. We can find an underlying order. An underlying order is essentially characterized by the movement of the system within phase space.

Chaos theory says two things. First, that complex systems like weather have an underlying order. Second, the reverse of that—that simple systems can produce complex behavior. For example, pool balls. You hit a pool ball, and it starts to carom off the sides of the table. In theory, that's a fairly simple system, almost a Newtonian system. Since you can know the force imparted to the ball, and the mass of the ball, and you can calculate the angles at which it will strike the walls, you can predict the future behavior of the ball. In theory, you could predict the behavior of the ball far into the future, as it keeps bouncing from side to side. You could predict where it will end up three hours from now, in theory.

But in fact, it turns out you can't predict more than a few seconds into the future. Because almost immediately very small effects—imperfections in the surface of the ball, tiny indentations in the wood of the table—start to make a difference. And it doesn't take long before they overpower your careful calculations. So it turns out that this simple system of a pool ball on a table has unpredictable behavior.

Is there a place for so-called "conservative" artists? Well, if you're talking about the kitschy paintings of Thomas Kinkade or the juvenile political functionalism of Jon McNaughton's "Liberalism is a Disease", I'd take a hard pass.

There are the curious (and somewhat meticulously obsessive) conservative religious artists such as the obscure American James Hampton's religiously themed The Throne of the Third Heaven of the Nations Millennium General Assembly, which took him 14 laborious years to create. He lived, worked, and died in obscurity as a janitor. His piece was discovered in a D.C. storage unit posthumously and transferred to the Smithsonian.

But maybe the time is ripe for conservative artists to find their place. After all, decades of modernist chaos, destruction, revolution, and perversion *ad nauseum* has created a dearth of order, goodness, and beauty in the world. Isn't it perhaps time to re-introduce it in a way that touches the soul and infuses grace and hope?

I remember when *The Passion of the Christ* came out in theaters; it was not a film, but a work of art. And yet, it was thoroughly "traditional" through-and-through. Mel Gibson, of course, had taken some creative license, drawing on the visions of Bl. Anne Catherine Emmerich. The cinematography was beautiful, the acting impeccable, and the ability to conjure not only the emotions but the spirit of those who watched it was, quite simply, what good art sets out to do.

I once watched an interesting interview with music producer Rick Rubin (founder of Def Jam records) who can't play any instruments and doesn't know how to use a mixing board. Self-admittedly, his "only real talent is listening." His Malibu recording studio *Shangra-La* is completely minimalist and painted all white. Generally speaking, according to Rubin, the creative process is subtractive. You have to remove as many distractions as possible. There's not a television, there's not a clock...it's like a blank canvas. Rubin notes:

> The goal is to create a setting where an artist can be completely vulnerable and feel completely free to be themselves one hundred percent. No shame or feeling of needing to perform a certain way, and no expectation...really, a safe place...to be naked, basically.

The "bearded super-producer" Rick Rubin takes the opposite approach of most record producers in that he doesn't try to interject himself into the albums but take himself out of it. The more invisible, the better. So, really, his only role (and the secret to his creative success) is being a kind of guide to accompany others into themselves:

> If you really listen to what people say, usually...they tell you everything. I just really pay attention to what people say and through that I can then reflect back thoughts that they've told me about themselves that they don't know about themselves...and allow them to unlock those doors to get to the places they want to go artistically.
>
> It's like fishing. You can go out fishing, but you can't say 'I'm going to catch three fish today.' You have very little control over this process. It's magic, really.

The lack of control can be scary for conservative-minded people sometimes. But interjecting such control into art is akin to trying to catch and cage a dove. The creative infusion of the Holy Spirit in the life of grace lends itself to a lack of control, in which you are following the wind where it leads, which is where creativity in art comes from.

ON WRITING

A man must be free to choose sin for his love to be authentic. An artist, likewise, must be free to explore the depths of his soul in order to bring it to the surface. Removing judgement and condemnation (which comes from the Enemy, the Great Accuser) may do wonders for any person of faith seeking to touch the Spirit of God which is within them. We all have that place within us. God sets the fence around the edge of the mountain so the children can play free from fear. The Devil, by contrast, cannot create, and so he resorts to legalism. Legalism is boring, predictable—the opposite of what makes for good art.

Chesterton said, "The Catholic Church is the only thing which saves a man from the degrading slavery of being a child of his age." An artist is one who has learned to bring to the surface for the world to see and enjoy, free of charge, the beauty of God within. Not only that, but also what it means to be truly human. This is the great mystery of the Christian faith—how the Eternal, Omnipotent, and Omnipresent Eternal God of the Universe also stooped to enter into the fray of time and space, and human existence as a man. There must, also then, be a place for Christians to be great artists in post-modern society. Barbara Nicolosi, a Catholic filmmaker I greatly admirer, said it well:

> People are thirsty for story, because, as Aristotle noted, human nature is driven to it and they are going to the movies to find something to feed them. But most of the time, when we go to the movies hungry, we come away still hungry and also disgusted. So why doesn't the church step in and fill the vacuum? Why don't we teach people how to make story? That's what we should be doing. The Church should serve the culture.

Amen.

REASONED ORDER AND CREATIVE MESS

Attending a large R1 research institution as an undergrad, I was surrounded by engineers. My parents were math teachers. My brothers are engineers. My roommate was an engineer. We hate what we don't understand, and for the life of me I couldn't understand or relate to the left brain and so loathed it on campus.

For a quick general breakdown, those who are predominately left or right brain might be characterized by the following:

Left Brain:

- Logical
- Focused on facts
- Realism predominates
- Planned and orderly
- Math-and-science minded

Right Brain:

- Emotional
- Focused on art and creativity
- Imagination predominates
- Occasionally absentminded

- Enjoys creative storytelling

The thing is, when I became Catholic my freshman year and joined the Newman center, obviously there were a mix of these "logical, fact-focused, math & science planned and orderly realists" among people of faith in the Catholic community. And of course there are degrees of both hemispheres in individual people.

As a predominately right-brained person, I feel a little self-conscious in a more traditional community because of the way I am. But I have grown to appreciate the order and predictability of the Old Mass, and have no tolerance for liturgical "creativity" that I experienced in the Novus Ordo. I find liturgical dance, spoken word, improvisation and such things cringe worthy. I never felt at home in the Charismatic movement, or Praise & Worship type services.

I'm in a strange period now where I am leaning on the order and predictability of the ritual and assent to faith while grinding through a creative and imaginative dry spell—in writing, in my worship and prayer life, and just my life in general. And thank God it's there. I don't get off on it the way left-brain Catholics who geek out on liturgical nuances or theological tit-for-tats might, but I appreciate it. I may be checking the boxes, but I'm ok with that for now.

Albert Einstein once said, "The intuitive mind is a sacred gift, and the rational mind is a faithful servant. We have created a world that honors the servant but has forgotten the gift." I find this to be true in what the world values.

In the movie *Romero*, the Archbishop is invited to the home of a well-to-do couple. Pleasantries are exchanged, and then the businessman husband/father lays into Archbishop Romero in the kitchen:

> You religious people...You live in your souls. You do not understand what we do...producing, selling, bringing dollars in...Capital, to develop the country, to create jobs...to build a prosperous economy. That is what affects people. But for that we must have law and order.

Succeeding in the world is a wholly pragmatic affair, one I never really caught on to, as I'm sometimes reminded. I never did any internships, got a useless degree, for ten years I thought I would be a monk, I never made much money and never really cared, don't have much to show for a career. But I've always prayed, and I know God is faithful. I know it is not a futile endeavor...but that itself takes faith.

My primary sins, as a right-brained creative/imaginative type, often comes by way of impulse—if I fall, I fall hard but don the sack cloth and ashes in tears as well. I live in my heart, not my head. This is why I love the King Davids over the King Sauls, and the Peters over the Thomases. Were I to be tempted by apostasy, I think it would be at the hand of hurt, rather than issues of belief or doctrine.

Although it is only speculation (since I have a hard time understanding them), I wonder if the sins of the left-brained type people differ in nature. What are their primary temptations? Do they struggle with reason? With Pharisaism? With the 'sins of certainty?'—of thinking that "If I just do X, God will do Y"? Of the logical progression of right belief+right worship=sanctity? I don't know! I want to ask them!

In the early centuries of the Church, most of their heresies revolved around the nature of Christ. Adoptionism, Docetism, Apollinarianism, Arianism, Monophysitism among others wrestled with how GOD could become MAN and possess two distinct natures, which are united but not combined.

Christ as perfect man had a distinct sex (male) but embodied the totality of human nature as well: he wept, he longed to gather his people as a hen gathers her chicks, he expressed tenderness and empathy. He sought to short-circuit the law-minded ways of thinking (by his teaching, by parables, by his witness in washing feet and healing on the Sabbath) to raise the disciples' heads to the work of grace.

St. Paul for his part was a radical zealot of the law who became the Apostle of grace. Grace is messy! Not always neat and orderly! Paul's road to Damascus moment was a blinding subjective encounter with Christ which literally knocked him from his (high?) horse. The law counts for nothing, according to Paul.

And yet for Traditionalists, there is comfort in the spiritual equations: if I say A, I merit B. If I practice X, my children will grow up Y. If I believe and check the right boxes, I can rest assured in certainty that God will not abandon me. Perhaps this is the 'sin of certainty' that leaves no room for the creative action of God to actualize our reality in a way that doesn't make logical sense. You see the antithesis to this line of reasoning in the life of David in 2 Sam 12:21-23:

> His attendants asked him, "Why are you acting this way? While the child was alive, you fasted and wept, but now that the child is dead, you get up and eat!"
>
> He answered, "While the child was still alive, I fasted and wept. I thought, 'Who knows? The Lord may be gracious to me and let the child live.' But now that he is dead, why should I go on fasting? Can I bring him back again? I will go to him, but he will not return to me."

But sometimes God does leave us alone, withdrawing from us and leaving us to the mystical 'dark night,' which for the left-brained can (I imagine) be a bit of a disconcerting place to be. In the same way I have no affinity and cannot understand St. Thomas Aquinas as a right-brained creative, a left-brained believer may struggle to relate to the boundary breaking ecstasies of the St. John of the Cross's and St. Teresa of Avilas.

I think for right-brained, creative types, it is good to learn and establish order and right worship from the beginning to learn how to 'color within the lines.' If you look at Pablo Picasso's early work, he was a realist—it was only later, after learning the rules and form of art, that he began to branch out into more experimental work.

I think it can be difficult for left-brained people, though, to do the same with their 'weaker arm.' That is, perhaps in the life of faith, practicing more contemplative ways of praying or just "being" with God in adoration rather than always "doing." Or journaling or something, to discover how God is speaking to them. I don't know. I'm not one of these people. But I think it's healthy to work on the things that don't come to us as part of our natural disposition.

For myself, I struggle with the sin of envy in my self-consciousness—that I invested all my capital in a spiritual economy, rather than a practical one, and so I'm behind the curve in my career. And so I envy those left-brainers who the world values and pays accordingly, who can provide well for their families as lawyers or engineers or scientists or accountants or whatever. And so it comes out in anger and envy, because I feel dumb, broke, emotional, exposed, and impractical (though this is highly exaggerated in my mind). As a result, I hate the way God made me—to be feeling, intuitive, creative, etc. These are "bad" things. I judge others, and I judge myself, and harshly so. This is my sin (among others).

But this is how God made me. I try hard to rest in that. It can be hard to accept yourself, and just let yourself be loved sometimes, the way you are. God didn't make me with a logical brain. He didn't make me a planner or a reasoner. But I'm not a reject, a 2nd quality fruit; I have to trust that. Although I haven't had a good cry in years, I always welcome it when it comes. If anything, I may even have a degree of buoyancy and elasticity to take the unexpected things God throws us and not be broken by them. Maybe it is my term insurance against apostasy. Faith and reason, works and grace, the human and divine nature of Christ—there is always this tension in the life of faith, and sometimes one is prioritized and weighted more above the other. But we have two hemispheres of the brain for a reason, even if one tends to dominate. It's what makes us humans, not pre-programmed cyborgs.

LETTER TO A HOUSEWIFE

I have a friend who I have been corresponding with for a year or so who is curious and exploring the Faith. She, like me, was not raised in a religious household, and I have been so edified in her openness to Christianity, coming from a secular Jewish background. She has been reading a Bible I sent her, and we talk from time to time about the things of faith. I am so encouraged by her and pray for her regularly.

We all are looking for meaning in our existence here on earth. Before I came to faith in Christ, the emptiness and futility of life here on earth was palpable, and I was often filled with despair. Followers of Christ are often chided to having a "crutch" in belief, but I have found in my own life that without faith, without the transforming power of Christ, it is true: nothing really matters, and nothing makes sense.

But the fact is, through the eyes of faith, you begin to see that EVERYTHING MATTERS. From the smallest detail to the largest life decision—when we are living for the Lord, our lives matter. They matter to Him, and they matter to the world. The smallest act of faith is larger than the greatest secular accomplishment, and nothing escapes His view. The "reason for our hope" can sometimes be hard for Christians to articulate if they do not have a real, meaningful relationship with the risen Lord but instead sit back in the comfortable hollow veneer of cultural Christianity or religion devoid of belief. But once you have encountered the living God, you cannot remain unchanged.

The following is from a conversation with my friend, in which I offer some meager advice on how to see the ordinary things of life, our every day duties and responsibilities, as a way of serving God and finding joy:

> That's the beauty of Catholic Christianity. Jesus was both 100% human and 100% God. No other religion can claim this. Our humanness and everything that comes with it, including chores, work, the everyday drudgery of life can be transformed and sanctified when given over to His purposes... In the Eucharist, ordinary bread and wine become the actually body and blood of Christ... In the sacrament of matrimony we are given the supernatural grace to live our vows...
>
> Remember: Mary lived a very ordinary and unassuming life of everyday things: nursing, changing diapers, making a home. And she was the Mother of God! These were not the things that 'got in the way' of the life of faith...they were sanctified through faith. Everything she—and you and I—do matters. St Joseph too worked as a humble carpenter to provide for his family...
>
> St. Benedict has a saying about prayer and work (I will link good article). They go together... Living by faith is not a futile or meaningless exercise. When we suffer, we suffer for the Lord... When we have joy, we give thanks and praise, and eat the fruit of gratefulness, which transforms our attitude and dispositions. But it's all only POSSIBLE by faith...I would encourage you to set aside a few minutes of quiet time each day to thank God for where He is leading you, and ask very specifically for what you want Him to give you, and He will do it, as long as it is in accordance with His will and good for you spiritually speaking...The next time you have an opportunity to love and serve your husband, remember St Joseph and the Blessed Virgin, the Holy Family. Ask for their intercession in

your marriage...The next time you are feeding your boys or doing laundry, offer it as a sacrifice to God who notices all things done in love...

When you are feeling downcast and lonely, remember our Lord in the garden before his crucifixion. He is RIGHT THERE with you. This is not make-believe, this is real life, not counterfeit... I promise you it will transform how you approach even the smallest detail of your life as a housewife. Pray from the heart, be honest, but make everything known to the One who knows you so intimately that He knows every hair on your head... Confess your sins and failings, and trust that you are forgiven before the words leave your lips...

There is a reason Christianity is a religion of JOY. We have been saved from death and meaninglessness by Christ's death and resurrection. Hallelujah!

God bless you.

Made in the USA
Las Vegas, NV
21 January 2024